THE HEALING
NATURE TRAIL

THE HEALING NATURE TRAIL

Forest Bathing for Recovery & Awakening

TAMARACK SONG

Snow Wolf Publishing

Snow Wolf Publishing
7124 Military Road
Three Lakes, Wisconsin 54562
www.snowwolfpublishing.org

Snow Wolf Publishing

Snow Wolf Publishing is a division of Teaching Drum Outdoor School

Song, Tamarack, 1948 –
The Healing Nature Trail: Forest Bathing for Recovery and Awakening

ISBN-13: 978-0-9894737-4-3
1. Forest Bathing 2. Natural Healing 3. Trauma Recovery

Text design and layout by James Arneson ~ JaadBookDesign.com

To send correspondence to the author of this book, mail a first class letter to the author c/o Snow Wolf Publishing, 7124 Military Road, Three Lakes, Wisconsin 54562, and we will forward the communication, or email the author at info@snowwolfpublishing.org.

Visit the author's websites at www.healingnaturecenter.org, www. teachingdrum.org, and www.snowwolfpublishing.org.

References to Internet websites (URLs) were accurate at the time of writing. Neither the authors nor Snow Wolf Publishing are responsible for URLs that may have expired or changed since this book was published.

CONTENTS

PART III
PREPARING TO WALK THE TRAIL

PART IV
A WALK ON THE WILD SIDE

CONTENTS

To all of Nature's voices, especially Wolf, Eagle, and Owl
who guided the birthing of the Trail

To the Spruce Bogs, Beaver Ponds, and Elder Pines
who provided the sanctuary for the Trail

To you who trusted in Nature to guide your healing
then lent your stories to the Trail design

This book is dedicated, that it may nurture
your continued well-being

PART I
FINDING OURSELVES IN NATURE

AS A CULTURE, we have forsaken our relationship with the Land and the Water, the Trees and the Birds. In this book section, we explore what that elemental loss has cost us healthwise, and the deep loneliness it has left us with. Yet the intrinsic allure of Nature persists, which has inspired a beautiful way to re-engender that most profound and heartfelt of all relationships. Healthcare providers have a unique opportunity with the Healing Nature Trail to incorporate Nature's healing touch into their practices.

CHAPTER ONE

A Book, a Doorway, an Invitation

I n select nooks of Nature, there are trails specially designed to maximize the healing properties of flowing water, Elder Trees, and Wildflower essences. Chipmunks scamper about, a Fox gingerly weaves her way across the Meadow, and a sprightly Warbler alights on a branch in front of you. In such company, merely walking barefoot, breathing the air, and drinking in the setting become healing exercises. Panoramic vistas encourage new possibilities, and the trill of Frogs and Crickets bears words of wisdom. The book you hold in your hands is a doorway to that world.

The type of trail presented in this book is found nestled in a sanctuary reserved exclusively for those seeking Nature's guidance and healing touch. Healthcare practitioners bring their clients, and people of all persuasions come to restore body, mind, and spirit. Others are looking for a peaceful place to meditate, and still others yearn to renew their relationship with Nature. "Forget not that the earth delights to feel your bare feet," says Kahlil Gibran, "and the winds long to play with your hair."[1]

This book serves as a comprehensive guide for all categories of trail users, and a source for Healing Nature Trail philosophy, benefits, usage, development, and maintenance. You'll find indepth sections that give:

- A multidisciplinary overview of the healing power of Nature.

- An introduction to Healing Nature Trails.

1

- ▶ A guided tour of a representative Healing Nature Trail.
- ▶ A workbook for establishing Healing Nature Trails.
- ▶ A description of Trail certification and Trail Guide degree programs.

The integrative approach of the Healing Nature Trail, which is drawn from Zen practice, the Nature-based healing methods of the world's indigenous cultures, and contemporary research on the curative powers of Nature, will be new to many readers. Consider progressing slowly through the book, to give time for assimilation and reflection.

Native people generally regard all living beings as people: there are Deer people, Raven people, and Cedar people. The human and nonhuman people converse and ask each other for guidance. Healing Nature Trails are designed to encourage the same type of relationship between you and the animals and plants you'll meet there. In honor of their kinship with us and the valuable roles they can play in our Healing and Awakening Journeys, you'll find their names capitalized in the text. You will see other select terms capitalized as well, to give emphasis to the significant roles they play in renewing our relationship with Healing Nature.

Yet a book, with as much as it might have to offer, is only cold print on lifeless paper. Nature is relationship, and the only way to be in relationship and benefit from it is to immerse yourself in it. Take this book outside with you, so that you are surrounded with what you are reading about. Or sit next to a window with an outdoor view. The book will then come to life, and you are bound to come more to life as well.

An Invitation

When you have pain
When sorrow nearly drowns you
There is a place where you can go
A haven tried and true
Where you'll find comfort for your soul
And the vision to start anew

When bitter trauma haunts you
And you struggle to move on
When you're trembling under fear
And depression's got you down
There is sweet solace oh, so near
Come walk on hallowed ground

When you are lost and lonely
And no longer know yourself
When you need to sit and ponder
And forget the daily grind
Hear the voice that calls from yonder
Come and let your nerves unwind

When you yearn to smell a Flower
Sweet and wild as your secret self
And dip your feet in a gurgling Stream
That whispers, "Set your soul a-sail"
Come home to renew your dreams
On the Healing Nature Trail

CHAPTER TWO

Getting Lost, and a Way Back

Thousands of tired, nerve-shaken, over-civilized people are beginning to find out that going to the mountains is going home; that wilderness is a necessity. ~ John Muir[1]

We know that humans have always had an intimate and complex relationship with the natural realm. And we know that Nature is there waiting for us. Yet we tend to forget that taking a walk outside is one of the most natural and beneficial things we can do for ourselves. More and more of us are migrating to large urban areas, and we are spending less and less time outside. It is a global trend: we are becoming an indoor species.[2] This is creating a crisis. Our connection with our natural habitat is rapidly becoming endangered, and in some areas, it has already reached the brink of extinction.

With the exception of a few rapidly dwindling Nature-based cultures, along with a handful of outdoor-oriented professions, many people's exposure to Nature is whittled down to an occasional camping trip or a yearly seaside vacation. Outdoor recreational sports such as hunting, fishing, and canoeing fill the gap for some others. Yet with each new generation, fewer and fewer people have a relationship with Nature.

Perhaps there is no longer a need for direct connection with Nature. After all, we have created a utopia: climate control, the eradication of pests, daylight on demand, doorstep food delivery, instant gratification of needs, and animals bred for indoor companionship. More and more, we have the freedom to work, communicate, and transmit information and resources to and from nearly anywhere at any time. Modern medicine now maintains our health, and the marvels of media allow us to experience the world from the comfort of our couches.

Yet there is the fragile underbelly of our accomplishment, which Jiddu Krishnamurti exposed when he said, "It is no measure of health to be well adjusted to a profoundly sick society." We are suffering because we have lost our connection with the natural rhythms of the sun, moon, and earth. Many of us have an increasing need to take time for self-reflection and renewal. Many more of us yearn for a bridge to connect our disjointed minds, bodies, and spirits. We find it near-impossible to meet these needs in the context of life as we have created it.

Most of us know that Nature can help us rediscover ourselves and heal. Many of us have experienced—at least temporarily— the connection to ourselves and our surroundings that takes place during a walk in the Woods or along the Seashore. We have felt how physically and psychically beneficial it was. It improved our mood; we stepped lightly and gained a positive outlook; we felt our stress melt away.

Yet with our busy, insular lives as they are, we are unable to bridge the gap between self and Nature. We are not able to avail ourselves of all that Nature has to offer. Why is this?

Our Main Barriers to Connecting with Nature

▶ **Rapid Urbanization.** 54 percent of the human population now lives in urban areas; and by 2050, it is projected to be over 65 percent.[3]

▶ **Inadequate Green Space Planning.** Some older cities are fortunate to have green corridors, along with community gardens and Flower beds. Many of these oases were set aside by early visionaries who wished to preserve the natural beauty that first attracted people to the area. However, most cities are now growing so rapidly that economic considerations are often favored over long-term planning to assure green space.[4]

▶ **Accessibility.** For economic reasons, many city dwellers do not have access to public natural areas. Any Nature-immersion experience available to them would have to be within range of public transit.

▶ **Shrinking Forests.** Although 31 percent of the planet's land area is currently forested, over half of the Earth's Forests have disappeared over the last 10,000 years, with the majority vanishing over the past fifty years. Currently, around 50,000 square miles of Forest disappears each year.[5]

▶ **Lifestyle.** A 2001 survey by the US Environmental Protection Agency revealed that US citizens spent an average of 87 percent of their days indoors, and an additional 6 percent in vehicles.[6, 7] We have truly become indoor dwellers.

The Consequences

The injurious effects of our isolation from Nature have been labeled *Nature Deficit Disorder* by social environmentalist Richard Louv.[8] We can now identify some symptoms, yet there are probably far more than we can currently recognize; and long-term repercussions will undoubtedly surface. Nature writer Robert Michael Pyle postulates that we will diminish our lives and our culture immeasurably if we fail to renew our relationship with Nature.[9] A compilation of scientific and medical studies from around the world points to these core health issues that are the direct consequence of our lost relationship with our natural habitat:

▶ Stress that is detrimental to mental and physical health.[10]

▶ Feelings of isolation.[11]

▶ Diminished sensory acuity (reduced awareness of surroundings).[12]

> Shortened attention spans.[13, 14]

> Impaired ability to think clearly.[15]

> Decreased productivity and creativity.[16]

The Benefits of Reconnecting

Yet we cannot—and will not—rest with that. "Deep inside," says biomimicry consultant Janine M. Benyus, "we still have a longing to be reconnected with the nature that shaped our imagination, our language, our song and dance, our sense of the divine."[17]

The restorative benefits of reconnecting with Nature are likely so far-ranging that they defy the imagination. As our nature *is* Nature, what we stand to gain could be as complex as Nature herself. And as beautiful and deeply satisfying.

Part of the beauty is that we do not need to earn the privilege of reconnecting, nor is there any question of deserving it, as we were born into it. As such, it is our heritage and birthright. Charles Cook, founder of Wild Earth Adventures, expresses it well: "Your deepest roots are in Nature. No matter who you are, where you live, or what kind of life you lead, you remain irrevocably linked with the rest of creation."[18]

Many of the greatest minds of our era have expressed the same. Albert Einstein said, "Look deep, deep into nature, and then you will understand everything better."[19] Yet that is often not enough. We need to justify our actions—especially when they require energy and challenge convention. Medical and social science studies have identified benefits in the following areas:

> Physical Health.[20]

> Mental well-being.[21]

> Intelligence and creativity.[22]

> Relaxation and sleep.[23]

> Social bonding.[24]

▶ The capacity to empathize and share.[25]

▶ The ability to envision and experience awe.[26]

A Way Back

Here in the West, we are fortunate to have indigenous Nature-healing traditions from which to draw. Many American indigenous cultures have survived into recent times, and they are repositories of healing wisdom that has been largely lost in the rest of the modern world. In Europe, some Nature-based Druidic, Norse, and Saami healing practices were transcribed before they were forgotten. Remnant practices from all these traditions persist to this day.

The 1800s saw a resurgence in Nature-based healing. Henry David Thoreau reflected this when he said, "I believe there is a subtle magnetism in nature, which, if we unconsciously yield to it, will direct us aright." Physicians of the time often prescribed convalescent time at health resorts or sanatoriums in pristine natural areas such as the Swiss Alps, Germany's Pine Forests, and the United States' Adirondack and Rocky Mountains. A popular medical hypothesis of the era was that Pine Trees released a healing balm into the air, which helped cure many ailments[27] (for more on this topic, see chapters 9 and 10).

For help in returning to respectful ways of being in relationship with the Earth, some people are adopting a *gods of place* approach. Nearly every bioregion has its sacred sites, which range from groves of Elder Trees, Mountains, and Volcanoes to geological formations in the shape of legendary beings. Other gods of place include plants, animals, and minerals who serve or served as guides and protectors for a region's indigenous people.

In contemporary consciousness, the gods of place are resurfacing in the concept of *co-intelligence*, which posits that collective aptitude outpaces that of a single enlightened voice.[28] In Nature, many voices come together synergistically to bring us insight and healing energy.

Designed by Nature

From these traditions came the Healing Nature Trail. It is a homegrown concept, rooted in indigenous Nature-healing wisdom. The Trail's founders learned how to listen to Nature's guiding voices for healing and self-discovery firsthand from living in the wilderness, apprenticing to American Indian Elders, and from experience with indigenous cultures around the world. One of the Trail's founders was trained while being raised by her Mayan Curandera grandmother, and the other founder learned by living with a pack of Wolves.

Our sister organization, the Teaching Drum Outdoor School, had a wealth of collected data and experience to draw from on trauma and relationship-healing approaches that worked in high-stress situations. The data came from having run outdoor skills and yearlong wilderness immersion courses for thirty-plus years. Add contributions from contemporary neuroscience research, the Zen tradition, and specialists in a variety of healing and self-discovery disciplines, and you have the parent stock that bore the Healing Nature Trail.

The first Healing Nature Trail was developed at the Coldfoot Creek Natural Area in northern Wisconsin in 1971 (more on that in chapter 28). The Trail continued to evolve over the next fifteen years, with prototypes being established in different locations around the Natural Area. During that time, word of its existence slowly spread through the Northwoods and beyond.

Then around 1987, the momentum increased dramatically. Mental health practitioners learned about the Trail, and they started to bring their clients for Nature-based therapy. More and more individuals came for a serene place to reflect or walk out their troubles in Nature's soothing presence. Others were looking for a deeper connection with themselves and Nature. It soon became apparent that the need had outstripped the Trail's ability to meet it. A new, more expansive location was needed.

There were several other outstanding trails in the region, such as *Scott Lake*, which looped through a magnificent stand of old-growth White Pine, Hemlock, and Yellow Birch; *Giant White Pine,* which featured the oldest Trees in the Headwaters Wilderness; and *Sam Campbell,* established by the namesake renowned *Philosopher of the Forest* (see chapter 17). Yet those trails lacked many of the special Nature-immersion features of the Healing Nature Trail.

Hence was born the Trail's sponsoring organization, the Healing Nature Center, which purchased suitable land to relocate and expand the Trail, along with establishing the organizational structure to support the Trail and related facilities (a welcome center, along with lodging and workshop space).

Meanwhile, in the East ...

Along with Westerners, many urbanized Southeast Asians were increasingly suffering from Nature Deficit Disorder. This spawned a parallel evolution of solutions. Over a thousand years ago, the Japanese, Chinese, and Koreans began to bring the serenity of Nature into their busy lives by creating elaborate landscaped gardens. Bonsai, a meditative exercise based on the practice of potting and tending to miniaturized Trees, spread throughout the region as well.[29]

Over the past several decades, the practice of therapeutic walks in the Forest took hold. It is based on the premise that spending time immersed in the sights, sounds, and atmosphere of Nature is highly effective as preventative and curative medicine for both physiological and psychological health. In 1982, the Japanese Ministry of Agriculture, Forestry, and Fisheries named the practice *Shinrin-yoku,*[30] which translates to *Taking in the Forest Atmosphere,* or *Forest Bathing* for short.[31] The practice is also known as *Nature Therapy, Forest Therapy,* and *Nature Healing.*

The supportive research and positive results of Forest Therapy have catalyzed a resurgence in the use of Nature immersion in medical practice. Both Japan and Korea have integrated this modality into their medical systems, and it is covered by insurance.

In 2004, Japan founded the Association of Therapeutic Effects of Forests to document medical evidence supporting claims of the benefits of Forest immersion on human health. As of April 2016, there were 1,055 Recreation Forests and fifty designated Forest Therapy Trails in Japan alone. They are visited by millions of people every year.[32]

Shinrin-yoku, the Japanese form of Forest Bathing, officially landed on the California coast in 2012 with the founding of The Association of Nature and Forest Therapy Guides and Programs.[33]

The Global Revival

Nature-based healing gained worldwide recognition with the launching of the International Society of Nature and Forest Medicine (INFOM) in September of 2004. The organization was born out of the desire to broaden understanding of Nature Healing through medical practice, along with supporting related scientific research.

Advocating worldwide through international cooperation and influence, INFOM contributes to the advancement of Nature-oriented health, welfare, and integrated medical care. INFOM has made significant contributions in the areas of Nature-based stress reduction and Natural Killer (NK) cell activation by collecting supportive scientific data. Influenced by INFOM, Finland launched a government-supported taskforce on Forests and human health in 2007.

In 2014, INFOM launched the Physicians in Forest Medicine Certification Program. This directly resulted in New Zealand establishing Green Prescriptions (GRx), which are written prescriptions for patients to increase physical activity and improve nutrition.[34, 35, 36, 37] They are now used by over 80 percent of the nation's general practitioners. Green Prescriptions (GRx) include follow-up calls or appointments for further patient support.[38]

As disconnected from Nature as we might feel we are at times, and as forlorn as that might make us, we can take solace in the fact that we are detached only in our minds. Nature is everywhere—literally everywhere—as she is our inner nature as well.

To access Nature, inner or outer, for our healing and our comfort, we can feel further relieved by the fact that there are no boundaries. As the mother of all, Nature is here for all, regardless of culture or belief. She speaks the universal language, so everyone can understand her. As you ply the pages of this book, you will see that all you need to do is listen. As William Shakespeare said, "The earth has music for those who listen."

CHAPTER THREE

What Are Healing Nature Trails?

A bove all, they are gateways to the wilds—the hidden realms of Nature and the inner reaches of our bodies, minds, and spirits. The animals are messengers, the plants provide restoratives, and the landscape serves as a metaphor for our Healing Journey. Through the Trail experience, Nature becomes a doorway to our inner nature. They are designed with these words from John Muir in mind: "In every walk with nature, one receives far more than he seeks."[1]

Nature trails are typically classed as either *hiking trails* or *interpretive trails*. A noted hiking trail is the Appalachian Trail, which runs for 2200 miles up the backbone of the Appalachian Mountains in the eastern United States.[2] Interpretive trails, which are usually associated with Nature centers and parks, feature signage to aid in the identification of plants, animals, and geological features. The Sam Campbell Trail, which is described in chapter 17, is a classic example.[3] Healing Nature Trails fall in the third class: *therapeutic trails*, which also include *Forest Therapy* and *Forest Bathing Trails*. In this class of trails, the general environment and specific natural features are utilized for inspirational and health-engendering purposes.

Healing Nature Trails also fall under the general classification of *Healing Gardens*, and the specific category of *Therapeutic Landscapes*. Healing Gardens are green spaces designed to improve the well-being of a general population, and Therapeutic Landscapes are intended to meet the needs of specific groups. *Sensory*

Gardens, Learning Gardens, and *Gardens for Solace and Comfort* are examples of the latter.[4, 5] Being designed by Nature and fashioned by humans, Healing Nature Trails can potentially meet a wide variety of needs.

The Trails' users include people on their Personal Journeys of Healing or Self-Discovery. Many come for Walking and Sitting Meditation. Therapists and certified Healing Nature Guides bring their clients, and others come to deepen their relationship with the natural realm. The next chapter expands on this theme.

When *walk* is used in relation to Healing Nature Trails, it is capitalized because it is a special kind of walking. It is not a process, but an experience, done with consciousness and intention. There is no need to do anything; it's all designed into the Trail. Nature, like all mothers, has an intuitive sense for what we need. All she asks is that we listen.

The name *Healing Nature* is a double entendre: we come to Nature for healing, and at the same time we help Nature heal. Native Elders from many cultures affirm that giving is receiving, which means that in order to open the channels for receiving, we must first be willing to give. This is the premise behind Healing Nature Trails being dedicated to healing Nature as well as us.

If only one term could be used to describe Healing Nature Trails, it would be *sanctuary*. Most Trails are located in parks, preserves, restoration areas, or private holdings that are set aside for the protection of native habitat and the welfare of its indigenous plants and animals. Along with that, the effort provides refuge and respite for us humans. When we help Nature heal, she has more strength and integrity for providing safe haven and sharing her healing gifts with us.

The sublime and sheltered feeling that drifts over people on Healing Nature Trails is conveyed in the enchanting song "Sanctuary" by Donna De Lory (from her album *Sanctuary*). She has graciously consented to let us adopt it as a Trail theme song.

Foundational Philosophy

The Healing Nature Trail concept is based on the philosophy of *Emergence*, which can be summed up in one phrase: the whole is greater than the sum of its parts. Since the time of Aristotle, scientists and philosophers have been exploring and developing Emergence theory. (The Healing Nature Trail founders were most inspired by University of Michigan professor of psychology John Henry Holland.[6])

Emergence principles have been applied to the social sciences, the humanities, economics, religion, and many of the hard sciences. Of most application to the Healing Nature Trail is Emergence Biology, where molecular components coalesce into life-forms, and Emergence Psychology, where woundedness and confusion lead to clarity and healing.

The Healing Nature Trail founders turned the Emergence approach on itself, by merging its offspring: Emergence Philosophy, Biology, and Psychology, into what might be called *Emergence Nature Healing.* The offspring—represented in plant pheromones, ion-charged air, Trail geometry, landform features, Conscious Breathing, Barefoot Walking, the elemental forces of Fire and Water, the Labyrinthine mind, and the voices of Nature—were all combined to form a whole greater than the sum of its parts: the Healing Nature Trail experience.

Healing Nature Trail Features

The four cornerstones of all Healing Nature Trails are that they be:

1. aesthetically appealing;
2. free of noise and distraction;
3. easy to navigate; and
4. designed to provide a sense of safety.

Each Trail offers a variety of topographical features, to provide the varied metaphors needed for the Healing Journey. In addition, special features have been incorporated into the Trails to act as catalysts for the healing process. These features typically include:

- A Gateway Labyrinth, for unwinding and centering before Walking the Trail (see chapter 18).
- A ritual cleansing, with incense, essential oil, or water (see chapter 19).
- A place for symbolic offerings, such as a Cairn, well, or a place to tie them (see chapter 31).
- An entrance threshold, which could be a bridge, arched gate, or transition zone between diverse habitat types (see chapter 19).
- A pathway suitable for Barefoot Walking (see chapter 8).
- Unexpected turns, forks, and changes in elevation (see chapter 20).
- A free-form maze (see chapter 23).
- Portable Finger Labyrinths (see chapter 9).
- Alcoves for private reflection (see chapter 22).
- Trailside Benches, nestled between boulders or Elder Trees, or adjacent to Water (see chapter 8).
- Group meeting areas (see chapter 22).
- Accommodations for the physically and mentally challenged (see chapter 25).
- A nook for reflection at Trail's end, preferably with a fire pit (see chapter 24).

Some Trails have special features, such as Japanese-style Zen Gardens, cabins for private retreats, Tree canopy experiences, and decks for evening wandering through the cosmic Labyrinth.

Trails do not typically allow Dogs or other pets, out of concern for the safety of Trail Walkers and the equanimity of the Trail environment. Additionally, the scent of Dogs tends to keep wild animals at bay.

All Trails that bear the registered name *Healing Nature Trail* are certified to use the name by the Healing Nature Center of

Wisconsin (www.healingnaturecenter.org), which is the parent organization. To qualify for certification, trails and their sponsoring organizations must meet established standards for responsible administration, environmental stewardship, site suitability, Trail design, and safety. For more on this topic, please see chapter 33, *Trail Certification.*

A Place for Ceremony

Imagine the enchantment of a wedding centered around a Labyrinth. Bride and groom walk the Labyrinth to the center, with the wedding party and guests following. The couple exchange vows in the center of the Labyrinth, with those in attendance witnessing the ceremony while standing in concentric circles on the Labyrinthine Path around the couple.

Another option has walking a part of the Trail as the wedding procession, with the exchange of vows taking place in the couple's favorite reflective nook, grove of Trees, or Wildflower Meadow.

On the original Healing Nature Trail in Wisconsin, the Cosmorinth (see chapters 18 and 31), with its log spiral staircase and breathtaking overview of the Labyrinth, provides a ceremonial site that is both moving and deeply symbolic. Picture an evening wedding on the Cosmorinth, with a warm, pastel sunset opening the ceremony and the spangled grandeur of the boundless galaxy witnessing the exchange of vows.

Reunions, anniversaries, green funerals, and other rites of passage are additional possibilities.

CHAPTER FOUR

Why People Come

When nineteenth-century naturalist John Burroughs was asked what drew him to Nature, he replied, "I come here to find myself; it is so easy to get lost in the world."[1] Trail Walkers give a similar answer when asked what brings them to the Trail. More specifically, here are the six reasons most often given:

- Touch
- Healing
- Sanctuary
- Reflection
- Self-Discovery
- Relationship with Nature

Finding common ground with others can help us better know ourselves and find support for our Life Journeys. The better healthcare practitioners and Trail Guides understand their clients, the better these professionals can address their clients' needs.

Two other groups that benefit from understanding what motivates people are Trail designers and staff. Designers can use the information to create Trail features that meet the needs and match the skill levels of prospective Trail users. Staff utilize the information to help them reach the people who could benefit from the Trail (see chapter 32 for more on outreach).

To gain the information needed to accomplish all of those ends, let's take an in-depth look at the six main reasons why people are drawn to the Healing Nature Trail experience.

Touch

"To touch the Earth" is one of the core reasons many people give for coming to spend time on a Healing Nature Trail. Nearly everyone knows how important touch is in early childhood development, and for maintaining physical and psycho-emotional health throughout life. Yet many don't realize how pervasive lack of touch is in American culture. Three out of four adults affirm that we suffer from what is also known as *skin hunger*.[2]

Begin now to be what you will be hereafter, said St. Jerome.[3] The effect of touch is immediate, and its impression is long-lasting. As the most elemental of our senses, it is the most critical to our well-being. Lack of touch can lead to depression, reduced immune function, increased cardiovascular stresses, and more.[4] Because of our isolation from Nature, many people are not aware of the fact that being touched by Nature is equally as important to our health as human touch.

Yet anyone who has walked barefoot on damp moss, held a stone warmed by the sun, wrapped your arms around a Tree, or pressed your fingers into soft, punky wood knows the intrinsic value of Nature's touch. Being kissed on the face by wind and rain and getting brushed by Fern fronds and overhanging branches are some of the nurturing ways Mother Nature reaches out to touch us. In Part II of this book, we further explore Nature's touch.

Healing

"Nothing can befall me in life—no disgrace, no calamity ... which nature cannot repair," said Ralph Waldo Emerson.[5] Some people who Walk the Trail are dealing with major health issues, such as cancer, stroke, or the effects of a debilitating accident. Others struggle with depression or relationship issues, and still others have been battered, physically or emotionally. Many of them are traumatized.

They may have heard that they could heal up to one-third faster if they spent some time in Nature (see chapter 5). Or they might know that Conscious Breathing in Nature (see chapter 7), Barefoot Walking (see chapter 8), and Forest Aromatherapy (see chapter 11) act as healing catalysts. Then there are some who simply feel an intuitive draw, as though they were responding to a primal calling.

And there are some who are generally skeptical of alternative healing approaches and modalities. Yet they show an intrinsic trust in Nature.

On the other extreme are those who come not in trust, but out of desperation. They've tried everything else, and nothing has worked. Nature is their last resort.

Whatever the case, there is magic afoot. With no referral needed, no forms to fill out, no pills to take, and no copayments, all they have to do is step onto the Trail, and the healing alchemy begins. They often express how that simple physical act alone helps them feel empowered—sometimes for the first time on their Healing Journeys. They have taken personal responsibility, and they are exercising it by coming to the primal source of all life and wellness—Mother Nature.

They describe how the Trail features that you are going to read about in the next chapters have transformed them: walking the Gateway Labyrinth has brought calm and centeredness, crossing the Threshold Bridge has helped them leave stress and trouble behind, viewing panoramic vistas has opened them to new possibilities, sitting in a grove of Elder Pines has relaxed their feelings of abandonment, Conscious Breathing has reintegrated them with life, walking the Zen Untangle has released pent-up feelings, Grounding has faded the pall of depression, and tending the Zen Garden has shredded the stories that have kept them oppressed.

(See chapter 17 for more on why people come to experience the Trail's intrinsic healing power.)

Sanctuary

The first thing deeply wounded people often need is a sense of safety—a place where they can relax their self-protective boundaries and allow themselves to be who and how they are. Once they can breathe easy, they can regain the wherewithal to trust again in themselves. The next step is to renew trust in their surroundings, and many of them find encouragement to do so in the Cradle of Nature that the Trail provides.

They know that Healing Nature Trails are havens reserved exclusively for people like them who need shelter from the storm of life's travails. They feel protected by the fact that registration is required for using the Trail, and that only a certain number of people are allowed on the Trail at any one time.

With the sense of well-being that the Trail experience instills, some people walk away with uplifted spirits and a new lease on life.

Reflection and Self-Discovery

There are those who just need a place to go from time to time where they can quiet the mind and listen. They are looking for solace—a quiet island in the rolling sea of life. They want to unwind and have some personal space, free of distraction or interruption, in a supportive environment. To make her point, one Trail user quoted Henry David Thoreau: "I have an immense appetite for solitude, like an infant for sleep, and if I don't get enough for this year, I shall cry all the next."[6]

Others have hit a dead end in life. They are lost, and troubled, and they need support, direction, and answers. A few others state that they are on a noble quest—they want to find the essence of all philosophies, all guidance, all voices, and they think Nature might hold that nugget.

One option for the reflective space they all seek is to reserve one of the tucked-away nooks along a Trail for a half-day or day-long retreat. Others spend an hour or two in Sitting Meditation, or a Walking Meditation. Some Trails have facilities where rooms or hermitages are available for private retreats. Whatever the arrangement, people appreciate the quiet and privacy that is engendered by the Trails' dedicated purpose.

They say they are grateful because when outside voices are quieted, inner voices can be heard, along with Nature's gentle guidance. The wisdom of the Ancient Ones comes forth in the whispers of the Trees and the murmurs of the Waters. The plants share their healing ways, and the animals show how to Walk in Balance.

For these people, the Trail could be called the *Forest Reflection Trail,* which is a double entendre in the sense that the Forest provides a place for reflection as well as the Forest being a reflection of themselves.

Relationship with Nature

"The goal of life," says mythologist Joseph Campbell, "is to make your heartbeat match the beat of the universe, to match your nature with Nature."[7] Quite a number of people come to the Trails for that express purpose, which they often express as a desire to renew or deepen their connection with Nature. "I don't know where the yearning comes from," said one Trail user. "It just seems to be innate."

That yearning to commune with Nature draws people for many and diverse reasons. Imagine an outdoor wedding, such as those described in the previous chapter under *A Place for Ceremony,* or a focus group/business team sitting on split-log benches arranged in a circle under towering ancient Pines. Imagine families reuniting and friends meeting at the Trail for a Walk together.

Another group of Trail users have a relationship history with Nature. Most of them see their relationship rooted in one of these sets of experiences:

1. Youth Programs

Historically, Nature-connection programs in the United States have been geared primarily toward enriching childhood development through outdoor experience. These programs, most notably the Boy Scouts and Camp Fire Girls, made their appearance in 1910, with the Girl Scouts following two years later. Nature-based summer camps followed in their footsteps. More recently, preschool and primary school programs have been developed that center on Nature observation and unstructured outdoor play.[8, 9]

2. At-Risk Programs

In the 1950s, wilderness-immersion programs for at-risk youth first made their appearance. Due to their success, they have proliferated to the point where programs can now be found across the United States, Canada, and Europe. Both staff and participants in such programs have become Trail users.

3. Environmental Groups

With the dawn of the environmental movement in the late 1960s, many adult-oriented organizations, such as the National Audubon Society (founded in 1905) and National Wildlife Federation (founded in 1936), gained prominence.[10] In recent decades, activist groups such as Defenders of Wildlife and Greenpeace, and preservationist groups such as The Nature Conservancy and land trusts, have joined the traditional organizations on center stage.

4. Nature-Based Professions

With the increased attention on outdoor recreation, conservation, and environmental crises over the past forty years, careers in the natural sciences have become viable options for increasing numbers of people,[11] which is reflected in the high number of Trail users and staff with such backgrounds.

5. Outdoor Recreation

Add to the above the growing popularity of camping, back-packing, ecotourism, national parks, resort areas, and regional Nature centers,[12] and it's not hard to see where another large group of Trail users originate.

One of the intrinsic beauties of the Healing Nature Trail experience is that whatever the reason people state for coming, and whatever the involvement of staff, designers, or developers, everyone benefits from Nature's healing touch.

CHAPTER FIVE

The Healing Power of Nature Immersion

Eighteenth-century French philosopher Voltaire said that the art of medicine consists in amusing the patient while Nature cures the disease.[1] As evidenced here, Voltaire was known as a humorist as well. Yet the gist of his quip is ringing more and more true in contemporary times with the advent of Healing Nature Trails and similar practices. Nature reconnection for overall medical and psychological health is now being addressed on both a therapeutic and visceral level for people of all ages. This chapter highlights the science behind the design features of Trails that support and catalyze the Awakening-healing-reconnecting experience.

Studies are currently being conducted in several countries around the world to evaluate the benefits of people spending time in Nature. The International Society of Nature and Forest Medicine (INFOM) is documenting these studies, compiling research, and helping to assure that future research meets scientific and medical standards of study.

In addition, INFOM is:

 ▶ Collaborating with the International Union of Forest Research Organizations (IUFRO) and related academic institutions to further the study of Forest and Nature medicine.

 ▶ Collecting and editing documents on the topic of Forests and human health.

⬧ Providing a platform for enterprises, universities, and governments involved in Nature and Forest medicine, for promoting the effective uses of Forest resources for stress management, health promotion, disease prevention, and rehabilitation.[2]

Following is a category-by-category synopsis of Nature's major contributions to human well-being, as can be gained by the Healing Nature Trail experience.

Preventative Medicine

Benjamin Franklin said that an ounce of prevention is worth a pound of cure.[3,4] In this sense, the best medicine may often be no medicine per se, but rather gaining a level of overall health and well-being that resists infection and disease.

Reconnecting with the natural world has the power to bring both our physical and psycho-emotional systems back into balance. A system as complex as Nature regulates the equilibrium of each of the organisms within her realm far better than we can comprehend, much less replicate.

When we engage all of our senses simultaneously to attune to the sights, sounds, smells, and tactile sensations of a natural environment, our bodies and minds are therapeutically adjusted and brought back into balance. Our primal senses are innately attuned to the natural realm, which gives us intimate knowledge of that world. This provides comfort and assures our safety by alerting us of danger.

Knowing intuitively that we can rely upon our sensory input helps us to remain in a state of calm. We then have the energy, wherewithal, and stable baseline for strengthening our immune systems and psycho-emotional resilience. This occurs spontaneously—we only need to be present and receptive.

Regular exposure to Nature's energies, in particular full-spectrum sunlight, regulates our body's activity-rest cycle.[5] We are then more likely to get quality and timely rest and exercise, which may be the most valuable preventative medicine prescription.

A Healing Balm for Stress

With our fast-paced modern lifestyle, many of us are vulnerable to the effects of low-grade chronic stress. As a result, we risk overexposure to the stress hormones cortisol, adrenaline, and noradrenaline. The resulting ailments include anxiety, depression, heart disease, weight gain, and memory/concentration impairment.[6]

As a counterpoint, exposure to Nature stimulates the parasympathetic nervous system, which allows our minds and bodies to relax. Randomized studies conducted in Japan on people following a walk in the Forest revealed the following:

- The average concentration of salivary/urinary cortisol was reduced, as were concentrations of adrenaline and noradrenaline.[7]
- Parasympathetic nervous activity was enhanced by 56 percent on average, which indicates a state of relaxation.[8]
- Just gazing upon Forest scenery for twenty minutes reduced concentrations of salivary cortisol to 13.4 percent under that of people in urban settings.[9]
- Similar results were found when comparing those taking walks in natural settings with those walking in urban settings.[10]
- Exposure to phytoncides (antimicrobial organic compounds released by plants), which are components of Forest air, significantly decreased concentrations of adrenaline and noradrenaline (for more on this, see chapter 11, *Primal Aromatherapy*).[11]

More Brainpower

Apple co-founder Steve Jobs had a reputation for conducting walking meetings. Facebook's Mark Zuckerberg is also known to hold meetings on foot. And you as well may have paced back and forth when you needed some inspiration.[12] If you prefer to think on your feet, research conducted in 2014 at Stanford University shows why you are in good company: A person's creative output and the free flow of ideas increase by an average of 60 percent when walking. Furthermore, the researchers found that those who walked in Nature were able to generate twice as many creative responses as those seated inside.

Here we see the benefits of utilizing Nature immersion along with the body-mind connection (see chapter 20 for more on this) to accelerate healing and Awakening. The ability to integrate what is gained is increased as well, as creative juices continue to flow for a period after an outdoor walk.[13]

A Calming Chorus

Noise pollution, especially in urban environments, is a major contributor to stress. Noises over 60 decibels can increase the risk for cardiovascular diseases, and a car can emit a noise level of 70 decibels. Imagine the cumulative effect of city traffic, along with the myriad noises from other sources. Such a constant barrage of noise triggers a stress response, which releases a flood of hormones that can ultimately damage the heart. People with diabetes or high blood pressure are particularly vulnerable.[14] The World Health Organization states that "noise is an underestimated threat that can cause a number of short- and long-term health problems," such as sleep disturbance, various cardiovascular conditions, poor work and school performance, hearing impairment, and more.[15]

The sounds of Nature, on the other hand, create a calming chorus. Professor Josh Smyth of Penn State University studies the calming effects of Nature sounds on human heart rates and hormones. He recommends a twenty-minute daily immersion in Nature's choral performance. When it's difficult to get outside, Professor Smyth suggests listening to recordings of birdsongs, wind, or waves.[16]

Immunity Boosting

Lymphocytes, commonly known as *natural killer* (NK) cells, defend us against tumors and viruses. Several studies indicate that time in Nature increases NK cell activity, along with increasing levels of intracellular anti-cancer proteins. Here is a summation of the study results:

▶ A 2007 study found that men taking two-hour walks in the Forest over a two-day period had a 50 percent increase in NK cell levels.[17]

▶ In 2008, a study of thirteen female nurses on a three-day Nature excursion showed an increased level of anti-cancer proteins that lasted more than seven days after the trip.[18]

▶ NK cell activity was enhanced by 56 percent on the second day of the nurses' excursion. After returning to urban life, NK cell activity remained enhanced 23 percent.[19]

▶ Another study showed higher levels of NK cell activity, along with a decrease in stress hormones, for test subjects visiting a Forest, as opposed to those visiting a city. With both male and female subjects who visited the Forest, the increased NK cell activity lasted more than thirty days.[20]

Faster Healing

A recent study revealed that exposure to Nature—even if it's just a view from a window— accelerated recovery from surgery or illness.[21] Another study using a matched comparison control design found that, compared to surgical patients with rooms facing brick walls, surgical patients whose rooms had windows overlooking natural landscapes had:

▶ Shorter postoperative hospital stays.

▶ Fewer negative evaluations by nurses.

▶ Less need for potent painkillers. [22]

Complements to Pharmaceuticals

The side effects of prescription medications, along with their high cost, limited availability to many people, and environmental concerns around their disposal, make many wish there were other options.

Fortunately, there is a nontoxic, environmentally safe, and often low-cost alternative that is potentially available to everybody. Phytoncides such as alpha-pinene and limonene are volatile oils produced by Trees and released into the atmosphere. Several studies made over the last decade have shown these oils to have beneficial effects on humans. The studies compared people walking in Forest environments with people taking urban walks. Here are the relative effects on the Forest contingent:

- A 12.4 percent decrease in the stress hormone cortisol after viewing the Forest, and a 15.8 percent decrease after walking in the Forest.[23, 24]
- A 7 percent decrease in sympathetic nerve activity.[25]
- Significantly lower blood pressure (systolic and diastolic).[26]
- Increased heart rate variability, indicating that the circulatory system can respond well to both stress and the calming parasympathetic nervous system.[27]
- Significantly decreased pulse rate.[28]
- Decreased blood glucose levels in diabetic patients following a three-to-six-kilometer Forest walk.[29]

Another way that time in Nature reduces reliance on pharmaceuticals is the lowered risk of certain types of cancer due to increased levels of vitamin D from exposure to the sun's rays.[30] Still another of Nature's drug alternatives might be exposure to *Mycobacterium vaccae,* a ground-dwelling bacteria that shows promise in helping those with autoimmune disorders such as Crohn's disease and rheumatoid arthritis.[31] We can expose ourselves to beneficial earthen bacteria by walking barefoot or sitting on the ground (see chapter 8).

PRESCRIPTION: NATURE

Pediatrician Dr. Robert Zarr of Washington, DC, is considered the US pioneer in the Nature Prescription Movement. His Park RX Program, started in 2013, is supported by multiple government agencies. He has written prescriptions "to get outside and play" for hundreds of young people suffering from asthma, obesity, ADHD, and depression.[32]

Mood Enhancement and Relief from Depression

There is a deep and intrinsic truth embedded in these words spoken by Holocaust victim Anne Frank: "The best remedy for those who are afraid, lonely, or unhappy is to go outside, somewhere where they can be quite alone with the heavens, nature, and God. Because only then does one feel that all is as it should be and that God wishes to see people happy amidst the simple beauty of nature.... . I firmly believe that nature brings solace in all troubles."[33]

One of the primary reasons that Nature offers a comforting balm is her negative ion–charged atmosphere. The air in natural environments is kept clean and fresh by negative ions. They are statically attracted to airborne mold spores, pollutants, dust, viruses, and bacteria, which gives them a negative charge and causes them to settle to the ground or attach to a nearby surface.[34]

Refreshing, negative ion–laced air is a mood lifter.[35] Negative ions are generated by Trees and moving water,[36] which is one reason why we feel so good near Rapids and Waterfalls, at the beach with its rolling waves, and in the Forest. It's the same reason so many people feel invigorated when breathing the fresh air after a Thunderstorm.[37]

The University of Pennsylvania's Positive Psychology Center, Stanford University, and Chiba University's Center for Environment, Health and Field Services studied the psycho-emotional effects a walk in the Forest had upon people, and here are their observations:

▶ Significantly less negative moods.

▶ Increased energy levels.

▶ Enhanced feelings of health and robustness.

▶ Decreased fatigue, anxiety, and confusion.

▶ Increased levels of joy.

▶ Reduced psychological stress.

▶ Decreased symptoms of depression.

▶ Diminished hostility.

▶ Less overthinking and negative self-talk.

▶ Considerably higher incidence of positive emotions.[38]

GET DIRTY, FEEL GOOD

Mycobacterium vaccae is a soil bacteria that causes our cytokine (a protein that helps cells interact) levels to rise, which elevates our serotonin (a neurotransmitter hormone) levels, making us happier and more relaxed. Exposure to the bacteria has been found to increase cognitive and concentration abilities of laboratory rats. These soil microbes may also serve a potential role in the treatment of autoimmune diseases such as Crohn's disease and rheumatoid arthritis.[39] (For more on the benefits of getting dirty, see chapter 8, Grounding in Nature.)

Better Sleep

Natural, full-spectrum light helps reset our diurnal rhythm regulator, which improves sleep and lessens symptoms of depression. Studies found that two hours of Forest Walking had the following effects on those experiencing nocturnal sleep issues:

▶ Lengthened sleep time.

▶ Increased immobile minutes of sleep.

- Self-rated improved depth of sleep.
- Overall better sleep quality.

The study found that afternoon Forest Walks were more effective than those taken in the morning.[40]

Improved Relationships, Empathy, and Sense of Awe

Awe is the sense of wonder we feel in the presence of something far greater than we can grasp.[41] A study of the awe experienced by astronauts viewing Earth from space points to how both perceptual vastness (the microscopic view of a drop of Pond water) and conceptual vastness (our place in the Cosmos) can inspire awe in humans.[42] Experiencing the sights, sounds, and smells of Nature can arouse similar feelings. "Nature inspires awe in doses both large and small,"[43], says Paul Piff, a psychologist at the University of California. Feeling a sense of awe, he says, "causes people to want to share their positive experiences collectively with one another,"[44] thus nurturing relationships.

The Benefits of Awe:

- Deepened friendships.
- Diminished focus on the self.
- Heightened sense of joy and well-being.
- Increased flow of life energy.
- Broadened social contexts.
- Enhanced collective consciousness.
- Decreased feelings of entitlement.
- Increased ethical considerations.
- More displays of generosity.
- Greater feelings of compassion and empathy.[45]
- Higher levels of feeling fulfilled.[46]

Studies show the positive influence of Nature immersion on social bonding and neighborly ties.[47] People living near green space, which is defined as an open area where people can gather without cost or discrimination, expressed feeling less lonely than those lacking green spaces in which to spend time. The percentage of green space in people's living environments has a direct relationship to perceived general health.[48]

WE BECOME WHAT WE SURROUND OURSELVES WITH

Merely being in Nature helps to rewire our neural synapses for greater compassion and less self-absorbedness. We are surrounded by spontaneity and continual adaptation to ever-changing conditions, which challenge our modus operandi of habit and pattern-based lives. In this way, we are supported in establishing wellness and relationship-nurturing thought patterns.

Enhanced Focus, Creativity, and Memory

We tend to think of memory, creativity, and attention span as mental processes. It turns out that this is only partially true. Actually, we perform better in all three areas when we approach them from an integrative body–mind perspective.

Indigenous people exhibit skills of perception and ingenuity that can baffle many of us Westerners. Aleut Elder Larry Merculieff explains why: "The intelligence of a real human being comes from the entire body where we use all of our senses, all of the time.... When we don't think, then it seems like the senses of the body come alive in a way that most people living today who are in the mind don't understand, but it's a way our people would connect with all of creation."[49]

We find this awareness manifest in the exploratory play of children, which is especially dynamic when it occurs outdoors in Nature. As a body–mind exercise, free-form play establishes critical neural pathways and develops core motor skills. Several studies of the effects of three to four days of Nature immersion, with a corresponding disconnection from media and technology, showed a 50 percent increase in the areas of creative expression and problem-solving.[50]

Healing Nature Trails are designed to encourage development of the body-mind connection. The unstructured nature of a Trail Walk further enhances the development of whole-being function.

Research shows that regular integrative experiences with Nature result in:

▶ A significant increase in memory span.

▶ Deeper and clearer intuitive expression.

▶ Increased creative performance.

▶ A greater ability to communicate with animals, plants, and natural habitats.★

▶ A restored attention-holding ability.[51]

★For more on this topic, see *Becoming Nature* by Tamarack Song.

Help for Autism, Schizophrenia, and Alzheimer's

An exciting area of new research involves the role Healing Nature Trails and other outdoor-immersion experiences may be able to play in the prevention and treatment of brain-related conditions such as autism, schizophrenia, and Alzheimer's. Acknowledgment of the pivotal role the body-mind-Nature connection plays in our well-being opens up new avenues for exploration and development.

Immersion in Nature has been shown to enhance our ability to tap into the brain's limbic processes, which are known to be disrupted in schizophrenia, autism, Alzheimer's disease, and perhaps other associated conditions and diseases. Further study into how limbic function correlates with such disorders is just beginning,[52] and it presents a new and expansive frontier of possibilities.

CHAPTER SIX

A Note to Mental and Physical
Health Practitioners

A disorder caused by a deficiency of vitamin N (for *Nature*) has reached epidemic proportions. This year, nearly half of the US population, around 150 million people, will not partake in outdoor recreation.[1] And it's getting worse—it's falling at the rate of around 1 percent per year.[2] Recent research shows that involvement in outdoor activities peaked a generation ago, after steadily increasing for more than fifty years.[3] The decline started in the 1980s,[4] and there is no end in sight.[5]

Along with those trends, there has been a corresponding increase in obesity, diabetes,[6] cardiovascular disease, depression,[7] and other stress-related conditions. At this point, we can only speculate on the correlation between the two trends.

Yet much is known about the health benefits afforded by Nature:

▶ Faster and more complete recovery from injuries.[8]

▶ Low levels of vitamin D, which afflict many people, increase with sun exposure.[9]

▶ As little as fifteen minutes per day outdoors strengthens immune systems and improves outlook.[10]

▶ Outdoor activities improve focus, encourage creativity, and boost energy levels (as covered in chapter 2).

According to many health professionals, fifteen to twenty minutes of outdoor time each day, doing whatever satisfies your soul, goes a long way toward improving overall physical and mental health. Please encourage your clients/patients to spend more time outdoors.

And if there is a Healing Nature Trail near you, please contact the director to find out how you can utilize the Trail to augment your healing approach.

THE CONSUMMATE HEALER

Nature has one guiding principle: function. When immersed in a natural environment for an hour or more, most distressed people come to at least the vague realization that Nature provides neither tolerance nor support for relational dysfunction, denial, or forms of externalizing such as blame and criticism. Nature would grind to a painful halt if all of her children were not fully and functionally engaged in their lives. Anything out of balance sticks out like a sore thumb, which is a blessing for those of us who come to Nature for healing. Some therapists do little more than accompany their clients on a Trail Walk, and they let Nature do the rest.

How the Trail Experience Contributes to Other Therapeutic Approaches

The Healing Nature Trail concept is based on mental mechanics and processes, as presented by current neurobiological research. Going under various names, such as the *Relational Neuroscience Model*, the *Dual Attunement Model,* and the *Interpersonal Neurobiology Model,*[11] the approach employs Nature's healing powers as a catalyst for fundamental change through awareness-raising and neural reprogramming.

This is orchestrated for clients by their therapist or Guide (or by Nature herself, which the therapist/Guide represents) entering into direct relationship with the client's core neuro-somatic sources of confusion, pain, trauma memories, or dissociation, rather than addressing the client's resultant behavioral patterns. The relationship fosters a sense of innate support, trust, and nurturing presence in clients, which relaxes the self-protective boundaries that create the denial, suppression, and numbing that they established to survive and function. A doorway then opens to the deeper self, where essential Awakening and fundamental healing occurs.

With the Healing Nature Trail both implementing and supporting this process, the Trail experience can be used as a therapeutic modality in and of itself, or it can be used as an adjunct to other approaches.

Mind-Openers: SRT and SRM

We are accustomed to stereoscopic vision and hearing, which we rely upon to navigate. If we could see out of only one eye, we would lose depth perception; or if we could only hear with one ear, we could not determine the directional source of a sound. Our orienteering abilities would be compromised, perhaps severely. To compensate, we would have to make adjustments by being more consciously engaged in normally routine and intuitive procedures, and by relying more on our other senses.

Our mental processes work in the same way: we become accustomed to the thought patterns and behavioral habits we have developed over time. Sometimes they serve us well; yet at other times they keep us entrenched in outmoded—and even hurtful—decision-making patterns and behavioral dynamics.

Knowing how this process works, and knowing the strength of the body-mind connection, we can manipulate our senses in order to breach the established protocols of our psyches. The resulting disorientation gives us the opportunity to step in where convention once ruled and become consciously engaged in transforming our mental processes. Knee-jerk behaviors, crippling coping mechanisms, and outmoded boundaries then become grist for the mill. This is called the **Sensory Reduction Technique** (SRT), which was developed by Healing Nature Trail cofounder Tamarack Song for use on Healing Nature Trails and in other natural settings. SRT is similar to the *Ganzfeld Technique* and *Sensory Deprivation*, all of which fall under the general category that is known in research as *Restricted Environmental Stimulation Therapy* (REST).[12]

Here are the demonstrated health benefits of REST:

❱ Stress reduction[13, 14]

❱ Pain reduction[15, 16]

❱ Decrease in anxiety[17]

❱ Reduction in smoking[18, 19]

❱ Treatment for headaches[20]

❱ Opening to new ideas, perceptions, or insights[21]

SRT may be viewed as a Nature-based form of REST. The Healing Nature Trail is designed to actuate SRT by disrupting conventional sensory—and thus cognitive—patterns, in these ways:

❱ Abrupt turns, T-intersections, panoramic vistas, changes in elevation, and transitions from one habitat type to another (such as Forest to Marshland).

❱ Artificially creating monoscopic vision and hearing with the use of eye patches and earplugs.

❱ Blindfold Trail Walking (see chapter 15).

Combinations of the above three methods can create synergistic effects that precipitate even greater opportunities for releasing or reconstructive work than any one method could alone. Because of the potential for unexpected reactions, such as the surfacing of trauma memories or the release of repressed emotions, we recommend that the combined approach be employed only under the guidance of healthcare practitioners.

Along with SRT, **Sensory Reception Modulation** (SRM) was developed by Tamarack Song for increasing sensory acuity and strengthening the body-mind connection in natural settings. SRM is practiced by methodically switching sensory impedance from one side to the other, or from one sensory organ to the other, such as:

- Block the right ear, then the left, then the right, and so on.
- Block the right eye, then the left, then the right, and so on.
- Block sight, then hearing, then sight, and so on.
- Block the right eye and ear, then the left, and so on.
- Block the right eye and left ear, then the reverse, and so on.

Modulating intervals typically range from five seconds to one minute. Experiment with your client to determine which variation works best.

Healing Nature Guides are trained in leading clients on Blindfold Trail Walks, and healthcare practitioners can take a short workshop to get trained as well. Out of concern for physical safety, anyone participating in Blindfold Trail Walking must be accompanied by a responsible partner, a Healing Nature Guide, or his/her healthcare practitioner.

Trauma Recovery in Nature

Healing Nature Trails, particularly those that are certified for trauma healing (see chapter 34), are specifically designed to act as catalysts and adjuncts for working through the haunting legacy of trauma. Along with that, the Trail experience can help manifest trauma's gifts and teachings.

Chapter 34 gives guidance on using Healing Nature Trails to work with clients in recovery from trauma. With its custom-designed features for supporting recovery, the Trail becomes a metaphor for the Trauma-Healing Journey.

When disturbing trauma memories surface during a Nature-immersion therapy session, direct physical contact with the Earth can impart a significant calming influence. (For detailed information on Grounding as a therapeutic tool, please see chapter 8.) Lush and varied sensory connections, which can include auditory, visual, tactile, and olfactory, work in harmony with Grounding to help restore stability and reduce stress. The uplifting effects of negative ions and Aromatherapy (see chapter 11) further contribute to a supportive and restorative environment for trauma work.

Tools of the Trade

Intrinsic to the Trail experience are counterparts to a number of approaches and modalities that you may already be using. By being aware of the equivalents, you can utilize them in your Trail sessions and take advantage of their synergistic effects with your tools. Here are the four most common Trail parallels:

1. **The Body-Mind Connection.** Abrupt turns and changes in Trail elevation, along with the sights, sounds, and other sensations of Nature, have effects similar to EMDR (Eye Movement Desensitization and Reprocessing), Brain Spotting, EFT (Emotional Freedom Technique), and various pressure point/meridian manipulations such as acupressure and acupuncture. Parallels to EMDR and Brain Spotting, which are based on shifting visual and auditory cues, occur spontaneously in Nature, where cues continually fluctuate in direction and intensity. A waft of breeze moves through the treetops; a Warbler sings on one perch, then flies to another and sings; a Beaver swims across a Pond; a Butterfly flits hither and yon. (For more on the body-mind connection, see chapter 20 and *The Trail as a Healing Metaphor* in chapter 34.)

2. **Direct Touch.** Grounding, the Labyrinthine experiences, Forest Aromatherapy, sunshine and wind, and negative ion bathing complement massage therapy, chiropractic, osteopathy, myofascial release, shiatsu, craniosacral release, and other hands-on therapies (more under *Touch* in chapter 4).

3. **Talk Therapy.** Naturespeak (the language common to all of Nature's creatures) and the awakening of inner voices add depth, substance, and perspective to the client-therapist dialogue.

4. **Trust and Openness.** The sheltered setting and openness-encouraging components of the Trail help clients relax and support them to be candid and expressive—prerequisites to emotional release and deep healing, regardless of setting.

On Tool Selection

Regarding the importance of setting and the use of compatible tools, there is the story of Western therapists who went to help survivors of the 1994 Rwandan genocide recover from the trauma, told by Andrew Solomon, professor of psychology at Columbia University and author of *The Noonday Demon: An Atlas of Depression* (Scribner, 2015).

He met a mental hospital worker in Kigali, the Rwandan capital, who said, "Foreign mental health workers who came here after the genocide … caused a lot of trouble … their practice didn't have any of the strengths of the ritual… . They did not identify the illness as an invasive external thing. They did not get the entire village to come together and acknowledge it together and all participate in trying to support the person who was getting treated. Treatment was not out in the bright sunshine where you feel happy. There was no music or drumming to get the heart running as the heart should run. Instead, they took people one at a time into sort of dingy little rooms for an hour at a time and asked them to talk about the bad things that had happened to them. Which, of course, just made them feel much worse, almost suicidal. We had to put a stop to it."[22]

Here we see the importance of matching the tools with the task. In the next section of this book, you'll find a thorough description of the Trail's components that are available to you as tools. You'll then be able to match the Trail tools with your methodologies. If you'd like help with this, please consult either the Healing Nature Center Director or one of the certified Trail Guides.

A Walk for Renewal

Soon after we opened the current Wisconsin Healing Nature Trail, we noticed that some counselors, massage therapists, nurses, social workers, chiropractors, and medical doctors came not with their clients or patients, but rather for their own benefit. College professors, architects, carpenters, and other professionals came as well. One MD told us about how understaffed his clinic was, and about how hard it was to get timely referrals to specialists. A psychologist and a nurse bemoaned the bureaucratic hoops they had to continually jump through. A chiropractor was saddened by how mercenary his profession was becoming.

Some of them said they came to the Trail for the stress release that quiet time in Nature afforded them. Others came to regain perspective on their careers, or to renew their sense of purpose. Still others hoped to recharge their batteries by drinking in Nature's nurturance.

At the same time, many came just to relax and bask in Nature's beauty, or to meditate. Whatever the case, Nature in all her splendor, and with all her gifts, is here for you.

PART II
HOW NATURE HEALS

"The physician treats, but nature heals," said Greek physician Hippocrates, who is known as the father of medicine. Here in the book we explore the many and wondrous ways that the plants, animals, earth, water, fire, and the very air we breathe, bring us to wellness.

CHAPTER SEVEN

The Gateway: Breathing in Nature

Breath is life—not only our life but that of our mother planet and our entire solar system. Perhaps you weren't aware of the fact that our solar system breathes. Our planet and all of her sibling celestial bodies are awash in a continuous flow of charged particles that the sun exhales. Without it, our planet would have no life.

Our sister planet Mars may once have harbored life—at least until she lost her atmosphere, her ability to breathe.

The Earth breathes in several ways:

Trade winds circle the planet in the equatorial zone, bringing moist Ocean air landward to create lush jungles.

▶ The jet stream screams high overhead at hundreds of miles per hour. It corrals air masses and directs weather systems across Land and Sea.

▶ Low pressure cells inhale while high pressure cells exhale. This continual circular breath creates the yin and yang of our weather: sun and cloud, cool and warm, wet and dry, calm and blustery.

▶ At night, warm Ocean air rises, which draws the land's cool air onto the water. By day, the reverse occurs, with the sun-heated land inhaling the Ocean's relatively cooler air. On the beach, you would experience this twenty-four-hour-long inhale-exhale as an onshore wind by day and an offshore wind by night.

It is this planetary breathing that brings nourishing carbon dioxide to the plants, which they convert to oxygen and exhale as a waste product. In turn, we animals make the plants' breath our breath by inhaling it—which to us is life-giving oxygen. We then exhale our waste product, carbon dioxide, which the plants inhale.

This is Breathing in Nature: all of Life sharing one breath.

Conscious Breathing

Breathing in Nature becomes Conscious Breathing when we realize that we do not breathe alone—we cannot breathe alone.[1, 2] "Between a human and a tree is the breath," said conservationist Margaret Bates. "We are each other's air." In a conscious breath, we come to realize that we are all related through breathing the same air—we are one interdependent family. My breath is shared with you, the other animals, the plants, the planet, and even the sun, the Cosmos, and all of its beings.[3, 4] Breath *is* life, in the grandest sense of the term.

How can we then not be respectful of our fellow beings and care for their welfare? Breathing consciously gives honor and respect to all life. We come to realize that every breath we take is a gift from Mother Earth and her children, and every exhale is an expression of gratitude for the breath given.

To breathe is to feel. We can think of how we breathe as a touch point to our feeling self. When we sigh or take a deep breath, what is our emotional state? Do we hold our breath when we are in a state of fear or anxiety? Or when we feel so good we can hardly stand it?[5]

When we breathe consciously, we find that we breathe as we believe. If our approach to life is based on scarcity and fear, our breaths tend to be short and interrupted. On the other hand, if our lives reflect abundance and trust, we likely breathe slowly and deeply.

And we breathe as we talk. In its essence, voice is breath. The more consciously we talk, the more consciously we breathe.

In the fullest sense, the practice of Conscious Breathing is the enactment of the Zen principle: *question everyone and everything that has occurred before you came along.* A fresh breath can cleanse the past and lend it new perspective. With Conscious Breathing everything is on the table, and no voice is ignored.

Breathing on the Trail

The Healing Nature Trail experience is centered on Conscious Breathing, which gives depth and dimension to nearly every Trail-related practice. Nature comes alive when we mindfully breathe with her. Sharing the same breath with the animals brings us all the closer to sharing the same language. Conscious Breathing strengthens the body-mind connection and energizes the healing process.[6] This form of breathing can take us deep into our subconscious selves and encourage what lies there to surface.[7]

All Trail Walkers are given a handout on Breathing in Nature, so that they can gain maximum benefit from their time on the Trail. The first thing Trail Guides do is give their clients instruction in Conscious Breathing. It is the basis of Primal Aromatherapy (see chapter 11), and it is an integral part of walking the Labyrinth, Grounding (see next chapter), meditation, and many of the healing modalities integrated with a Trail Walk.

As a tool to take on the Trail, Conscious Breathing can be particularly helpful to:

- Be more present.[8]
- Heighten sensory awareness.[9]
- Work through physical or mental discomfort, or reduce pain.[10, 11]
- Empower an experience or exercise.[12]

Some Healing Nature Trails offer special programs, such as Tree-climbing Canopy Meditations and Full Immersion Groundings (see next chapter), where Conscious Breathing is an important component. Many Trail users also appreciate learning Conscious

Breathing because it is a practice they can take home with them to enrich their lives in general.

Finding Nature's Breath

Conscious Breathing as it is practiced and taught on Healing Nature Trails traces its origins back to what the Trail System's cofounder, Tamarack Song, learned from the practices of indigenous cultures, and directly from Nature. In his words:

"I first became aware of breathing rhythms when I was a child watching wild animals. Often the only movement I could detect from them was their breathing. When a Dove was frightened by a Hawk passing overhead, she would huff, then momentarily hold her breath. A Fox slowly stalking up on a Pheasant would freeze, and his breathing would become slow, shallow, and spaced as accurately as if guided by a metronome. Wanting to remain invisible, a frightened Rabbit would crouch in the grass, yet his twitching nose and vibrating sides caused by his rapid breathing could be detected by a sharp eye.

"Over time, I learned to read animals' breathing to the point where it often told me what they were feeling, thinking, and doing. The ability helped me integrate into the Wolf pack I lived with for several years when I was a young adult. Wolves, who are social beings like us, have complex personalities. I had to learn their often-silent language, which was based on nuances of facial expression, posture, tail/ruff positioning, and variances in breathing. Whoofs, pants, quick exhales, and short, sharp inhales each had their own meanings, which were elaborated upon by the way they were executed.

"Shortly after I left the pack, I was taught more about Conscious Breathing by the Ojibwe, Menominee, Hopi, Blackfoot, Iroquois, and Lakota Elders with whom I apprenticed. I learned the benefits of breathing through the nose by holding mouthfuls of water for extended periods of time while doing other activities.

54

"The most demanding—and rewarding—lesson came from having to run with a mouthful of water. In order to maintain the blood oxygen level I needed to keep me going, I had no choice but to make every breath count as much as possible. It's hard to pant through your nose, especially for any period of time, so I had to slow my inhale and breathe deeply, to completely and fully fill my lungs. Then I had to exhale completely, to make room for the next full breath. I found that as my technique improved, I slowed my breathing even more, as it kept me better oxygenated than did short, partial inhales.

"In time, I naturally fell into a rhythm where I took full, deep inhales, all the way down to the bottom of my lungs, which were followed by full and complete exhales.

"I also learned breathing techniques associated with the Sweat Lodge Ceremony, which is a sacred steam bath used for body-mind-spirit revitalizing and healing. The Ceremony runs some parallels with traditional Scandinavian saunas and Turkish steam baths. Here is some of what I learned:

▶ If it gets uncomfortably hot, keep breathing slow, deep, and steady, through your nose. Do not hyperventilate.

▶ If the hot air irritates your throat, cup your hands and breathe through them.

▶ If you get lightheaded, put your head down between your knees and keep up slow-and-steady Conscious Breathing.

▶ When the ceremony concludes, remain seated for a time and keep breathing consciously, until your blood pressure normalizes and you're sure you will not faint when standing up.

"From this phase of my training, I came to realize what a potent role Conscious Breathing could play in centering, stress release, trauma healing, and metabolic stabilizing.

"Makwa Giizis, the Ojibwe Elder who guided me on my Vision Quest (a rite of passage into adulthood where one fasts alone in the wilderness to find one's life's direction), showed me how to breathe with Trees. 'Go to the Elder Tree who calls for you,' he would say. 'Wrap your arms around her. Hug her close and feel her heartbeat. Breathe into her bark, and she will breathe with you.'

"'What did she tell you?' he would ask when I came back.

"When I had nothing much to say, he would encourage me to 'Go back and breathe with her. Then listen.'

"From there, I came to feel the heartbeat of the Forest, and I started to breathe spontaneously in sync with its pulse. Thanks to my childhood training in animal observation, I came to realize that all the other creatures were doing the same as me. Like clouds parting from the sun, it dawned on me one day that we all shared the same breath! Even more so, I realized that breath wasn't just giving me life; breath *was* life.

"That awareness sent me into a trance, from which I never fully returned. I go to the Forest and breathe, and before long, I have lost myself to the sway of the Trees, the calls of Birds, and the flicker of Butterflies' wings. But really, I have not lost myself— they have found me."

You'll find training for Conscious Breathing later in this chapter.

Breath for Healing

Just as *Healing Nature* is a double entendre (we help Nature heal as she helps us heal), so is *Breathing in Nature*: we inhale Nature's healing essences while we are immersed in Nature.[13] More than 2,500 years ago, the Buddha elaborated on this double meaning for *Breathing in Nature* when he said, "There is a most wonderful way to help overcome directly grief and sorrow, end pain and anxiety. One remains established in the observation of the feelings of the body and of the mind by going to the Forest, to the foot of a tree, sitting down and holding one's body straight, and establishing mindfulness. By breathing in, one is aware of breathing in. Breathing out, one is aware of breathing out. Breathing in, I am aware of my whole body. Breathing out, I am aware of my whole body. Breathing in, I calm the activities of my body. Breathing out, I calm the activities of my body."[14]

Conscious Breathing in Nature may be the most accessible and easy-to-use healing modality.[15] Our breath is always with us, we are always using it, and we can channel it for an intended purpose at any time.[16] A Tree to breathe under, as the Buddha and Makwa Giizis suggest, is usually not too far away. Yet if there is too much concrete between you and Nature, a video or recording can bring Nature to you, as suggested in chapter 5.

Another consideration is that less is often more, and this is especially true with healing. In essence, it all starts and ends with the breath, from our first labored inhale at birth to our last exhale when leaving this life. We might not have anything or anyone else with us, and it may not be possible to practice other modalities or exercises; yet we have our breath: its deep warmth and calming cadence are always with us.[17]

FOR FAST STRESS RELEASE

Has anyone ever suggested that you to take a deep breath when you are stressed or anxious? Do you sigh when you are stressed? If you do, you know a highly effective technique for mental and physical stress reduction that works quickly and is always available to you.[18, 19]

The therapeutic benefits of Conscious Breathing are far-reaching. It affects us deeply and somatically, in ways that verbal and hands-on techniques cannot.[20, 21] When we tap into the Rhythm of Life with our breathing, that energy becomes available to us for healing.[22] Whether our imbalance be physical or psycho-emotional, this life-energy is essential to core healing.[23]

The life-energy released by Conscious Breathing covers such a broad spectrum that it can be used for either relaxation or arousal. The breathing exercises found later in this chapter can address anxiety, panic attacks, stress, and many other conditions that involve interaction between breath and emotional distress.[24] Depression is successfully treated with Conscious Breathing,[25, 26] as are issues relating to self-consciousness.[27]

With all of that, what yet may be most important is the fact that Conscious Breathing actively engages us in our own healing process.[28] In fact, it can be no other way, as we are our breath. As such, we empower ourselves by becoming both the methodology and the client in our healing process.

The Character of Healing Breath

As breath is not just air, breathing is not just taking in and expelling air. Tamarack Song described in his personal story how the nuances of breathing have everything to do with its effect and what it conveys. Here is an overview of breathing, based on tempo:

Slow Breathing

▶ Is comprised of around five breaths per minute, usually through the nose.[29]

▶ Encourages reflection and gaining perspective.[30]

▶ Causes the heart to beat slow and strong, blood pressure to drop, and vessels to dilate, which brings nourishment to the brain and body. This clears and activates the mind, which encourages a state of mindfulness.[31, 32, 33]

▶ Expands breath capacity, which helps oxygenate the system.[34, 35, 36]

▶ Arouses the parasympathetic nervous system, which aids digestion and constricts the pupils: a sign of a relaxed, introspective mind. Indicates that you are not stressed or in pain.[37, 38, 39]

▶ Reduces stress,[40] promotes relaxation, and encourages conflict avoidance.[41, 42]

▶ Supports a sense of safety, nurturance, and well-being.[43]

Fast Breathing

▶ Is comprised of six or more breaths per minute, and up to thirty, usually through the mouth.

▶ Is highly arousing.[44]

▶ Triggers the fight-flight response, which encourages thoughts and feelings oriented toward self-preservation.[45]

▶ Causes adrenaline to course through the system, which tenses the muscles.

▶ Helps in entering the trance state.

▶ Aids in breaking through emotional and mental holding patterns.

▶ Increases vital energy, to support physical and psycho-emotional healing.[46]

Understanding these differences between fast and slow breathing helps make breathing a conscious experience.[47] The more we realize how breathing affects and reflects our psycho-physical state, the more our breathing can become an Awakening and healing process.[48]

A Short Course in Conscious Breathing

For this training, all you need to do is find a quiet place, where there is just you and your breath. Conscious Breathing works best on an empty stomach.[49]

Step One: Connect with Your Breath

Relax and loosen your jaw, which reduces pain and anxiety,[50] and helps you to breathe easily. Then inhale, imagining that you are taking your first breath. Feel it coming in through your nose, then back out through your nose. Is it cool, or is it warm? Can you hear it? Smell it? What are your chest and gut doing? Is your breathing fast or slow? Do you pause between breaths? Does your head move when you breathe?

Now envision that you have become your breath, going in and out, in one continuous motion. Let your breath take you where it will: into your body, your blood, your muscles, your mind. Your breath is your guide for this Journey.

Feel your feet, solidly rooted. Let your breath travel down the length of your body, through your knees and calves and out through your feet, straight into the ground. With every exhale, your breath flows through every organ and muscle—through your very bones—in a continual stream into the Earth.

Become aware of how the Earth, steady and strong, beckons your breath and all that it carries. Again feel your breath, tumbling like a Waterfall in through your nose, into your lungs, and down, down through you. It washes you like a wave, catching everything: what wants to be seen and heard, what wants to be forgotten, what you don't know exists. Your thoughts, your laughter, your pain ... everything gets swept away like froth on the crest of a wave.

After five or ten minutes, bring your attention back to your basic breathing. Close your eyes and let your breath fill you, then let it empty you.

Step Two: Establish Circular Breathing

1. Breathe a bit faster than normal for the situation.
2. Balance your inhale and exhale by giving equal time and presence to both.
3. Let your inhale flow into your exhale, so that there is no interruption between them.
4. Imagine your inhale coming up your spine, your exhale flowing down your chest, and your inhale again rising up your spine, in a circular fashion.

As goes the breath, so goes the body. When you breathe in a circular fashion, your senses keen and you become present within your body. Your mind grows vibrant and active, processing and synthesizing the increased input. You feel ready for anything or nothing.

Circular Breathing should come easy, as it's the natural way to breathe.[51] The goal is to eventually release yourself from conscious involvement in the mechanics of your breathing, and just allow the rhythm and cadence of your breathing to take over.[52] It's like learning how to ride a bicycle. After a while, you don't think about balancing or pedaling anymore because you have integrated it and you are then free to give your attention to other things.

If you have any difficulty, make sure you are breathing through your nose, which is called *Nasal Breathing.* It supports your breathing in circular fashion by regulating the speed at which air can be inhaled and exhaled. Along with that, regulated Nasal Breathing is central to healing with breath, as it stimulates the limbic brain,[53] which is the seat of emotion, memory, and behavior. The olfactory-limbic connection, then, gives us the means to use Conscious Breathing for accessing and healing emotional, memory, and behavior-based issues.[54] In addition, Nasal Breathing affects cognitive functions,[55] which make it a viable tool for strengthening the body-mind connection (see chapter 20).

Step Three: Create a Rolling Breath

1. Inhale into your gut.
2. Continue the inhale by expanding into your chest.
3. At the top of your inhale, let your chest relax and contract.
4. Your gut will follow, then seamlessly begin to expand with your next inhale.

After a few breaths, the rhythm should start to come naturally, as this is the typical way we breathe when we are centered, relaxed, and in good physical shape. It's called *Rolling Breath* because of the rolling motion of the gut and chest as they go in and out. Your diaphragm is actually doing most of the work, billowing down into your abdomen, then up into your chest.

Rolling Breath accomplishes these three things for you:

▶ Enlivens your senses.[56]

▶ Prepares your lungs and metabolism to absorb the healing essences of Nature, particularly negative ions and phytoncides (which were covered in chapter 5).[57]

▶ Massages your internal organs, which strengthens and stimulates them, making them more capable of metabolizing the healing elements ingested through lungs and skin.[58]

Step Four: Integrate Your Breathing

Here you merge your breathing seamlessly with whatever you are doing, so that it can serve without distracting or interfering. To others, your Conscious Breathing should become invisible.

This synching of breath and movement tends to happen naturally. Have you noticed your tendency to inhale when something stimulating or shocking occurs, then exhale when it's over? We see this reflected in the sayings, *It took my breath away, It's a breathtaking view,* and *It helped me breathe easy.*

Everything has its rhythm, and integrating your breathing helps you find it and become one with it.[59] This is particularly true outdoors, as Nature's rhythms are strong and we as a species evolved to be sensitized to them. As you become practiced at integrating your breathing, you will likely find it easily falling into sync with the sway of the Trees, the movements of the animals, and the general rhythm of the life around you. You will be moving with them by breathing with them.

One beautiful thing of this training is that you don't have to learn something before you can Breathe, or before you can heal. Your training *is* the breathing, and it *is* the healing.

IF YOU STRUGGLE WITH THE TRAINING

There may be times when you get distracted and your breathing falls out of sync with your surroundings or involvements. Just take a moment to reconnect with your breath (see Step One), then with your surroundings. The important thing is to adapt the training to fit who you are and how you live, so that you don't have to continually focus on your breathing in order to keep it in sync.

Here are a few more suggestions, from someone who spent time at a Thai monastery:

- *Stop what you are doing and simply feel your breath coming in and out through your nose.*
- *When your mind wanders, let whatever comes up drift away like a wisp of cloud crossing the sun.*
- *"What you practice, grows stronger," said a monk. "This foothold is all you need."*

The Forgotten Breathing Organ

The skin is our biggest organ, yet we seldom recognize it as such. It excretes toxins and waste products, and it absorbs nutrients such as sunshine-generated vitamin D and elements from the air, including oxygen.

Along with sensitizing yourself and practicing Conscious Breathing, you can prepare your skin for a Trail Walk in these ways:

- Wash it, but do not strip it completely of natural oils, which are essential for vitamin D production.
- Keep it fragrance free, to not interfere with absorption, or with your olfactory sense.
- Wear loose clothing, to allow the skin to breathe.
- Expose as much of your skin to the air and sunshine as weather permits.

Conscious Breathing in Everyday life

As a standalone tool, Conscious Breathing can be used part-and-parcel to whatever you are doing. Everyday activities take on a new dimension as you become more present and engaged with them. Many people express a newfound sense of presence—even joy—in their involvements after starting to Breathe along with them.[60]

Most folks like to integrate Conscious Breathing with something active, such as walking, jogging, yoga, bicycling, dancing, washing the car, or gardening.[61] Any activity works when it involves some movement. Breathing along with reading, conversing, or watching a movie can be challenging, as the high degree of focus they may require detracts from being present with your breathing. Yet if you're able to combine the two, you will gain the same benefits of active involvements.

Remember that there is no one right way to Breathe. Some people go slower than others, and some go faster; some are vigorous, some are gentle. Let the situation and what works best help you determine how to Breathe. The only general guidelines to keep in mind are:

▶ Conscious Breathing is typically deeper and more rhythmic than normal breathing.[62]

▶ Keep your breath moving freely with every inhale and exhale.[63]

▶ Honor your breath as the Breath of Life, and help keep it clean.[64]

CHAPTER EIGHT

Grounding in Nature

"It was good for the skin to touch the bare Earth," said Oglala Lakota chief Luther Standing Bear. "The old people liked to remove their moccasins and walk with their bare feet on the sacred Earth. . . . They sat on the ground with the feeling of being close to a mothering power. The soil was soothing, strengthening, cleansing, and healing."[1]

Standing Bear's people were practicing what is now commonly called *Grounding*. It involves direct skin contact with the surface of the Earth. Along with sensory contact, Grounding connects us with the Earth's electrical field. Direct contact with the Earth grounds our bodies, inducing favorable electro-physiological and psycho-emotional changes that promote optimum health.

Many people use the terms *Earthing* and *Barefooting* synonymously with *Grounding*, yet we prefer the latter, as it carries the double meaning of becoming grounded in both yourself and Earth energy.

Research has found that Grounding yields positive health benefits to such an extent that it has been called "electric nutrition."[2] It has been found to boost human immune response by minimizing inflammation and accelerating wound recovery.[3] The practice enhances sleep quality, balances cortisol levels, activates the parasympathetic nervous system, and reduces pain and stress, among other health benefits.[4] Simulated Grounding with specialized electrical devices is used in neonatal intensive care units to help protect preterm infants from the damaging effects of stress.[5]

The immune system, circulatory system, biorhythms, and other physiological processes function optimally when the body has an adequate supply of electrons, which are easily and naturally obtained by Grounding. This makes it appear that we are designed to live close to Mother Earth and touch her directly, on a daily basis. Grounding may be the most effective, essential, affordable, and accessible antioxidant there is.

Grounding can be accomplished in a number of ways: with the hands or feet, lying flat on your back or face down, sitting, kneeling, or crawling, or through artificial methods involving electrical conduction.[6] Water Grounding is another option (see *The Role of Water* later in this chapter).

Make It an Everyday Experience

The science of Grounding is raising our cultural awareness of its benefits, yet the practice was the way of life for our hunter-gatherer ancestors, and for indigenous people worldwide. Indeed, for most of our evolutionary history as a species, we have had continuous physical contact with the Earth. Most of our daily activities brought us in contact with the Earth. We lived largely outdoors, hunting, collecting firewood, gathering edibles, preparing food, and eating. Childcare, socializing, crafting, storytelling, and nearly every other activity were conducted on the ground.

We have disrupted this nearly constant contact in several ways, most notably through our footwear. Our ancestors went barefoot whenever possible; and when they needed foot protection, it was light and flexible. Modern rubber and plastic-soled shoes act as electrical insulators, blocking the flow of beneficial electrons from the Earth to our bodies.

The largely indoor lifestyle characteristic of modern cultures further prevents us from contact with the ground. We spend the vast majority of our lives in insulated, above-ground buildings and vehicles.[7]

Yet all is not lost. Even those of us who live in modern towns and cities can learn from Native people's example by incorporating the following practices in our lives.

For Daily Grounding

- Wear light, thin-soled footwear without heels.
- Walk to nearby locations rather than biking or driving.
- Walk off-pavement whenever possible.
- Sit on the ground when outside, rather than using a bench or lawn chair.
- Touch and hug Trees.
- Plan social and recreational activities around being outdoors.
- Have more picnic lunches and cookouts, even if they are just outside in your backyard.
- Adopt hobbies that take you outside and off-pavement.
- Take vacations to natural areas.

Grounding is a whole body-mind-spirit experience. Healing Nature Trails and other natural areas are conducive to Grounding because the setting and the energies at play encourage the deep relaxation and sensitizing of the entire being that is supportive of the practice.

Yet it is possible to Ground nearly anywhere the soil is not paved over. Your backyard, a park—even that strip of grass beside your place of work—provide opportunities to Ground. To fully gain from the practice, all it takes is being fully present, which can be accomplished quickly and easily with Conscious Breathing (see previous chapter). The two work together synergistically, as attested to by one Trail Walker who had just completed a rocky section of a Trail, "It's as though the rocks shape-shifted to fit my feet."

Grounding on Healing Nature Trails

Visitors are encouraged to walk barefoot on the Trails, if they are able to do so and if weather permits. Along with the therapeutic effects, walking barefoot or with minimal footwear promotes healthy feet and legs, along with good posture.

Though some weather conditions are more conducive to Grounding than others, the regenerative effects of the practice can be experienced in any weather. Dampness of any form increases conductivity, with walking barefoot in the rain giving the strongest connection. Exposing some of your skin to the rain enhances the experience even more. Snow is a moderate insulator from Grounding energy, yet there is typically enough of a benefit to make a Trail Walk worthwhile.

The Grounding experience on the Trails can be amplified in these ways:

- Note the differing sensations underfoot: wet or dry, cool or warm, rough or smooth, brute, stone, needle, sand, moss, or sticks.

- Embrace an Elder Tree or spend extra time sitting beneath her, with your back resting against her.

- Lie down on the ground, anywhere along the Trail that is open, out of the way, and does not harm vegetation. You'll experience the fringe benefit of increased sensory awareness.

- Practice the *Rooting* exercise found later in this chapter.

Along the Trails, you'll find benches periodically spaced for rest and reflection. People who are not able to sit on the ground or traverse the entire Trail due to injury, mobility impairment, or other reasons can rest on a bench and Ground themselves there. (You'll find more on special needs Trail features in chapter 25, *For Those with Special Needs*.)

Some Trails have benches made of large-diameter log sections lying directly on the ground. Their mass and substance make them effective conductors of the Earth's Grounding energy. Those not able to sit or lie directly on the Forest floor can then Ground themselves by sitting on these special benches. When a bench sits adjacent to a Tree, resting one's back on the Tree increases the Grounding effect.

On Trail webpages and in Trail literature, Walkers are encouraged to bring light moccasin-type footwear, with thin soles made of nonrubber material and no heels. On some Trails, leather moccasins are available on loan. Walkers also are encouraged to wear light clothing that permits some bare-skin contact with the soil, Trees, and other plants.

Most people adapt readily to the Grounding experience, as we evolved in environments where people were continually being Grounded as a matter of course in their daily lives. Yet now some people find themselves highly sensitive to Grounding energy and need to take it in small doses initially, just as with someone who is not used to being out in the sun. If you start to feel lightheaded or overly stimulated, it may be best to don the footwear you were encouraged to bring along with you on your Walk, or to take a short break on one of the readily available benches.

Shamanic Grounding

Healing Nature Guides follow in the tradition of shamanic practitioners by helping facilitate a client's Grounding experience. Prior to the Trail Walk, Guides interview their clients to determine what type of Grounding would best serve their needs:

- Barefoot or light footwear?
- Over all or particular parts of the Trail?
- Sitting, lying, or crawling?
- Incorporating a Grounding ritual, such as *Rooting* (found later in chapter)?

Guides monitor their clients, to assure that they get a full Grounding experience without overdosing. Clients with special needs, such as those in recovery from physical injury, working with psycho-emotional issues, or on Journeys of Self-Discovery, are given customized Grounding experiences by their Guides.

In shamanic traditions around the world, a more advanced form of Grounding that involves full-body immersion is practiced, for both physical and psycho-emotional healing purposes. Earth, water, and vegetation are the most common covering mediums. The rituals are known by various names, such as *Toltec Earth Embrace*, *Burial Extraction*, *Ritual of the Sacred Burial*, the *Death Rebirth Ritual*, and *Earth Swaddling*.

Full Immersion Grounding is a powerful transformative technique that should be practiced only under the guidance of a seasoned shamanic practitioner. Without proper preparation and oversight, a person risks psychic overload and physical harm. For these reasons, Full Immersion Grounding is not a regular part of the Healing Nature Trail experience.

If a Healing Nature Guide or other healthcare practitioner is trained in Full Immersion Grounding and receives prior approval from the Center Director, the ritual can be practiced as part of the Trail Walk experience.

Rooting: An Exercise for Stronger Connection

Grounding occurs spontaneously when walking barefoot or with minimal footwear, or when sitting/lying on the earth. Yet the experience can be magnified with various practices. A very effective one that can be used nearly anywhere is called *Rooting*. Here's how it is done:

1. **Find a quiet, shaded place** with sparse ground vegetation, preferably in a grove of Elder Trees, amongst Boulders, or in a recessed area such as a depression or ravine.

2. **Remove footwear** you may be wearing (weather permitting), so that your feet can be in direct contact with the Earth.

3. **Spread your feet** to the width of your shoulders, and stand with knees slightly bent.

4. **Relax your eyes** and let them partially close, so that you are looking softly and not focusing on anything. Let your eyes close if they so choose.

5. **Breathe slowly and consciously,** following the guidance in the previous chapter.

6. **Continue until you feel rooted.** A deep calm will come over you, and you may experience a slight tingling sensation. Go no longer than a half-hour.

7. **End with several deep inhales** and long, slow exhales. Then gently continue your Walk.

If you do not feel any change, it may be because you were already Rooted. Otherwise, you can Root more strongly by resting your back against an embankment, rock face, or Elder Tree, or by finding a location more conducive to Rooting.

After you have become accustomed to Rooting, practice it blindfolded and see what difference it makes (there is more on Blindfolding in chapter 15).

Another option is *Deep Rooting,* which gives your feet more solid contact with the bare Earth. First, clear away the underfoot debris, then work your feet into the Earth an inch or so. When you have finished, please remember to restore the site, so that you leave no trace.

Water Grounding

Native people hold Water sacred. It is the blood of the Mother Earth, essential to all life; and it is one of the four sacred elements, along with Earth, Air, and Fire.[8] Water plays a central role in the cleansing and healing rituals of many cultures. Purification through ablution (the washing of hands and sacred vessels) is an essential component of Islamic prayer rituals,[9] Baptism by Water is a traditional Christian practice,[10] and the Seven Sacred Rivers are central to Hindu practice.[11] Like most American Indians, the Ojibwe people of northern Wisconsin (where the original

Healing Nature Trail is located) hold Sweat Lodge Ceremonies, where Water plays a central healing and cleansing role.[12]

We can become Grounded in ourselves and in Earth energy most viscerally through *Water Immersion*, which is commonly referred to as *Water Grounding*. It provides an amplified Grounding experience because the human organism is itself mostly water, developed *in utero* in an aquatic environment, and lives on a planet whose surface is 71 percent water.[13] Serving as a longstanding healing modality for indigenous peoples, Water Immersion is growing as a form of therapy and recreation in modern cultures.[14]

The impact of Water Grounding is largely on the *autonomic nervous system* (ANS), which serves a crucial role in how the body regulates itself, including cardiovascular, gastrointestinal, renal, bladder, and other biological processes. The ANS is divided into two distinct systems: the *sympathetic nervous system* (SNS) and the *parasympathetic nervous system* (PNS). The SNS regulates limbic processes, including the fight–flight response system. The PNS controls the relaxation response.

Stress, fear, and trauma stimulate the SNS, while activities such as meditation stimulate the PNS and calm the body-mind.[15, 16, 17] Water Immersion has been found to promote activation of the PNS, which induces relaxation.[18, 19, 20, 21] This results in lower anxiety,[22, 23, 24] better memory, and better focus, [25] along with decreasing cortisol and other stress hormones,[26] and balancing out serotonin—the feel-good neurotransmitter.[27] Depression, chronic fatigue, and cancer treatments may be successfully augmented with Water Immersion.[28]

For best effect, use cold water. It is more effective than warm water because we have several times more cold receptors than warm receptors on our skin surface.[29] Splashing cold water on the face is particularly invigorating because of the face's high density of nerve receptors.[30, 31] The most significant effect is achieved with exposure to cold water over an extended period of time.

Partial or Full Immersion

Water Grounding can be achieved through either partial or full immersion. Many of us have felt the draw to wade into the shallows of a Lake or Stream, or the Ocean. It may be because standing in water (called *Shallow-Water Grounding*) is the most effective partial-immersion method. Yet dangling one's feet in the water while sitting on a dock or bank also works well. Foot immersion has been shown to encourage relaxation by decreasing the SNS stress response.[32]

Full-immersion water rituals were found in the ancient Egyptian, Greek, and Judaic worlds, and beyond.[33] In this day, Hindus immerse themselves, their idols, and the ashes of their dead in the sacred Ganges River,[34] and Full Immersion Baptism is practiced by a number of Christian denominations.[35]

Yet Full Immersion Water Grounding, like Full Immersion Earth Grounding, is not a regular part of the Healing Nature Trail experience. The practice, which can be very potent, ought to be undertaken only under the watchful eye of a shamanic practitioner, Healing Nature Guide, or healing-arts practitioner well-familiar with the process. This is for the sake of both avoiding harm and gaining the most from the practice.

A Healing Nature Guide who is trained in the practical and ritual aspects of the practice can incorporate it into a Trail Walk with prior approval from the Center Director.

CHAPTER NINE

The Labyrinthine Experience

In this day, not many people are familiar with Labyrinths. A few of us know about the Labyrinths of medieval cathedrals and courtyards, or the classical Labyrinths of ancient times. Most of us who are familiar with Labyrinths came upon them as children in the form of Mazes. Our childhood activity books had them— a tangle of trails, with dead ends and looming danger that we had to find our way through in order to get to a buried treasure or escape from a castle dungeon.

Labyrinths have made a comeback. They are helping transform the lives of many people across Europe and the Americas, and they figure prominently in the Healing Nature Trail experience. Let's get to know Labyrinths anew by taking a look at their origins and what they have to offer.

Genus and Species

The Labyrinthine experience fits into the general class of practices known as *circumambulation*, which *Webster's Third New International Dictionary* defines *as walking or going around an object of worship or reverence in a ritual circular course.*[1] Circumambulation is practiced in virtually all cultures, both Native and contemporary.

Many Native people refer to circumambulation as the *Circle Way*.[2] They practice it in many ways: when dancing around a fire with drummers or chanters in the center of the circle; in the way they conduct ceremonies and councils (which some American

Natives call *Talking Circles*);[3] and in following the Path of Life, the circle of the seasons, and the orbits of Sun and Moon.

Circumambulation is commonly found in traditional religions.[4] Zen Buddhists practice *jundo,* which refers to any form of ritual circumambulation. Jews dance around the Torah Scrolls,[5] and circular dancing is a part of Sikh and Jewish weddings.[6] Walking around a shrine is a common form of Hindu prayer.[7] In Catholicism, priests circumambulate altars while wafting them with incense.[8] Muslims circumambulate their most sacred site, the Kaaba;[9] and Bahá'í circumambulate around shrines and on holy days.[10] Freemasonry degree candidates circle lodge altars.[11]

In walking a Labyrinth, one circles around its center until reaching it, then spirals out in reverse until returning to the beginning point. The circling takes the form of a meander, which is the back-and-fourth motion similar to that taken by a river making its way down a broad valley. In doing so, the river finds equilibrium and proper pacing. We benefit in the same way from a Labyrinth's meandering pattern, which is a form of Nature's pendular geometry.[12] Later in the chapter, we'll explore how the pendular geometry of meanders (which is intrinsic to all forms of Labyrinths) is supportive of healing.

As a pendular circumambulation practice, walking a Labyrinth stands as a ritual on its own. The ritual is found as a component of many traditions, from ancient Middle Eastern, South Asian, and Scandinavian to medieval European and Native cultures in the southwestern United States.[13, 14]

A Historical Overview

To understand what Labyrinths have to offer as meditative and transformational tools, it helps to know where they originated and their original intent. The Labyrinths of classical times were constructed and used for these reasons:

> ◗ As divining mediums, often in conjunction with the astrological courses of celestial bodies.

- To prepare for battle or a long journey.

- To atone for sins or escape karma and the cycle of reincarnation.

- As a symbolic pilgrimage, stroll through an enchanted Forest, or walk on the Path of Life.

- To attain clarity or find relief from suffering.

- As a vehicle to progress from numbness to Awakening, or from the secular to the sacred.[15]

The oldest surviving Labyrinths exist as petroglyphs on boulders and cave walls.[16] They are hard to date accurately. Remnants of ancient outdoor Walking Labyrinths with stone or elevated sod-bordered Pathways have been found in China, Europe, and the Middle East, where they may go back 3,500 years.[17] Labyrinths appear in Greek mythology, and on coins from the fifth century BCE.[18] Archaeologists have unearthed tiled Labyrinths associated with the early civilizations of India, the eastern Mediterranean, and southern Europe.[19] Many of Europe's great medieval cathedrals have Labyrinths designed into their floors, walls, and courtyards.[20] Numerous other Labyrinths survive to this day, only they go unknown, as they have been obscured by renovation.[21]

With all that Labyrinths had to offer, they fell out of favor with the dawn of the Age of Reason in the 1800s. The Hedge Labyrinths of Elizabethan England were the last holdouts.[22]

The Resurgence

Over the past thirty years, Walking Labyrinths have made a revival. Yet as recently as a few years ago, only a handful of people knew anyone who had seen a Walking Labyrinth, much less used one. This is changing rapidly, with increasing numbers of Labyrinths—including ours—appearing around the Western world.

Labyrinths have returned to the popular consciousness in part because of the contemporary interest in antiquities.

Simultaneously, archeological research is showing the role of Labyrinths in bygone cultures.

A growing segment of our population is coming to realize that organized religion, rationalism, and allopathic medicine can be complemented by alternative modes of healing and awareness-raising, and the Labyrinth experience is meeting some of those needs. In the words of Melissa Gayle West, author of *Exploring the Labyrinth: A Guide for Healing and Spiritual Growth,* "Walking the Labyrinth fulfills six important contemporary needs: deepening spirituality; inwardness and connection to soul; access to intuition and creativity; simplicity; for integration of body and spirit; and intimacy and community."[23]

Here are the most common reasons Healing Nature Trail Walkers give for using Labyrinths:

- Curiosity.
- A pilgrimage.
- A refuge.
- Walking Meditation.
- An inward journey.
- Unraveling mental and emotional entanglements.
- Stress release.
- Deep trauma work.
- Life-transition support.

Whatever the reason for walking a Labyrinth, it is an apt metaphor for a Healing Nature Trail-guided Journey to Wellness and Awakening. Here is the three-leveled Labyrinthine experience offered by most Trails:

The First Level: The Mind

The regions, folds, and neural pathways of the mind form the quintessential Labyrinth.

The Second Level: The Trail Itself

It provides the body-mind connection for negotiating the Labyrinth of the mind. Every turn in the Trail brings up new possibilities in the mindscape, and every Side Path presents another choice.

The Third Level: Trailside Labyrinths

Nearly all Trails offer Labyrinthine experiences in addition to the Trails themselves. Most common are traditionally styled Turf (or Grass Path) Labyrinths and Finger Labyrinths, though you might also see Cosmorinths, Aquarinths, and other forms (as described in chapters 18, 23, and 31). Each one provides a unique doorway to the pathways of the Labyrinthine mind.

Labyrinth Design Origin

The most popular theory on the origin of the Labyrinth is that it was inspired by the spiral: a pattern that can be found throughout the natural world.[24, 25] The spiral can be seen in whirlpools, snail shells, and the arms of galaxies. The form is mathematically represented in the *golden ratio*, which is also known as the *divine proportion*.[26]

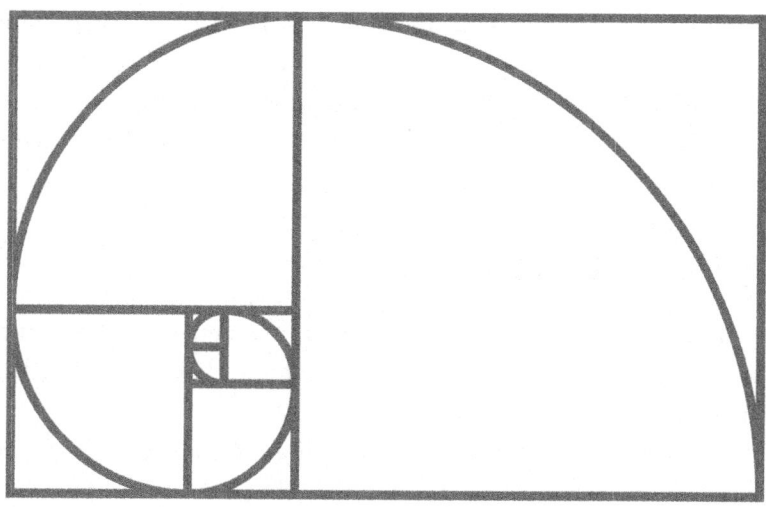

With classical Labyrinths, the spiral origin is apparent, as every Labyrinth is based on the geometric form. This roots Labyrinths in what is referred to as *sacred geometry,* which is the reverence for patterns and numerical ratios that are reoccurring and universal.[27, 28, 29] As such, sacred geometry is connected to the belief that by exploring these patterns, one may gain insight into the very structures of the Universe. For this reason, many sacred sites throughout our known history—including some incorporating Labyrinths—have been designed along the principles of sacred geometry.[30]

Further steeped in symbolism are the ancient seven-circuit Labyrinths, an example of which is the Cretan Labyrinth (illustrated later in this chapter). The design consists of seven concentric rings that correlate with the essence of the number *seven*, which is found throughout Nature. During the medieval period, walking such a Labyrinth was likened to moving through the Cosmos, as the seven circuits were equated to the seven visible planets. The number *seven* recurs in numerous significant places: the days of the week, the colors of the rainbow, musical tones, and chakras.[31] These are some of the reasons that seven has come to be considered a sacred number in many cultures.[32] On that note, it is worth mentioning that seven Labyrinths are components of the original Healing Nature Trail in Three Lakes, Wisconsin.

One modern view of Labyrinth design is that its resemblance to the human brain is one of the reasons for its healing properties.[33] Based on the body-mind connection, walking a Labyrinth stimulates both the right and left hemispheres of the brain, which encourages mental balance.[34]

Types of Labyrinths

Let's start by defining the two general categories of Labyrinth: *unicursal,* which means *having one route,* and *multicursal,* which means *having more than one possible route.*[35]

Unicursal Labyrinths, also known as *Meanders,* are by far the most common type. They are comprised of single circuitous Paths with serpentine turns, which start at entryways and lead to center points. Often the Paths meander out toward the perimeters of the Labyrinths, then back in toward the centers. Examples of unicursal Labyrinths are the *Man in the Maze* and *Chartres* styles found later in this chapter.

Multicursal designs, commonly known as *Mazes,* are complex systems of interconnected Paths or tunnels. They are rife with dead ends and detours, through which one has to navigate in order to reach the goal—should it be reached at all.[36] In some ancient cultures, Mazes were positioned at dwelling and public building entryways, to confuse evil spirits and negative energy and thus keep them from entering.[37] Examples of Mazes are found in children's activity books and the Cornfield Mazes popular in some rural areas in autumn.[38]

Labyrinth Types and Healing

The two types of Labyrinths have different psychotherapeutic effects. This is because unicursal Labyrinths (or Meanders) are Pathways to a center, while multicursal Labyrinths (or Mazes) present obstacles to mount.[39]

With their multiple switchbacks and directional changes, Meanders can be complex and engaging. This encourages deep exploration. At the same time, the Meanders' Paths are well-defined and show no variance, which helps people clarify their Healing Journeys and shed distractions. Solidly guiding walkers to a well-defined center, the Paths support walkers to find centeredness within themselves. According to the Reverend Dr. Lauren Artress, canon of Grace Cathedral in San Francisco and a leader in the Labyrinth resurgence, "The set path takes you to the center; that you know you will get to the center helps focus and quiet the mind."[40]

The Paths then lead walkers back out, to continue their Journeys with the guidance of their Heart Centers to accompany them.[41]

Negotiating a Maze's wrong turns and dead ends takes both presence and astuteness—just what is needed for the nooks and crannies of the psyche that Mazes lead one into. These are often places where we don't want to go, but we know we have to. Once we have entered the bowels of a Maze, the only way out is through the tangle.

To serve a wide range of healing needs as well as supporting people on their Awakening Journeys, Healing Nature Trails incorporate both types of Labyrinths. Meanders are represented by gateway and Finger Labyrinths, and the Trails themselves are Mazes. Some Trails feature Zen Untangles, Cosmorinths, and Zen Gardens as well, which could serve as either Mazes or Meanders, depending upon how they are used. (You'll find these latter Labyrinths described in chapter 31, *Options: Cairns, Cosmorinths, and Coneflowers.*)

THE LABYRINTH THAT SPEAKS TO YOU

There is another special and intimate Labyrinth that we each walk every time we hear the song of a Bird or the rustle of a leaf. You can find out about it in chapter 15 under Blindfold Listening Guidance.

Labyrinths throughout History

Now let's take a closer look at what we know about Labyrinth origins and evolution. It will help us relate the Labyrinthine experience to our cultural heritage as well as better understand the function of Labyrinths as transformative and mindfulness tools.

Labyrinths of the Classical Era

In Greek myth, Queen Pasiphaë, daughter of the god Helios and wife of King Minos, became enamored with a beautiful white bull. Unable to overcome the curse of her unusual affection for the animal, the queen called upon the famed craftsman Daedalus, who constructed a wooden cow for her to hide within, so that she could consummate her desire for the bull.

The coupling resulted in the birth of the famed Minotaur: a monstrous creature who was half human and half bull. Minos could not bring himself to kill the beast, so instead the king also called upon Daedalus—this time to construct a Labyrinth to contain the Minotaur.[42]

The Labyrinth Daedalus built for the purpose is fabled to have been so complex that he, himself, was hardly able to navigate a way out. Known as the *Knossos*, or *Cretan Labyrinth*, this mythic structure was a well-established icon in the mythos of ancient Greece.[43] Its imagery is found on coins from the era.[44]

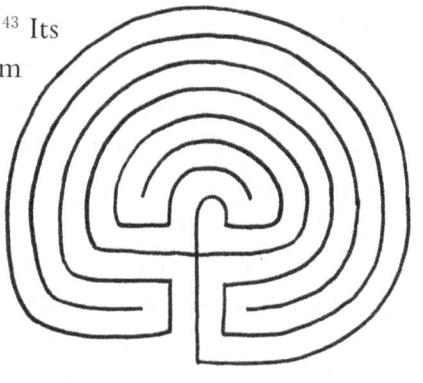

Even with its fame and history, the Cretan Labyrinth is far from the first representation of the Labyrinthine form. Early examples can be found throughout the world, making them a universal symbol rooted in the cultural,

Cretan Labyrinth

spiritual, and initiatory practices of antiquity. Labyrinths and depictions thereof—some dating back 4,500 years—have been found in India, France, Scandinavia, Crete, Italy, Sumeria, Egypt, Russia, the Far East, and the Americas.[45]

Yet there is no specifically known time or place of origin. One of the popular theories is that the motif is archetypal, meaning that it arose from the innate, collective imagery contained within the human psyche.[46] Another well-held theory is that the spiral form commonly found in Nature (which we covered a few pages back) is the original inspiration.[47] The earliest examples of the Labyrinthine image appear as simple Maze-like designs in the stone carvings of the Neolithic Age.[48] In Italy, Labyrinths have been found carved into rock faces, most notably at Val Camonica.[49] The

Usgalimal petroglyphs, located on the rock banks of the Kushavati River in Goa, India, contain archaic carved designs of the classical Labyrinth. They are dated at approximately 2,500 BC.[50] A Labyrinth lies etched in the Earth among the famous Nazca Lines in Peru,[51] and the classical Labyrinthine design is carved into boulders throughout the southern United States and Mexico.[52] The motifs of Bronze Age pottery often include depictions of Labyrinths.[53]

Egypt was the location of what may have been the earliest Labyrinthine compound. Though lost to time, it was described by a number of ancient chroniclers,[54] including the Greek historian Herodotus. After viewing the facility, he wrote: "Greater than words could tell, for, although the temple at Ephesus and that at Samos are celebrated works, yet all the works and buildings of the Greeks put together would certainly be inferior to this Labyrinth as regards labor and expense . . . The Labyrinth surpasses even the pyramids."[55]

A number of Labyrinths constructed of large boulders can be found in Arkhangelsk Oblast, Russia. Located on Bolshoi Zayatsky Island, these structures are roughly 2,500 years old and are believed to have been used for ritual purposes.[56] Scandinavian sailors once walked a Labyrinth to encourage fortuitous weather and successful fishing.[57] The *Yantra*, a variation on the Labyrinth form, was used as a Hindu meditation practice. It was thought to help relax women during childbirth.[58]

In the Americas, Labyrinth motifs are found in the basket-weaving designs of some indigenous peoples, most notably the Tohono O'odham of the Southwest. Their *Man in*

Man in the Maze Labyrinth

the Maze design consists of a man standing at the entrance of a unicursal Labyrinth, thought to portray a person's Path of Life.[59]

Labyrinths of the Middle Ages and Renaissance

In medieval Europe, the Labyrinthine form grew complex. It continued as a metaphor for the Path of Life, only with the overlay of portraying the difficulties and complexities of navigating a life without sin. Walking those Labyrinths was viewed as a symbolic act of pilgrimage, and it encouraged religious contemplation.[60]

Labyrinths of the time were most commonly found inlaid in the floors of places of Christian worship.[61] The most famous of medieval Labyrinths is found at the Chartres Cathedral in France. Constructed of inlaid marble in the thirteenth century, it remains a site of pilgrimage to this day.[62]

Labyrinth at Chartres Cathedral

Dinner plate-size Labyrinths, commonly referred to as *Finger Labyrinths*, were a relatively common feature on the walls of medieval churches. For those unable to make the pilgrimage to Chartres or Jerusalem, Finger Labyrinths gave the devout an opportunity to metaphorically take the Journey by tracing the Path with the tips of their fingers.[63]

Due in large part to renewed interest in the cultures of antiquity, Labyrinths became increasingly popular in the Renaissance. Taking the form of extravagant sculpted gardens, these Labyrinths were modeled after visions inspired by the writings of classic historians such as Herodotus.[64]

Rather than serving a religious or reflective purpose, Garden Labyrinths were sites for social gatherings, dances, and contests.

Known also as *Hedge Mazes*, they persisted into Elizabethan times,[65] and they are now what come to mind when many people envision Labyrinths.

The Contemporary Use of Labyrinths

Many of us feel the increasing need for self-reflection and simplifying our lives. We yearn to live with a greater sense of wellness and fulfillment. The drive to reunite our minds, bodies, and spirits may be even stronger for us than it was for people in times past.

In our quest, some of us find that the therapeutic and spiritual techniques of our ancestors are just as pertinent today as they were back then. This may explain the resurgence of interest in Labyrinths, and why we are still able to experience their benefits, even though we no longer live in cultures where Labyrinths are commonly used.

The Labyrinths of most recent history, the Elizabethan Hedge Mazes, have been utilized recreationally, yet the Labyrinthine form remains intrinsically allegorical and spiritually symbolic. Throughout their existence, Labyrinths have been most often associated with sites of metaphysical significance, whether it be initiatory or funerary rites, a means for pilgrimage, or a metaphor for the Shamanic Journey into Death and Rebirth.[66]

In this day, Labyrinths are primarily used for exploring one of the most complex mysteries of all—the human psyche.[67] From the earliest days, the Labyrinthine experience appears to have been used to unveil the psyche by encouraging altered states of perception and consciousness. Once the veil is lifted, the Labyrinth walker holds the potential to connect with elements of the subconscious as well as the universal. Thus begins the meditative process toward integration and individuation of the self—the essence of the Path of Life.[68]

The Four Stages of Walking a Labyrinth

First: Preparation

Before setting foot on the Sinuous Path, take a moment to go over this list:

1. Take a few deep breaths (see *Step One: Connect with Your Breath* in chapter 7) to immerse yourself in the now.
2. Let go of expectations and relax into the experience.
3. Sensitize yourself by observing your surroundings, listening, and touching.
4. Go at your own pace. You can pass others and be passed.
5. Stay present with whatever emerges and breathe through it.
6. Take nothing literally. Everything is a symbol or metaphor for something deeper.

Second: The Inward Journey

As we enter a Labyrinth, we symbolically leave behind the pressures and stresses that so often keep us from the inner work—and mask the awarenesses—necessary for healing and personal evolution. Each bend of the Path strips away more of the world as we know it: more of who we *think* we are. In essence, we are ritually killing our old self.

We then stand alone, stripped down to our essential self. Before us lies the Hero's Journey. Shadow surrounds us, and the Void awaits to engulf us, perhaps on the next step. All we have to guide us through is reflection and nebulous voices.

Third: Entering the Womb

Out of the shadow emerges the sacred destination at the very center of the Meander. There awaits the Minotaur: the bastard spawn of our fragmented self. We must defeat (i.e., embrace and consume) the abominable beast in order to be reborn into ourselves.

Now is the time for Conscious Breathing, to imbue our new self with the Breath of Life. The first breath is for awareness, the second breath is for illumination, and the following breaths are for meditative listening.

We stay in the Womb until we feel complete and ready to enter the Birth Canal.

Fourth: The Return Journey

When we retrace our steps, we find that nothing looks the same from the backside as it did from the front. What was fragmented is now becoming integrated; what was disturbing has somehow become insightful.

As we walk the serpentine Path from birth to spreading our new wings before the fresh breeze that greets us at the Labyrinth's threshold, we use the time to integrate all that we have gained. Following are the potential benefits of that integration:

▶ Mental clarity.

▶ Reduced stress and anxiety.

▶ Revitalized sense of intuition.

▶ Improved state of well-being.

▶ Expanded self-awareness and capacity for self-reflection.

▶ The aptitude for Trance Journeying.

Finding a Labyrinth

All Healing Nature Trails offer one or more Labyrinthine experience options. The original Trail in Three Lakes, Wisconsin, USA has seven different types of Labyrinths threaded out along the Trail like a string of pearls: a Gateway Turf Labyrinth, a Cosmorinth, a Stump Labyrinth, an Aquarinth, a Zen Untangle, a Zen Garden Labyrinth, and handheld Finger Labyrinths. You'll find them described in Parts III and IV of this book.

In recent years, many indoor and outdoor Walking Labyrinths of traditional and contemporary design have been constructed by private individuals and various organizations. They can be found across North America and Europe, and in various other locations around the world. Locate them by consulting with like-minded

**The Gateway Labyrinth at the Healing Nature Center,
Three Lakes Wisconsin, USA**

people in your area, or by searching your area—or anywhere else—through the online *World-Wide Labyrinth Locator.*[69]

Yet you need not be limited to what your area has to offer. You can make your own indoor Labyrinth by taping the pattern on a floor, or an outdoor Labyrinth by mowing the Pathway in tall grass. Another option is to delineate the Pathway with rocks, rope, or another suitable material. If you'd like portability, full-size canvas Labyrinths are available online.

If you'd like help, professional Labyrinth designers and installers offer their services to individuals and groups. In addition, various designs, including a few of contemporary origin, are available in books and online.

For those who don't have the room or resources for a full-size Labyrinth, plate-size Finger Labyrinths can be found online and at the Healing Nature Center. Then again, you might like to make your own, which could be as simple as a photocopy. If you are craft-oriented, consider using clay, wood, or papier-mâché.

There are now active Labyrinth organizations, such as *The Labyrinth Society* and *Veriditas,* that can provide you with additional designs, along with a wealth of information and Labyrinth-related experiences.[70] In addition, there are a number of well-researched books on the topic[71] and a plethora of information available on the Internet.

CHAPTER TEN

How Plants and Animals Speak to Us

Indigenous hunter-gatherers the world round refer to the animals and plants they live with as their sisters and brothers. These are not just platitudes, or some hollow religious belief. Such people live in community with the plants and animals, where they rely on each other for their sustenance and welfare. In doing so, they come to know each other intimately. They live together in honor and respect, as true kin. When Native people call a Frog "Little Brother" or a Tree "Grandmother," they mean it literally.

With such an interdependent relationship, the humans, the other animals, and the plants get to know each other well. They come to know each other's needs and desires. They talk amongst themselves, asking each other for favors, and complaining when things don't go well. They communicate in the universal language, which is known by many as *Naturespeak*. (For more on the topic, see *Becoming Nature: Learning the Language of Wild Animals and Plants* by Tamarack Song, Bear & Company, 2016.) Kahlil Gibran gave a beautiful, poetic definition of Naturespeak when he said, "A single leaf turns not yellow but with the silent knowledge of the whole tree."[1]

Here is where some people get derailed. Nearly everyone agrees that at least rudimentary communication is possible between us and "higher" animals, such as the great apes and cetaceans. And many of us have spoken with Dogs, Cats, or Horses. But a Snake? Or a Cricket? Even better, when have you last met someone who has carried on a conversation with Grass, or a Bush?

Classical Roots

Let's start with plants. Peoples of many cultures throughout the ages have held Trees in high esteem. Their presence imparts a sense of comfort and protection, and walking amongst them uplifts the spirit. Since time immemorial, people have gone into the Forests to seek sanctuary, take retreats, and commune with the ethereal.

Classic Norse, Celtic, Hindu, Egyptian, and American Indian cultures recognized the life-giving power of Trees, as witnessed by their legends and religious texts. Buddhist scriptures describe the unlimited kindness of Trees: how they give generously and offer protection to all beings.

In this day, we see the same high regard for Trees. A potent example comes from the Veterans Administration, which chose a Forest setting for an innovative supportive community for veterans suffering from severe post-traumatic stress syndrome and traumatic brain injury. It's called Cabin in the Woods, and it is comprised of twenty-one cabins tucked in the Woods at the Togus VA Medical Center in Augusta, Maine.

Still, there is more to our relationship with Trees—much more—and to our relationship with plants in general. Traditional legends and Native Elders have elaborated on these relationships. Here, however, let's review how modern science is helping us reconnect with our innate knowledge of plants, and with the legends about our relationship with them.

Bridging the Plant-Animal Divide

One reason for our distant relationship with plants is that we consider them to be lower life forms than animals, and much lower than us humans. We see this perspective reflected in our beliefs and daily practices. We mow the grass without thought for countless plants we are tearing limb from limb, when we would never do so with a similar congregation of animals. We who are vegetarians seldom demonstrate the same sensitivity with broccoli or soybeans that we do with cows and chickens.

Yet unbeknownst to many, plants are sentient beings, in the full sense of the term. They have senses of sight, smell, hearing, feeling, proportion, and memory; and they process sensory input.[2] They do all this even though they do not have eyes, noses, and other sensory receptors like ours.[3]

Even though there is no apparent similarity in the sensory organs of plants and animals, the gene grouping responsible for the ability of each of them to determine if it is light or dark is the same.[4] Across the board, it turns out that genetic differences between plants and animals are not all that significant.[5, 6] Even more surprising to many is the fact that plants are more genetically complex than many animals.[7] Let's take sight as an example.

How Plants See

Plants can see you and me, which tells them when we come near, if we loom over them, and whether the shirt we are wearing is red or blue.[8] And they can see some of the colors we cannot, such as the ultraviolet light that gives us sunburns and infrared light that makes us feel warm.[9]

This in no way means that plants see in image-form as we do. Yet they can tell when light is very dim, such as from a candle; when it is mid-day or sunset, from which direction the light is coming; how long it has been light; and if another plant has grown over them and blocked their light.[10]

But they're just plants, you might say. *Why do they have such a phenomenal ability to see?* Blue light tells them in which direction to bend, and red light tells them the length of the night.[11] The last color they saw tells them when to bloom. The last light of the day is the red at the far end of the spectrum, which tells plants when to shut down for the night. The same red tells them when to wake up in the morning. They gauge the time between dusk and dawn to determine their rate of growth.[12]

As if that isn't impressive enough, plants have up to eleven different photoreceptors,[13] where we have only four.[14] For them, light is much more than a signal—they need it to eat. It takes a complex light-monitoring system to use light in converting water and carbon dioxide into the various carbohydrate compounds that feed all animals. When a plant sees that she is being shaded by other plants, she grows faster, to get back in the sun and continue eating efficiently. Plants need to see when it's spring, so they know when to start growing and hatching out of their seeds, just as many animals need to know the same in order to lay eggs and give birth. As the season progresses, plants see by the changing light when to flower, set seed, and go dormant for winter.[15]

Plants don't have a nervous system as we do, yet like us they are able to translate visual signals into physiologically recognizable instructions.[16] When a finger detects a sensation, our entire body responds. A plant does the same: when a single leaf sees something, the entire plant responds.[17]

How They Smell

The similarities between us and plants continue with the sense of smell. Plants communicate with us through pheromones they release (see chapter 11, *Primal Aromatherapy*), and they communicate with each other. A tree attacked by Caterpillars releases a pheromonal message that is picked up by neighboring Trees, who then increase the levels of compounds in their leaves that inhibit the growth of Caterpillars.[18] In the same way, a single attacked leaf warns the rest of the plant. This is plants' way of practicing empathy, both toward themselves and their neighbors.[19, 20]

We humans communicate with each other via hormones in the same way, even though we are typically not consciously aware of it.[21] Women living in close contact with each other synchronize their menstrual cycles as a result of odor cues in perspiration.[22] Men's testosterone levels drop, along with a corresponding reduction in sexual arousal, when they smell negative emotion-related tears obtained from women, even though the tears are odorless.[23]

Their Sense of Touch

Then there is the sense of touch, which in some plants is more acute than ours.[24] Over 2 percent of some plants' genes are devoted to touch response, which is a surprisingly high number. Plants react to a variety of factors that affect their survival, such as Insects landing on their leaves, animals brushing against them, and the wind moving them.[25] We react to something we touch that is unfamiliar or threatening to us by moving and so do plants; only plants do so by modifying their growth.[26, 27] When seen over time, their ability to move by growth modification could cause one to question the assumption that they are stationary organisms.[28] Windblown plants maintain a dwarf shape, leaves touched once too often wither and die, and plants continually browsed or injured on one side transfer their growth energy to the opposite side. A plant can transform herself so radically over time that if you hadn't seen her in a while, you might be convinced that you were looking at a different plant.

Of Minds and Memories

And now for the coup de grace: plants have memories. Here again, we share some characteristics with plants, and there are some that we don't. To begin with, memory—whether plant or animal—is based on sensory input.[29] A key component to memory is the ability to recall past events in order for them to influence present actions. Like us, plants are capable of this. They can remember a past experience and respond by changing their growth. I could have broken an arm in the past, and a Tree could have broken a branch. If at some point were the Tree and I to experience the same environmental conditions as when our limbs were broken, we would likely act differently than we did originally, in order to prevent another break. We are both relying on what is known as *morphogenetic memory.*[30]

Like us, plants retain trauma memories. A past wound on one side of a branch can cause the buds on that side of the branch to remain dormant, while those on the other side grow.[31] Even more amazing is plants' ability to pass trauma memories on to their offspring, which is another trait they share with us. This is called *transgenerational memory,* and it is based on *epigenetic* (or genetically transmitted) memories.[32] Here's how it works: A plant—or a human—experiences a high stress situation and reacts to compensate. The offspring act in the same way, even though they have not experienced the stressful situation.[33] The adaptive advantage is that if the offspring are able to act in the way their parent did to negotiate the trauma, they may be able to avoid being traumatized.

"But still, we are fundamentally different from plants," some of you must be thinking. "We have brains, and they don't." Even that is being put to question by recent research showing that neuro-receptors in plants function in cell-to-cell signaling in a way that is similar to how human neurons communicate with each other.[34, 35, 36]

There may even be an argument to support the fact that plants can be differentiated from each other by their unique and individual personalities. Trees have complex electrical voltage patterns that can be monitored, and they show individuation.[37]

Even Jet Lag?

If any of you are still holding out after all that's been covered, here is the game-changer: Plants experience jet lag, just like us. And they take a few days to recover, just like us. The reason we both suffer from the same affliction is that we both literally have the same circadian clock, which is the mechanism that governs when we get active or grow tired, and when we get hungry or feel the urge to relieve ourselves. In plants, the circadian clock tells them when to photosynthesize, and when to furl their leaves for the evening.[38, 39] The plants and us ended up with the same circadian clock because early in the evolution of single-celled organisms, they developed the circadian clock before they diversified to form the basis of the plant and animal kingdoms.[40]

The Gift of Relationship

Now we come full circle, back to the Elders who honor plants as kin and listen to their guidance. When we gaze up at the crown of a great Pine Tree, or look down upon a blushing Flower in the Meadow, we might now recognize distant relatives. We know that we both see, smell, and feel. We both have memories, and we are both capable of empathy. The Elders obviously know something that science is only beginning to rediscover.

In addition, it would serve us well to acknowledge that plants differ from us in a number of key areas. While the sensory experiences of plants and people run some strong general parallels, they are qualitatively different.[41] A plant can remember that she was touched, yet she cannot remember who touched her. You and I, however, can carry the memory of the plant on into our future.[42] Like us, a plant can react to injury, yet she cannot suffer from pain.[43, 44] Plants are aware—they are acutely aware of their surroundings—yet only we are self-aware.

These distinct differences, resting on a bed of familial similarities, are the basis of the plant kingdom's profound gift to us. We are related: We are born of the same mother and we live together on her bosom. We are descended from the same parent stock, and we speak the same language.[45] Yet we each see, feel, and move differently. Therein lies their gift to us—a unique vantage point that gives them perspective we do not have.

As giving is receiving, let us gift them in return. We can help Nature heal while Nature heals us.

How Animals Guide

When we step onto a Healing Nature Trail, we walk into the ways of our Native ancestors. Rather than an observational experience, we are immersing ourselves in a living diorama, vibrant with creatures large and small, vocal and silent, flying, crawling, walking, and swimming. Some inhabit the Trail environs, and others are just passing through.

Many of these animals have long served our ancestors as their most trusted guides and life companions. Let's explore that form of relationship, as it is available for us as well.

We tend to visualize the intimate connection between Native peoples and Nature primarily from a landscape perspective, with animals playing a supportive role as sources of food, clothing, craft materials, and shelter. Natives perceive themselves as living in a world of animals, with whom they have social and mystical relationships. Isolated pockets of Native peoples on every continent have survived extant into modern times, so we have been able to talk with many of them and listen to their stories. Nearly all of them have animals who are main characters in their lives.[46]

A Timeless Yearning

Our species' fascination with the other animals has been the connecting thread of the human lineage across the ages. Many of the earliest-known paintings, pendants, and pottery include references to animals.[47, 48, 49, 50] The same is true of the legends, manuscripts, and astronomical symbols we cherish from times past. Nowadays, tattoos, names, icons, and brands continue to draw upon animals for inspiration.

As significant as the endurance of our close association with animals is, it has changed over recent times. What we know from our hunter-gatherer ancestors, anthropologists, and Native communities today is that Animals and Humans once lived together in balance with Nature. This balance ended when we became sedentary agriculturalists. The ability to grow and harvest food diminished our need for hunting and foraging, which signaled the decline of our direct connection with animals—especially as guides. This rift was most deeply rent when we dominated over animals by domesticating them.

Yet our need—our yearning—for existential guidance is consistent across cultures. Organized religions are one way of satisfying the longing. The Guardian Angel of the Judeo-Christian tradition is a contemporary parallel that can help us understand the traditional Animal Guide relationship and how it functions on a personal level in daily life.

Religion, however, does not have a monopoly on civilized adaptations of the relationship. Our longstanding cultural affinities for oracles, divining methods, channeled entities, Aliens, Psychics, and other supernatural mediating figures are new twists on the old form.

Animals as Dodems

A commonly used term for the sacred bond between Humans and Animals (and plants) is the *Dodemic relationship*. It is our deepest relationship, closer even than our relationship with others of our kind. A Native might consider it to be so intimate that she views herself and her Animal Guide, or Dodem, to be of one life. In the fullest sense, the term *Dodem* means *the relationship from which one gains sustenance, sense of self, and meaning in life.* When a Native says, *Cougar is my Dodem,* she is essentially saying, *Cougar and I are of the same heart and spirit.*

When many Natives introduce themselves, they also introduce their Dodems. They consider acknowledgment of their Dodem as part of their name and identity. They may display the symbol of their Dodem outside their lodge and affix it to their shield, clothing, and other belongings. In these ways, others can come to know them in a complete sense; and those of the same Dodem can easily connect. Dodemic relationship also plays a big role in relationship dynamics, with the Dodemic connection sometimes being more highly regarded than the biological.

The Dodemic relationship is closely related to the shamanic traditions found in many Native cultures. Around the world, shamanic healers often transform into the animals who give them the power to Journey into the Netherworld to retrieve the lost part of a soul or to bring back a healing formulation or ritual.[51] This is known variously as *shapeshifting, animal transformation, skin-walking, otherkinning,* and *zoanthropy.*

Native dancers typically wear animal masks, skins, and Feathers while imitating animal movements. This is to both honor the animals and learn from them. The Ojibwe people who live in the vicinity of the original Healing Nature Trail have Snake, Deer, and Crow Hop dances. Native music follows the same pattern, with Ojibwe flute music being based on birdsongs and the calls of other animals.

Underlying the Animal Guide bond is our innate ability to communicate with all of life. Our Native ancestors practiced this ability daily. Earlier in this chapter, it was referred to as Naturespeak, and it is encoded in our DNA. All living creatures converse in Naturespeak. However, very few of us live immersed in Nature anymore, so we have no real need to communicate with animals. The thought of doing so might seem foreign to many of us, but only because our Naturespeaking ability has atrophied from lack of use.

Even so, nearly everyone can recall a special moment when we were in total conscious rapport with another animal. Most of us still find ourselves drawn to animals in many ways and we feel an intrinsic urge to communicate with them.

To learn more about Animal Guides, and for help in coming to know your own, you can consult with a shaman or Native Elder. In addition, several helpful books are available on the topic, including *Your Spirit Animal Guides* by Tamarack Song.

Yet it is not necessary to know who your Dodem is in order to receive the wisdom and guidance of animals on a Healing Nature

Trail. Whether Insect or Mammal, Reptile or Bird, Amphibian or Fish, they are all in regular communication with each other, and they would welcome you to join in on the conversation.

How to Listen

To avail yourself of the full transformative potential of the Trail, it is necessary to attune to Naturespeak. Sufi mystic Rumi referred to it as the "voice that doesn't use words."[52]

Fortunately, we have an intrinsic understanding of Naturespeak. Rumi went on to say that all we need in order to understand it is to "listen." Healing Nature Guides are trained to help you get your listening skills up to speed. In addition, you might want to enlist the services of an animal communicator or pick up a book or two on the topic.

As well, you can let your intuition guide you. Watch what creatures come your way and which plants draw your attention. Pay particular note to sounds and movements that appear to be just a bit out of the ordinary, as they are often the initial feelers put out by someone who has something to share with you. Note the voices that resonate with you most. Go ahead and reply, in whatever way comes to you. It could be silently, vocally, or by body language.

TO FOSTER RELATIONSHIP

Many animals are most active early and late in the day, and some are nocturnal or seasonal. The warmer the temperature the more active become plants and cold-blooded animals. Giving offerings, such as a hair from your head or the pinch of a Sacred Herb, helps open channels of communication. Meeting Nature humbly, and without preconceived notions, is perhaps the greatest thing you can do to prepare.

Voices can come from the strangest of places: a stone, a wilted Flower, or even an overhead cloud. Set foot in Nature with an open mind and heart, and there is a good chance you will hear the voices. Be open to plants of all ages, not just the Elder Trees, as they all have wisdom to share with us.

This is bound to strike some you as a foreign concept because our cultural perspective on growth and maturation is linear: from embryo to fetus, to newborn, then toddler, and so on, to the elder years. In many Native cultures, however, growth is viewed as a continuum, with each successive stage being added like the layers of an onion. We are then still that inquisitive toddler, rambunctious child, and confused adolescent, so we can use the mirroring and guidance of animals and plants of various ages.

With that perspective, you can potentially hear from any and all animals and plants. Otherwise most of us tend to romanticize—and only listen to—stately Trees, charismatic land animals, and great, soaring Birds. Yet some of the stories of the beautiful breakthroughs we have heard from Trail users have come from such seemingly unlikely sources as a blade of Grass being chewed on by a Grasshopper, a biting Mosquito, and an Acorn sprouting from a rotting Tree stump.

Much of the language of Nature is written in sign. Similar to the words you are reading and translating off of this page, you can read the "words" the animals have left behind for you. A footprint or claw mark, a Feather or tuft of fur, an eggshell or bone fragment . . . all are the beginnings of teaching stories. A Trail Guide can help you read them; and again, you can get training from an intuitive tracker, along with training yourself with the help of a good book on the topic (such as Tamarack Song's *Entering the Mind of the Tracker: Native Practices for Developing Intuitive Consciousness and Discovering Hidden Nature,* Bear & Company, 2013).

To accompany and empower you on this key component of your Trail Walk, consider taking an *Animal Token* or two along with you. Also known as *Talismans* or *Charms,* Tokens are pocket-size likenesses of Animal Guides that are typically crafted from wood, stone, or clay (more on Tokens in chapter 12, *Talismanic*

Voices). Bring your own from home, or you can find one in the Trail outfitting section of some welcome centers.

If at the end of your Walk you could use some help in interpreting any encounters you had, your Trail Guide is trained to assist. Your therapist may be able to help as well. Some Trails have staff available to consult.

Here is one Trail Walker's personal experience that shows how intimate plant and animal sharings can be: "My Guide said he was just going to stop and show me this Tree because it was very special—it was over five hundred years old . . . I closed my eyes and hugged the Tree and I could feel its branches hug me back, and it whispered . . . I began to cry."[53]

CHAPTER ELEVEN

Primal Aromatherapy

Robert Louis Stevenson said that "it is not so much for its beauty that the Forest makes a claim upon men's hearts, as for that subtle something, that quality of the air, that emanation from the old trees, that so wonderfully changes and renews a weary spirit."[1]

That "subtle something" can be as minute as a single molecule of an odor that a plant emits, as that's all it takes for the receptor cells in our noses to detect a new smell.[2]

Plants emit these odors to attract animals, which is why one of the first things we usually notice when we leave the city for the great outdoors is the refreshing scent of the air. Stepping into a Forest, Meadow, or Wetland opens our noses to a new world of essences. Some change as slowly as the seasons, and others as immediately as one step to the next. Sometimes the smells are totally encompassing, as when the Forest is in bloom. At other times the bouquet is subtle, inviting us to bend down and investigate which Flower it might emanate from. Or maybe it's the soil itself, so we bend even lower to test our hypothesis.

All of these aromatic curiosities represent one of the most ancient forms of communication. An alluring fragrance attracts a Bee or Butterfly, which carries the pollen from plant to plant helping them to reproduce. Another Insect begins to feast on a leaf, which triggers the plant to release a malodorous repellent. As we learned in the previous chapter, a Tree attacked by Insects can release an airborne scent signal for other Trees to detect, so that they can prepare themselves by producing repellents.[3, 4, 5, 6, 7]

We humans are just as enticed by the bouquet of beneficial aromas swirling around us. From the incense used in rituals to uplift our spirits, to the Flower essences that inspire us, to the perfumes that engender passion, our lives are both strengthened and enriched by the fragrances that grace the air we breathe.

Ancient Healing Essences

The first sense to evolve in animals was that of smell. Our olfactory nerves help us detect danger, forage for food, and find sexual partners. In addition, our ability to detect certain odors helps us remain healthy and recover from disease. It's based on a complex mode of olfactory communication with the plant world.

Our distant ancestors discovered that certain aromatic plants had positive effects on our physical and psycho-emotional well-being. Thanks to ancient literature and modern archeology, we know that we humans have long been extracting the beneficial compounds from numerous plants, in the form of resins and oils. The practice of using these compounds medicinally and therapeutically is called *Aromatherapy*.

Some of these plant-derived compounds were so valued in the era of early civilizations that entire economies were developed around their production and distribution. Frankincense and myrrh, aromatic resins from Trees found in the Middle East, were actively traded along what came to be known as the Incense Road, as they were highly prized in Rome, Greece, Egypt, and Israel. The resins were put to many uses:

> **Funerary**. They were burned to mask the stench of decay. The Roman Emperor Nero loved one woman so much that he burned an entire year's production of frankincense for her funeral, which disrupted the trade until the next year's harvest.

> **Medicinal.** They were used extensively in a variety of applications, including nausea relief and post-partum recovery. Smoke created by burning the resins deterred

malaria-infected Mosquitoes, thus preventing outbreaks of the disease.

▶ **Spiritual.** Frankincense was used as an offering to numerous deities across the Middle East. The resin found fame in the West because in Christian theology it was recorded as being given to Jesus at his birth.[8, 9]

Modern Application

With the advent of refined scientific methods and advanced technologies like the mass spectrometer, chemists have been able to create a vast library of remarkably potent essential oils derived from plants found across the globe. Scientists who have studied the chemical compounds found in specific oils have been able to give us a far better understanding of how each plant extract can help us.

ONE DOWNSIDE OF PHARMACEUTICAL RESEARCH

We have gone deep into the Forests of the world to extract medicines for a plethora of diseases. Unfortunately, this has often led to exploitation rather than conservation. A wave of bio-buccaneers are pillaging the intellectual and genetic property rights of indigenous cultures and their habitats, resulting in accelerated habitat loss and species extinctions.

Essential oils are currently used in Aromatherapy to:

▶ Strengthen the immune system.

▶ Reduce inflammation.

▶ Encourage the healing process.[10]

▶ Aid decongestion.

▶ Disinfect air and surfaces (antiviral, antibacterial, and antifungal properties).

▶ Repel biting and other parasitic Insects.

- ❱ Significantly decrease anxiety.[11]

- ❱ Lower perceived stress and depression.[12]

- ❱ Improve sleep quality.[13]

- ❱ Enhance mood.

- ❱ Improve memory.

There are numerous other applications as well.[14]

Our intent here is to gain a basic understanding of the practice of Aromatherapy, so that we can apply the knowledge by going straight to the sources of the essential oils and benefit from them directly, in their raw form. In addition, we'll gain from the synergistic effects brought on by Conscious Breathing, Grounding, and Nature's guidance (as covered in previous chapters).

Some benefits of Aromatherapy, whether administered by an aromatherapist, Mother Nature, or self-administered, are that it is an inexpensive, accessible, portable, and noninvasive mode of healing. And, as we shall see, practicing Aromatherapy can encourage a close relationship with Nature.

Here is a definition of the terms commonly associated with the practice:

- ❱ **Essential oil:** a volatile oil derived from the roots, bark, leaves, flowers, seeds, or fruit of a plant, which contains the vital fragrance of the plant material.

- ❱ **Synthetic oil:** artificial, chemically derived oil that does not have a botanical origin. Commonly used in air fresheners and laundry products.

- ❱ **Fragrant oil:** a synthetic oil with a pleasant scent. Found in perfume, personal care products, and candles.

- ❱ **Carrier oil:** a naturally derived, neutral-smelling oil used to dilute concentrated essential oils for proper and safe application to the body. Jojoba, grape seed, and certain nut oils are commonly employed as carrier oils.[15]

There are three general modes of Aromatherapy practice:

1. **Diffusion** is the movement of molecules from an area of high concentration to an area of low concentration. Essential oils are highly concentrated, which accelerates spontaneous diffusion. Appliances called *diffusers*, which regulate and sustain the rate of diffusion, are popular. In Nature, diffusion occurs in a controlled manner as well; it is regulated by the plants.

2. **Direct inhalation** is commonly accomplished by holding a bottle of oil under the nose, applying oil to the upper lip, or applying a couple of drops to a folded piece of cloth and breathing through it. In Nature, one crushes several conifer needles or aromatic leaves between the palms of the hands, then cups the palms around the nose and inhales.

3. **Topical application**. The oil is diluted with a carrier oil, then applied to the skin. This technique is often used by massage therapists and other hands-on practitioners who hold Aromatherapy certifications.[16, 17]

Diffusion and direct inhalation can work quickly, with our olfactory nerves relaying signals from the biochemical compounds in essential oils directly to the limbic system of the brain, which regulates our emotional functioning and houses our long-term memories.

Some of you may have experienced the effectiveness of topical applications after you inadvertently had a brush with poison ivy. Yet if you were fortunate enough to be aware of another nearby plant-based topical application, such as Jewelweed (*Impatiens capensis*)[18] or Sweet Fern (*Comptonia peregrina*),[19, 20] you could have immediately rubbed their crushed leaves over the affected area, which would have counteracted the effect of poison ivy's volatile oil.[21]

Preparing for Primal Aromatherapy

When in Nature, we are awash in what is literally the Breath of Life. The effectiveness of that regenerative essence is based entirely on how well we can assimilate it—how well we can make Nature's breath *our* breath. Review the guidelines and exercises in chapter 7, *The Gateway: Breathing in Nature*; and be sure to inhale slowly through your nose, to fully saturate the olfactory receptor neurons in your sinuses. Exhale slowly through your nose as well, to cleanse and moisten the receptor neurons in preparation for your next inhale.

Exercising your sense of smell enhances the experience of Aromatherapy. Whether you live in a rural or urban environment, and whether you are indoors or outdoors, make a practice of noticing the variety of smells you encounter. Describe the smells in words, and compare them with other familiar smells. Building your vocabulary for smells can help you distinguish nuances amongst even familiar odors.

Unfortunately, some of our modern eating and oral hygiene habits have the effect of dulling our sense of smell. Here are some suggestions for sharpening our olfactory abilities before engaging in Aromatherapy or Walking a Healing Nature Trail. Refrain from[22]:

- Smoking.
- Using toothpaste or mouthwash.
- Wearing perfume or cologne.
- Eating a meal with hot sauce or high salt content.

The Trail of Essences

Along a Healing Nature Trail, you have the opportunity to partake of the health benefits offered by a number of aromatic Herbs and Trees. There may be Wild Mints and Sunflowers, or Willows and Cattails, or Birch and Pine, or Cactus and Sage. Whatever the habitat and composition of the vegetation, there will be numerous members of the plant community continually diffusing their volatile oils into the air.

On many Trails, branches, Ferns, and Grasses are allowed to overhang enough that Walkers brush against them, which stimulates them to release their aromatic essences.

As you continue, you are likely to experience a peaceful—even euphoric—feeling. The Trees and other plants, along with the wind and running water, are generating negative ions that clean the air we breathe, boost our immune systems, and lift our moods.[23, 24, 25, 26, 27] (Find more on this topic in chapter 5 under *Mood Enhancement and Relief from Depression*.)

FULL-BODY AROMATHERAPY

Our skin is our largest organ. Among the many ways it serves us, it manufactures nutrients, emits toxins, and breathes. These functions are benefited by Aromatherapy; so on the Trail, wear loose clothing and expose as much of your skin to the air as is comfortable for you.

Makwa Giizis, an Ojibwe Elder with whom Healing Nature Trail System cofounder Tamarack Song studied, taught people about the cleansing, centering, and healing energy that comes from hugging Trees. He would take them into the Forest and have them choose an Elder Tree who spoke to them. Then he would have them hug the Tree, breathe into a cleft in the bark, and inhale the infused air the Tree gave back. You'll notice benches placed adjacent to Elder Trees along the Trails specifically for this purpose.

You may be surprised to hear that many plants along a Trail have Insect-repellent properties, which they produce for their own defensive purposes. However, we can take advantage as well, by crushing the leaves or needles and rubbing the extracted essence on your skin and clothing. **However, do so only under the supervision of a Healing Nature Guide,** to avoid the risk of skin irritation or poisoning from using an inappropriate plant.

Sunshine, moisture, and moving air are the primary stimulants for plants to release their aromatics. Hug a Tree on the side that the sun's rays have warmed, and do so especially after a fresh rain. In lieu of rain, the moisture from your breath has a similar effect.

Remember that you can get a more concentrated dose of a plant's healing essences by crushing the foliage. Again, do so only under the supervision of a Healing Nature Guide, to assure that you have selected safe and proper species.

CLEANSING YOUR OLFACTORY PALATE

Scents, like the flavors of foods and drinks, can overlap, blend, and numb your olfactory receptors. This diminishes both the pleasurable and medicinal effects of plant essences, a condition known as nasal fatigue. To refresh yourself, move well away from the source of the essence and take several long, full breaths through your nose. Inhale deeply, and exhale completely, through your nose. Another method is to smell your own clean skin.

Traditional Aromatherapy Techniques

Following are a few additional means for extracting beneficial essences from plants that are common with Native people. Although not particularly suitable for the Healing Nature Trail experience, you can practice them elsewhere and they will nurture your relationship with Nature.

- **Smudging.** Done by heating plant matter on a small bed of coals to create a rich smoke. Used as a disinfectant, Insect repellent, inhalant, and for ceremonial purposes.
- **Pulverizing.** Plant material is dried, then ground to fine consistency. Used as a disinfectant and Insect repellent.
- **Steam Extraction.** Plant material is boiled, often after being diced or crushed, and the resultant aroma-rich steam is inhaled.

BREATHING WITH THE BIRDS

One adaptation of a traditional technique offered at select Healing Nature Trails is Tree Canopy Aromatherapy. A Certified Recreational Tree Climbing Instructor takes you up into the Forest canopy, for a potent dose of the Trees' healing essences.

After the Trail

The end of your Trail Walk doesn't have to mean the end of your practice of Primal Aromatherapy. The human olfactory system is one of our most powerful mechanisms for maintaining and restoring wellness, and Aromatherapy is a highly portable modality. Following are suggestions for integrating Aromatherapy with your daily life, no matter where or how you live.

Essential oils are a highly concentrated form of Nature, which means they can be very effective. In addition, they serve a wide range of purposes, which we covered earlier in this chapter. To take full advantage of this potential, it is important to choose an oil (or blend) that is best suited for your intended use. If a particular scent resonated with you on the Trail, a Healing Nature Guide or licensed aromatherapist should be able to help you find the equivalent in a bottled essential oil.

Equally important to selection are considerations around proper dosage and safe usage. Here again, an aromatherapist can work with you to create an individualized treatment plan.

Essential oils can be purchased online, at holistic and naturopathic shops, and at many natural food stores. Some Trail welcome centers have bottled oils from the plant species found along their Trails. However, before purchasing or using any essential oil, take time to review the following information, which you'll find on the oil bottle[28]:

- Botanical name of plant
- Plant origin and processing location

- The carrier oil, if any
- Statement of purity
- Batch number
- Expiration date

CHAPTER TWELVE

Talismanic Voices

M any people believe there is no such thing as self-healing. Wherever we go, we take ourselves with us: the same awarenesses as well as the same blind spots, the same uplifting talents as well as the same crippling traumas. It's true no matter where we go—even back to Nature. There we find ourselves, alone. We try to go forward, yet we invariably come to realize that we're doing no better than a Dog chasing her tail.

We need other voices to mirror us, challenge us, inspire us. As social creatures, we need the comfort of companionship. We need the synergistic effect that comes from joining with others on the same venture.

Right away we think, "That means I need to involve somebody else in my process." Perhaps. And perhaps not. There is value in working with others of our kind, and there is value in truly detached, other-realm engagement.

Our kind who still live on their Mother's unfettered bosom recognize that all of the components of Nature possess life and spirit. This includes the forces of Nature, such as volcanoes, storms, and earthquakes; and it includes the primary elements of Earth, Air, Fire, and Water, and what comprises them. A stone, a Feather, a candle flame . . . they breathe and speak, just like you and me.

We know this intuitively, and we practice it when we give someone a farewell gift to take along with them, or when we take a book along with us on a trip. We wear amulets and carry keepsakes for the same reason.

In this chapter, we are going to look at who we might be able to bring along with us on our Trail Walk. We are each different in our current needs, and in whose voices we might best be able to hear. A variety of power objects, representations of Dodems and other animals, and centering tools will be presented here, so that we can each let our intuitive selves select the traveling companion (or companions) who can best serve us.

The Drum

Life starts and ends with the heartbeat. We breathe to the rhythm of the heart; we love and dance and cry to the rhythm of the heart. The Earth, and the very Cosmos, pulsate with their own heart-rhythm.

All of the sundry hearts know one rhythm—one heartbeat. It is the core of relationship. For when everything else is stripped away, we can feel it in everything and everyone. In this most fundamental of ways, we are all related. We all know the same language; we all know the same Way of Being.

When we fall out of sync with the Heartbeat, we get sick. It starts with stress. We feel disjointed, out of touch. Things quit working for us, and we struggle in our relationships. Physical ailments crop up, and the shadows in the dark reaches of our minds come out to haunt us.

We need to reconnect with the Heartbeat.

The Drum is the way of our kind to rejoin. In the beat of the Drum, we hear the fall of the hoof, the rumble of the storm, and the tremble of the Earth. Drum is the primal musical instrument, the first vehicle beyond voice to express our inner yearnings. Drum is so elemental to the Human experience that she is the only universal instrument. She is the heart of close-to-the-Earth peoples—the center of their social and ceremonial lives. She is so respected in some cultures that all activity stops when she is being played and needs attention.

Our birth mother was our first Drum: she drummed for us continuously for the first nine months of our lives, then comfortingly thereafter as we Cuddled and Nursed. To feel Drum's reverberation to our deepest core is to again be in the womb, immersed in the heart-throb of our mother. Drumming is a renewal of the mother-bond, a dying back to that base of Gifting to be birthed anew.

On the Trail, a Healing Drum may be best played softly, to let her resonance speak more than her volume. Hold her close to your body or put her on your lap, so that you can feel the vibration, feel her pulse. Your body then becomes an extension of the Drum—a conveyance of your heartbeat to your Mother Earth, and vice versa. And play the Drum slowly, one beat at a time, until you find the heartbeat of the Drum. On its own, it will then come into sync with your heartbeat, then the Universal Heartbeat, and you will return to Balance.

Other Rhythm Makers

Our bodies are Drums, which we can play by clapping hands, slapping thighs, stamping feet, or beating chests.

Rattles are Drum's younger siblings. Play them in the same way as Drum: slowly to find their heartbeat, then let them find the beat of your heart and bring it into resonance with the Great Heartbeat.

Scrapers, Rasps, and Claves can be used similarly to Rattles. They are preferred by some people over Rattles because it takes more conscious involvement to play them. Where those with short attention spans, or who carry overbearing burdens, might unconsciously choose a Rattle, the other rhythm makers hold a better chance of keeping these people present and engaged.

Rainsticks (also known as *Rattle Sticks*) are the most difficult of the elemental rhythm makers to play, and for this reason they can be the most effective. More often than not, Rainsticks are used to create an ambient background sound similar to the continual rustle of leaves in the breeze.

Another empowering technique is to use Rattles and Rainsticks in pairs.

Tokens

Known also as *Charms, Amulets, Talismans,* and *Fetishes,* Tokens are likenesses of Animal Guides, inscriptions, symbols, or any other representation that exercises a significant influence on a person's feelings or actions.[1] Typically in the form of rings, figurines, and engravings, Tokens are made of malleable materials such as stone, bone, antler, shell, wood, clay, and metal. Some people wear them as pendants, rings, or bracelets, while others carry them in a purse, pack, or pocket.

Indigenous people around the world carve small Animal Tokens from the materials listed above. These people consider the Tokens to be alive, in that the spirits of the animals live within them. Some Tokens are imbued with the spirit of the dream or vision that bore them. In addition, the memories of the Tree or antler from which they were crafted abide within them. As living beings, they are interactive—they speak, feel, grow, and change. People who have Tokens as companions and guides tend to treat them respectfully and cherish the relationship.

Some Native people's legends tell of a time when animals were turned into small stone or wood Tokens. Most of them were brought fully back to life, yet some were not. This is the origin of Tokens.

Many Tokens are unique unto themselves, such as found stones or pieces of driftwood that bear uncanny resemblances to power objects or animals. Some Token carvers search for stones or shells that already resemble the animals they are going to carve, because these raw materials already contain the spirits of the animals.

Other Tokens represent dream or Trance Journeying images, or indescribable intuitive impressions. Whatever the case, they are all meaningful companions on the Life Journey.

Many people like to carry more than one Token, or accompany it with a verse or book excerpt. This works as long as the addition is complementary to the original Talisman. Incompatible or opposing influences can wreak havoc—especially in circumstances like

Trail Walks, where the preparation involves relaxing boundaries to become trusting and receptive.

As we'll cover in chapter 14, Tokens can be empowering accompaniments on a Trail Walk—especially those symbolic of the voices of Nature.

Feathers

Here is a Token that appeals especially to those who have Birds for Animal Guides. Feathers can represent specific Birds, or Feathers in general can be valuable for those who see Birds as symbols and metaphors for aspects of their Life Journeys. For some people, Feathers represent *Guardian Angels,* who are cultural variations of Animal Guides. For others, Feathers are mementos associated with pivotal times in their lives, or gifts that carry meaning because of the contexts in which they were given.

The size, shape, color, and texture of Feathers create their personalities and hint at the gifts they have to share. Worn and stained Feathers show resilience and steadfastness. Brightly colored and iridescent Feathers are mirrors and magnifiers. Stiff-quilled Feathers encourage inner strength and seeking truth and clarity.

The part of the Bird's body from which the Feather originates has much to do with the gifts it has to share. Here is a general overview:

- **Wing Feathers** are for empowerment; for the ability to rise above situations and venture out on new frontiers.

- **Tail Feathers** are for direction and stability; to stay on course and focus, and to make abrupt changes when necessary.

- **Body Feathers** are for comfort and security; for easy flowing movement and a sense of self-knowing.

It is suggested that Trail Walkers bring significant Feathers with them. Some welcome centers have Feathers for loan.

Crystals

Nature's primary elements—Earth, Air, Fire, and Water—come together to create her skeleton of Stone. Embedded in the mineral composition and crystalline structure of Stones are the energies of those primary elements. Due to their makeup, some Stones have unique properties that can be called upon to support healing and Awakening. These Stones are commonly referred to as *Crystals*.

The vast array of Crystals gives the person drawn to use them seemingly endless choices. Yet as with Feathers, certain Crystals speak to certain people. Some Crystals appear seemingly by happenstance, and others come as gifts. In addition to their clarifying and regenerative properties, some Crystals hold commemorative meaning.

Crystals of a wide variety of sizes, shapes, and structures figure prominently in the original Healing Nature Trail, which you'll find described in chapters 18, 19, and 23. The Gateway Labyrinth, Cosmorinth, Cairn, Zen Untangle, and Zen Garden all feature Crystals.

Trail Walkers are reminded to bring Crystals with them that they find helpful. Some Trail welcome centers have a selection of Crystals available for Walkers to choose from and take along with them on the Trail, or to leave at the Cairn at the entryway to the Trail.

Manifesting Your Inner Token

Some of us are verbally oriented, and some of us have a strong tactile sense. Substantive objects such as Figurines, Feathers, and Crystals tend to work well for us. Yet that may not be the case for those who are visually oriented. They have no ready material representations of the mental images of Dodems or other helpers who they sometimes envision in dreams, while Trance Journeying, or in some other way.

Nor do they always have symbolic mirrors to stand before or traveling companions to talk with, as the rest of us more easily find. Sometimes the comfort of having somebody there with you is worth more than anything else.

Visually oriented people tend to prefer a way other than words to help convey a deep thought or feeling. The same can apply to journaling, or even to expressing themselves in the moment.

To meet these various needs, they often turn to self-rendered images. With many visually oriented people already being artists, or at least liking to sketch and doodle, they are encouraged to take some favorite art supplies along with them on the Trail.

Drawing or sketching can be therapeutic in and of itself, even for those who are not visually oriented. It provides a way to:

- Strengthen the body-mind connection.
- Navigate the Labyrinthine mind.
- Release troubled thoughts or repressed feelings.
- Work problems out graphically.
- Envision a new reality.
- Chart a course toward that reality.

For deeply wounded individuals, drawing provides a way to access trauma memories that cannot be voiced (or sometimes even recognized) because of fear, conditioning, or denial. However, Trail protocols require that such work be undertaken only under the direct supervision of an authorized therapist.

Bring Tools and Talismans

In the information packets sent out to prospective Trail Walkers, it is suggested that they bring from home any Drums, Rattles, Tokens, Feathers, and Crystals that they would like to use. Some Trail welcome centers have these items available, along with colored pencils, watercolors, crayons, charcoal, and sketch pads.

Consider taking some of these talismanic voices along with you any time you venture out into the Wilder Places.

PART III

PREPARING TO WALK THE TRAIL

This book section prepares you for Walking the original Healing Nature Trail, which is located outside of Three Lakes, Wisconsin, USA. A major part of the preparation is the Trail's acclaimed Turf Labyrinth and Cosmorinth, which are described here in detail.

CHAPTER THIRTEEN

Welcome to the Trail Complex

You are driving north on historic Military Road, which prior to Euro-American colonization was known as the Lake Superior Trail. Then, it was a footpath that meandered from the Chicago area up to the south shore of Lake Superior, which the Natives called *Gitchee Gumee*: the Great Waters.

Military Road is a quiet lane winding through northern Wisconsin's Chequamegon-Nicolet National Forest. Stately Pines close in overhead, which gives you the feeling of entering a portal to another world—a place where Nature lingered while progress marched on. How easy it is to be taken in by the pristine beauty and serenity along this designated Scenic Byway.[1]

However, it wouldn't be as picturesque now if a road "improvement" project had progressed as planned a decade ago. Thousands of Trees—including hundreds of great Pines and Oaks—were slated to be cut down in order to widen and straighten the road. *Preserve historic Military Road* became the rallying cry of the grassroots effort headed up by Healing Nature Trail cofounder Tamarack Song.

The conflict between developers and preservationists raged for months. It drew media attention from across the state and resulted in the election of local legislators favoring preservation. Yet the effort was not over until the state Department of Transportation, recognizing the historic significance of the road and its value to tourism, took control of the project.

In a real sense, the Healing Nature Trail experience begins when you first turn onto the Lake Superior Trail. Right away you benefit from the legacy of those who came together to keep this precious nook of Nature whole and healthy. Nature greets you with her healing gifts of uplifting vistas and restorative essences from the Elder Trees lining the road.

What You First Find

Pay attention as you come up Military Road, as there is no sign to mark the turnoff to the Trail. There is only an address number on a post at the base of a nondescript driveway, which could pass for the entrance to any normal residence. The unpublished address (which you know only because you preregistered), the discrete entryway, and the fact that only registered users are allowed on the Trail assures your privacy and sense of safety.

Yet there is one distinguishing feature that might catch your attention: the vibrant Wildflower beds on either side of the entryway. An informative sign tells you that pollinators—especially Bees and Butterflies—have been experiencing increased stress over the past decade. The loss of habitat due to agricultural practices, urbanization, climate change, and pesticides has caused a population crash among pollinators, along with compromised health for the survivors.[2]

The Healing Nature Center staff is engaged in a mutual healing relationship with Nature by planting a wide variety of native Wildflowers, along with shrubs such as Staghorn Sumac (*Rhus typhina*) and Red Elderberry (*Sambucus racemosa*), to support pollinator species. An increase in pollinator habitat leads directly to improved health and increased populations for Bees and Butterflies.[3]

Humans benefit as well, from the healing properties of floral essences and the aesthetics of blooming Flowers being visited by Hummingbirds and Butterflies. Planting the beds is therapeutic in and of itself[4]: it has a strong positive effect on mental and physical rehabilitation.[5, 6] The new flowerbed and the nectar sippers it has attracted serve as a metaphor for the healing that could potentially manifest anywhere; but here it hints at what is possible with your upcoming Trail experience.

Along with reintroducing Wildflowers, the Healing Nature Center is actively engaged in reintroducing, protecting, and monitoring endangered and extirpated animal species, such as the Eastern Cottontail Rabbit (*Silvilagus floridanus*), Thirteen-Lined Ground Squirrel (*Letidomys tridecemlineatus*), and Eastern Timber Wolf (*Canis lupus lycaon*), and various Bird species. In addition, the Center has an invasive plant species eradication program. It focuses on nontoxic methods to control or eradicate alien plants that outcompete native species and disrupt the ecological balance.

Pulling up the drive, you see the vehicle parking area immediately to the left, and on the right is a bicycle rack. There are picnic benches where you can sit and relax, and maybe have a snack while the nearby Gateway Labyrinth captures your gaze.

The main Trail is a half mile in length, with several side Trails forking off of it. The Trail is designed to bring you closer to Nature, which includes literally closer. One way that's accomplished is by the Trail's soft, smooth surface, which is suitable for Barefoot Walking (also called *Earthing* or *Grounding*—see chapter 8).

Here are the four main experiences that most Trail Walkers look forward to:

▶ **Walking/Sitting Meditation.** The serene setting of the Trail winding gently through stately Pines creates a classic setting for Walking Meditation. Whether you spend an hour or an afternoon here, the gentle slopes, scenic overviews, and route options engender a meditative experience.

Rustic benches and the soft, carpeted Forest floor under towering Elder Pines provide inviting private spaces for Sitting Meditation. In addition, nine off-Trail nooks overlooking expansive vistas rich with Wildflowers and Waterfowl can be reserved for solo and group meditation.

Everywhere, the Trail Guide says, is the uplifting energy of Earth, Sky, and Water, along with the companionship of your plant and animal kin. The Buddha asked us to join him by coming and finding a Tree to sit under, and here is a splendid opportunity to do so.

▶ **Day Retreats.** You have the option of spending a half or whole day out on a peninsula reserved just for you. Nestled in a sheltered grove of spruce and fir, you'll have a panoramic view of a classic Northwoods scene: a Beaver Pond and Bog bordered by Pine and Birch.

▶ **Healing.** Like all Healing Nature Trails, this one is designed for guided and self-guided healing immersions in Nature. Whether you come alone or accompanied by a therapist or Healing Nature Guide, Nature is there to renew you.

▶ **The Labyrinthine Experience.** Many come just to walk the Gateway Labyrinth or Zen Untangle, or to work in the Zen Garden. The Cosmorinth is popular for evening visits. With each, there are choices to make, impasses to confront, and the opportunity to feel the connection between self and Nature. Or you might prefer a plate-size Finger Labyrinth, which allows you to travel the maze in whatever space calls you.

The Healing Power of Water

The Trail is located on an island Nature preserve, which is bordered by Streams, Ponds, and floating Bog. The only easy access to the Trail is the Threshold Bridge, which helps to assure the privacy and integrity of the Trail experience. The Healing Nature Trail could be viewed as a large-scale version of the Healing Gardens found at many healthcare facilities. Another perspective is to imagine the Trail being set in a large-scale Healing Water Garden.

The water theme is carried through in the island's interior, with the Trail skirting five Ephemeral Ponds. Here is an opportunity to view Pond life up-close. In the spring and summer, Frogs and Turtles are busy tending to their affairs, while Birds and Dragonflies flit overhead. The Trail has been designed to keep you mostly in the shadows around the Ponds, so that you can observe without disturbing.

Water possesses tremendous healing power, which is one reason the Trail's founders selected this site. Wetlands are Nature's filter, taking the runoff from the highlands and letting it percolate slowly through its dense mass of vegetation, where excess nutrients are taken up by the plants. The water then gets further purified as it filters down through the soil to recharge the water table.

When you visit a Wetland, you can get taken in by this process, and it becomes a metaphor for your own cleansing and recharging. Water in itself has a calming effect. Remember how refreshing it is to dangle your feet in the water of a Lake or Stream? Just splashing water on your face can center you and lift your spirits.

The therapeutic properties of water amplify the effect of other healing practices and explain why water plays a central role in many ceremonies. We see it in the Christian baptism and holy water anointing traditions, and in the Water Honoring and Sweat Lodge Ceremonies of the Algonquin people of the Great Lakes Region where the original Healing Nature Trail is located. The Trail staff feel deeply blessed to have the Mother Water, with her supportive healing properties, as such a central component of the Trail.

Trail Features

Here is an overview of the therapeutic features of the Forest Pathways that fork and rejoin as they meander across Wetlands, around Ponds, over ridges, and through groves of Elder Trees:

- **Conifer Bough Smudge,** for cleansing before setting foot on the Trail.

- **Remembering Cairn,** for making an intention and placing an offering before your Walk, then taking a memento after.

- **Threshold Bridge**. Leave your baggage and cross the arch to enter the island preserve and trailhead on the other side, where you immerse in the trusting embrace of Uncharted Nature.

- **Numerous Foot Bridges,** which encourage fresh perspective.

- **Two Meeting Circles** in the Pines, with one having a Ceremonial Fire Pit.

- **Log Benches beside the Trail**, each nestled between a pair of Elder Pines.

- **Seven Labyrinths:** the Gateway Labyrinth with Wildflower-bordered Paths, Cosmorinth, Stump Labyrinth, Aquarinth, Finger Labyrinths, Zen Untangle, and Zen Garden. And the Trail itself functions as a Labyrinth when one stays on the main Pathways.

- **Nine Private Nooks,** for reflection, Sitting Meditation, and one-on-one therapeutic work.

- **The Water Therapy Beaver Dam,** for Water Grounding and bathing in negative ions generated by tumbling water.

- **Three Side-Trail Loops,** which serve as metaphors for the choices we face on our Healing Journey.

- **No Informative Signs** on the Trail proper, as language keeps you seated in your rational mind, which detracts from engaging in the Awakening and deep-healing work that falls in the realm of the limbic system—the seat of emotions, long-term memories, and intuition.

- **A Separate Trail** for the physically and developmentally challenged.

Regarding the last point, in the parking area, there is a space reserved for Trail users in wheelchairs. From that spot, users can access a separate wheelchair-friendly Trail crossing a Threshold Bridge spanning the nearby Pond, then meander through the adjacent Pine Grove and Prairie Wildflower Meadow.

Open Year-Round

Rain or shine, winter and summer, the Trail, Labyrinth, lodging, retreat space, and seminar-workshop facilities are available to individuals and groups. The Trail and surrounding Forest take on a new magic in the wintertime, and the form of the Labyrinth changes with every snowfall.

A Place of Reverence

Lastly, just before you cross the driveway to register at the Welcome Center, you read that over the years people have requested that their ashes, or the ashes of loved ones, be spread along Healing Nature Trails. Many Trails are located in Nature preserves, where final remains can lie undisturbed, and where they can be visited undisturbed. Some preserves accommodate Green Burials, for those who wish to lay their loved ones to rest in the unfettered bosom of Mother Earth, rather than in a traditional cemetery.

In Germany, *Bestattungswald,* or *Forest Burial,* is practiced in designated wooded areas adjacent to traditional cemeteries. A *Baumbestattung,* or *Tree Funeral,* involves burying a biodegradable urn at the base of a tree, in such a way that the burial site goes unrecognized by passersby.[7] In some jurisdictions in the United States and abroad, it is possible to have Healing Nature Trail sites legally sanctioned for Bestattungswald-style Forest Burials.

Some see having their ashes spread along a Trail as their final Healing Walk. They want to rest in the presence of others who, like them, came to abide in Nature's comfort. The parents of a child who died an untimely death wanted his last resting place to be on sacred ground, where he would become a part of something they felt good about. Another person wanted to return to the original mother who bore him—to Nature—when he died. In the ultimate sense, he saw his nature as Nature.

The traditional Tzutujil Maya of Central America share that perspective. They see both birth and death being midwifed, with us not releasing our loved ones, but helping them echo on through the soil and Wildflowers and animals, through the nourishing water and cleansing wind.[8]

Knowing this, many people Walk the Trail with a sense of reverence. The awareness that they stand in the presence of others who have come before them empowers their healing and Awakening Journeys.

CHAPTER FOURTEEN

Checking In at the Welcome Center

L eave your watch and handheld device behind, so that you can immerse yourself in the Trail experience, without distraction. To lose time is to become the moment and merge with your surroundings, and that's one of the reasons you came. On the Center door is a sign with posted hours:

**TRAIL AND LABYRINTH USE
BY RESERVATION ONLY.**

Summer hours: 8:00 a.m. to 6:00 p.m.
Tuesday–Sunday, May 15–October 15
Winter hours: By appointment.

Evening Cosmorinth use: By appointment.

For service, call 715-546-8080.

As you approach the Center door, you get distracted by the birchbark and thatch-covered wigwams that catch your eye under a large Pine at the far side of the Cosmorinth. This type of lodge was once used by the Northern Woodland Natives, and it makes you wonder about the region's heritage and ecology, and how the Trail fits in. You can learn about this history by touring the Trail History Museum inside the Center.

Check-In and Trail Fees

Right away, you're surprised that there is no set fee for Trail usage; but rather, the Trail is supported by freewill offerings. This policy is based on the shamanic healing principle that giving is receiving. Nature is the healer, so the more transparent we can be, the more we can step aside and let Nature do her work.

Setting a fee can create an expectation; and if that expectation is not met, resentment could result. And a mercenary edge could interfere with the body-mind connection. Being open and welcoming, with as few prerequisites as possible, fosters a sense of openness and feeling of trust, both of which are highly conducive to listening and receiving. Whatever you feel inclined to contribute after you complete your Walk is acceptable.

Yet there are some people who do not feel comfortable operating on a donation basis under this premise. They either want to contribute up-front; or if they wait until the completion of their Walk, they want a solid suggestion for what to contribute. For them, forcing an unfamiliar protocol could cause more harm than good, so the Welcome Center staff suggests a contribution amount.

Other people purchase an annual pass, so that they can come and use the Trail and Labyrinths as often as they like. Again, there is no set fee for the pass. Most professionals and institutions use the Trail on an annual contract basis.

Special Services

Certified Healing Nature Guides are available to take you on the Trail. They help you get the most from your Trail experience. Being professionals with extensive training, and having guided many people, they know the Trail and its features well. They have been vetted and trained to follow ethical guidelines, so you can feel safe with them.

Healing Nature Guides have received special training to guide the blind and clients in wheelchairs.

Trail usage contributions are separate from Healing Nature Guide or therapist fees. Guides and healthcare practitioners enter into their own contractual relationships with their clients.

Since this is your first time on the Trail, you want to get the most out of the experience, so you decide to go with a Guide. Her name is Sarah, and she has already given you an overview of what to expect and answered your questions regarding registration. The two of you then decide that it would be best for you to experience the preparatory process of the Gateway Labyrinth, Smudge, Cairn, and Threshold Bridge on your own. Quoting holistic healer Deepak Chopra, that "solitude is the great teacher, and to learn its lessons you must pay attention to it,"[1] Sarah adds that she's glad you're starting your Walk alone. She then says that she's going ahead to wait for you on Breathing Knoll, which is at the beginning of the Trail proper.

But first Sarah is going to conduct a Conscious Walking Workshop (see next chapter) for you and a couple of other Trail Walkers. You planned your arrival to coincide with the workshop, as you've learned through your Walking Meditation practice that Conscious Walking is a great way for you to bring your total being into a state of presence.

Clothing and Gear

The Welcome Center staff person gives you a weather report and checks to make sure that you are appropriately outfitted for the day and Trail conditions. Here are their general recommendations for how to dress and what to bring:

- **Lightweight Clothing.** Weather permitting, wear clothing that exposes some skin to the air and sun, along with allowing some bare-skin contact with the ground and plants.

- **An Extra Layer of Seasonally Appropriate Clothing.** Includes raingear in spring, summer, and autumn.

- **Footwear.** Wear light, flexible footwear, without rubber soles if possible, to allow for maximum contact with the ground (as discussed under *Make It an Everyday Experience* in chapter 8). Moccasins are ideal.

- **Insect Repellent.** Especially important in spring and summer.

- **Sun Protection.** Includes sunscreen and/or a wide-brimmed hat and protective clothing.

- **Notebook** and art supplies (for *Manifesting Your Inner Token,* as discussed in chapter 12).

- **Water.** We suggest that you bring water only on the Trail, as the flavors and odors of other beverages can interfere with the healing essences of the Earth and the Trees.

- **Food.** A snack for the Trail, and something for the Feast of Gratitude at the Trail's end (as mentioned under *The Last Sojourn: Healing by Fire* in chapter 24).

- **Small Backpack or Shoulder Bag,** to comfortably carry everything.

Trail Tokens

We encourage you to bring a Crystal, Feather, stuffed animal, picture, keepsake . . . any Token that you typically carry for empowerment, comfort, or security. For some people, such items are valued—even necessary—companions on significant steps of their Life Journeys.

Yet for others, it may be time to set old and familiar supports aside, in order to venture forth with a fresh sense of trust and openness. When we hold onto something, it can be hard to fully experience free flight. As helpful as our traveling companions have been, we sometimes need new voices and fresh inspiration.

Tokens can be left at the Trailhead Cairn, then picked up when you complete your Walk. Or you may realize that it is your time to fly, and you want to leave your Token at the Cairn for someone else. Other Tokens that are weather-sensitive or you want to be held securely can be left at the Welcome Center, to be reclaimed after your Walk.

You didn't bring a Token, as you typically shy away from what you consider to be primitive practices. But now something in the Welcome Center has caught your eye. Up on a shelf you see Bear, Turtle, Fox, Eagle, Dolphin, and Frog Tokens, among others, carved out of wood and stone. Along with them are brightly colored, fanciful creatures that the attendant says are *Alebrije* Tokens. Trail cofounder Lety Seibel is from the indigenous Oaxacan culture of southern Mexico where Alebrijes originated.[2, 3]

Next to the Alebrijes sits a similar hybrid animal, yet she incorporates aquatic features as well. This is a *Hodag*, who is the contemporary incarnation of the ancient Spirit-Keeper of the North Country Waters.[4]

The Token who originally drew your attention speaks to you, and for some unexplainable reason, you are not surprised. The attendant hands him to you, and you reverently tuck him into the breast pocket over your heart. (See chapter 12 for more on Tokens.)

A Gifting Shop

As an afterthought, you ask how much the Token costs. The attendant handed him to you so caringly that it seemed to be a sharing from the heart rather than a transaction, which made you momentarily forget your assumption that the items displayed in the Welcoming Center must be for sale. Yet as you look around, you see that most items are not priced.

"Nearly everyone is confused at first," explains the attendant. "But just like ours is no ordinary Nature trail, this isn't the type of gift shop people typically expect. It's more like a *gifting* shop, as nearly everything that's Trail related—Tokens, Finger Labyrinths, Drums, Rattles, art supplies—is available for use at no charge."

"But what if I want to take the Token home with me?"

"That's possible, and you can leave a donation for it to cover the Center's cost. If you need a suggested donation amount, we can do that."

Yet the real value of something like a Token or Finger Labyrinth goes beyond its monetary value—it comes from the many hands that have caringly held him and the awarenesses and healings he has witnessed. It's like an antique, which has a patina and an intrinsic value that no reproduction can match.

Welcome Center Stock Items

For Trail Use

- **Trail Maps**
- **Handouts** on Conscious Breathing, Labyrinth therapy, Trail meditations, pollinator restoration, and others
- **Moccasins**
- **Paddles and Lifejackets** for the Aquarinth
- **Drums**, Rattles, and Rainsticks
- **Sitting Pads,** basic and sheepskin, for use on the Trail
- **Finger Labyrinths** in three styles

- **Art Supplies:** colored pencils, crayons, charcoal, and sketch pads

- **Tokens** of Animal Guides, along with Crystals and Feathers

- **Earplugs, Eye Patches, and Bandannas** for the Sensory Reduction Technique (SRT) and Sensory Reduction Modulation (SRM) explained in chapter 6 under *Mind-Openers: SRT and SRM*

- **Backpacks and Shoulder Bags**

- Many of the above items are also available for purchase.

For Purchase

- **T-shirts** and hoodies with Trail and Labyrinth logos

- **Notebooks**

- **Insect Repellent and Headnets**

- **Aromatherapy Essential Oils** from Trees and other plants found on the Trail

- **Books** on waking to Nature, Labyrinths, Zen, trauma and emotional healing, and *The Healing Nature Trail*

- **Traditional Birchbark Baskets**

- **Notecards** by the late Ojibwe artist Moses (Amik) Beaver

- **Gift Certificates**

The Final Preparation

There is one more personal item that we suggest you consider. You've probably heard that *curiosity killed the Cat*, but you may not know the rest of the saying: that *satisfaction brought her back*. That is why Cats have nine lives. The same is true for us when we embrace our fear and let it be our guide to a new life. When fear controls us, we cannot open up enough to trust and listen.

Then why do we hang on to fear? Some of us dread what is inside of us, and some of us are concerned that others will control us. The irony is that we are already controlled by our fear.

Yet without fear as our companion, we are not ready to heal. As Indian mystic Osho said, courage is a love affair with the unknown—a love affair with fear.[5] Courage is nothing more than fear-infused curiosity, and this is what we need in order to be a trailblazer into our healing frontier.

Without fear, then, there are no love affairs—no love for the life we want to heal, and no love for our Mother Nature, who wants to help heal us. And let's not forget that love affairs are fun. The Healing Journey is an adventure, and healing makes us feel good. In the deepest sense, fear is fun in disguise. Why else would the Cat keep dancing out on her edge?

The Trail History Museum

Before you begin your Journey, the staffperson invites you to learn the story of the Trail's beginnings and familiarize yourself with the animal life on the island preserve and surrounding Forest. At the rear of the Welcome Center is the entrance to the Trail History Museum.

Upon entering the museum, the first thing you notice is a photo display chronicling the Center's cleanup of the island. Everything from a 1942 Chevy coup to the ornate cast-iron frame of an ancient treadle sewing machine was pulled out of the floating Bog separating the island preserve from the mainland.

Next your attention is caught by the canoe exhibit. There is a bulrush boat, wooden dugouts, a moose-skin boat, a birchbark canoe, and a contemporary lightweight canoe. With the new and old boats side-by-side, you can see how canoes have evolved, and how similar today's models are to their predecessors.

Rounding out the display are hand-carved paddles, sticks used for harvesting wild rice by canoe, and winnowing baskets for cleaning the chaff from the rice. All are representative of the boats and tools once used by Native people of this area.

Mounted beside the boats is a collection of traditional bows and arrows, birchbark and willow baskets, buckskin clothing, fur parkas, and stone tools, all of which give you a feel for how people once lived in balance with Nature. You marvel at the craftsmanship and ingenuity reflected in the display.

The final display is the region's most extensive collection of animal skulls and Bird skins, which represents most of the native species. Here you get a visceral feel for the animals you could see and hear—and who might be speaking with you.

An Island's Healing Journey

The artifacts you just perused give you a feel for the island preserve's natural and aboriginal history. After the Natives were coerced to abandon the area in the late 1800s, an era of exploitation began. Almost immediately, loggers came for the great Pines that held sentinel over the island, in order to satisfy the hunger for lumber to fuel our country's rapid growth. The ox- and horse-drawn sleighs, which took timber off of the island, were soon replaced by a railroad spur, which made for much quicker and more efficient log transport to the sawmills.

When the prime timber was gone, the loggers left, the railroad tracks were pulled up, and the land was allowed to heal. Seventy-five years later, one had to look very closely in order to find any sign of the wholesale leveling of the Elder Pine groves. The massive stumps had rotted away, as had most of the tin cans, worn-out tools, and other debris left behind by the loggers.

Sign of the old narrow-gauge railroad grade could still be found if you knew what to look for. With a metal detector, you might be able to come up with an old busted crosscut saw or cast iron cooking pot buried under the moss and Pine needles. Beyond that, the island looked close to the way it had for thousands of years. The medium-size Pines that the loggers passed up had now grown to take the place of their fallen Elders. Beaver returned to build dams along the Stream and flood the Wetlands, which gave all the more feeling of seclusion to the island.

Then about sixty years ago, a family from the state's biggest city wanted to move up to the Northwoods. They bought the island, along with an adjacent parcel that had a cottage on it. Five years later, a schoolteacher purchased an adjacent parcel.

What ensued can only be compared with the fabled Appalachian Mountain feud between the Hatfields and the McCoys. Unbeknownst to the teacher, the family had been waiting until the price dropped to buy her property, which fueled tensions that lasted for years.

Eventually an unspoken truce was reached. For three decades thereafter, each party went on with life as though the other didn't exist.

Then one day, the father of the family came over to the teacher's house and apologized for all that he and his family had wreaked upon her. She in turn took responsibility for any hurt she caused.

A year or so later, the teacher saw the neighbor man's elderly mother, who lived in the next house down from the family, standing at the foot of her driveway with a suitcase in her hand. Two hours later, she was still there; so the teacher, out on a walk, stopped to talk with her. She said her leave was up and she was waiting for the bus that would take her back to the field hospital, so that she could help care for the soldiers wounded in the battle to liberate Europe.

While they talked, the Elder related how she liked to see the teacher working hard to improve her property. "You don't see that much anymore," the old woman commented. This was a radical turnaround, as she too had been resentful of the teacher purchasing the property.

Around a month later, the Elderwoman's son went over to ask the teacher if she would be interested in buying their properties. He said his mother could no longer live alone, and his family was in the process of moving to another residence. His family and his mother would feel good about selling their properties to her, he said; and they would give her a good price. "I'll go only if my place goes to that teacher," the Elderwoman's son quoted her as saying, "because I know she'll keep it natural and do something good with it."

For the same reasons, the teacher offered to sell the land to the Healing Nature Center when she could no longer care for it. It was a proverbial dream come true, as not only were the island and buildings made to order, but the trauma history of the island and the healing history of the neighbor relationship established a tradition of deep recovery that the Center staff felt honored to adopt and continue.

The land remembers. The Elder Trees have stories to tell about rape and abandonment—and about how to not only survive it, but to learn from it, heal from the wounds, and again thrive. The legacy of the previous owners was a tradition we wished to keep alive as well. Their Healing Journey has left its imprint, and those who come to the Trail for healing will feel their presence and be empowered by walking in their footsteps.

Ready to Go

Now that you've toured the Museum and heard the story of the Trail, you pack up what you're taking with you on your Walk, and you're ready to go. The staff person asks that you take all trash out with you, including organic material. Wishing you a fulfilling Walk, she adds that you should have uninterrupted, one-on-one time with Nature, as no more than ten people are allowed on the Trail at any one time.

"Plan on about two hours for your basic Trail Walk," she says. "Of course, with the Gateway Labyrinth and any other features you take advantage of, you could easily double or triple that time.

"By the way," she adds, "did you grab a Trail Meditations handout from the shelf here? [See chapter 26.] You may not need it, but I suggest taking one anyway, just in case you hit a flat spot and need some inspiration."

As you step outside, you orient yourself by taking a look at the foldout Trail map you picked up in the Welcome Center. Getting the full picture of the Trail layout, you catch your breath as you suddenly realize that the Trail is a mosaic of the mind—and that you are about to take a metaphorical Journey into its inner realms! There it is: the Trail's folds and forks make it look like a giant Labyrinth, and you remember that Labyrinths may be patterned after the many-folded appearance of the brain.

You take a calming breath and head back across the drive to meet Sarah and the others for the Conscious Walking Workshop, then to begin your Walk at the Gateway Labyrinth.

CHAPTER FIFTEEN

Seeing Blindfolded:
A Conscious Walking Workshop

There may be no better way to encourage the body-mind connection than by walking, considering that our legs comprise nearly 40 percent of our body mass—and significantly more when including their cardiovascular, skeletal, and connective-tissue support systems in the torso. This compares to 13 percent of body mass for our arms, and 7 percent for head and neck.[1] In addition, walking improves brain functioning,[2] which Danish philosopher Søren Kierkegaard alluded to when he said, "Above all, do not lose your desire to walk. Every day I walk myself into a state of well-being and walk away from every illness. I have walked myself into my best thoughts, and I know of no thought so burdensome that one cannot walk away from it."

Regular walking is so effective at maintaining centeredness that it could be one of the main reasons people are drawn to Walking Meditation, and to walking in general. At the same time, the quality of an experience is based not only on what we do, but on how we do it. A conscious approach to walking can magnify its benefits.

Urbanized people are typically centered in their heads when they walk. They start each step by moving their head forward first, which causes them to lean into their steps. They then end up coming down heavily on their heels in order to continually catch themselves.

This plodding-along walking style keeps people head-centered and disconnected from the body. Also, such walking is hard on the feet, leg joints, and lower back, even though it works adequately for getting from point A to point B over prepared surfaces.

In Nature, however, no two steps are the same. To move smoothly and quietly—and to keep from tripping—we have to adjust every step to the terrain. And there can be a lot going on between points A and B, so we may need to quickly stop or change direction at any time. That all takes presence, sensory acuity, and functioning from our belly-centers rather than our heads.

Now we can thank the body-mind connection, as Conscious Walking's clarity of movement strongly encourages clarity of intention. As Thich Nhat Hanh says, "Walk as if you were kissing the earth with your feet."[3] Here's how it's done:

1. **Wear soft-soled shoes** or go barefoot.

2. **Stand up straight,** with knees slightly bent and arms relaxed at your side.

3. **Take a few deep, slow, centering breaths,** all the way down into your belly.

4. **Lift one foot,** as though you are going to take a step, and hold it there while you take another breath.

5. **Step forward,** shortening your stride by about one-third, and coming down on the ball of your foot rather than your heel.

6. **Take another step,** directly in front of the first, as though you were walking on a line.

7. **Proceed slowly,** as though you were stalking up behind someone.

8. **Let your body do the walking,** so that your head is free to observe, smell, and listen. Glance down only once every few paces, to see where you will be stepping.

When to Walk Consciously

Some people like to Conscious Walk the whole Trail. They say it slows them down and keeps them attuned to their surroundings. When they compare their Conscious Walking experience with times that they do not Conscious Walk, they realize that they notice more, and they feel a deeper sense of satisfaction with their Walk overall.

Here are some other times when Conscious Walking can be helpful:

- **As a Walking Meditation.**
- **When you want to move quietly** and not create a disturbance.
- **When walking the Labyrinths.**
- **When *Wolf Walking,*** which is how Wolves conserve energy when negotiating deep snow. The leader breaks trail, and the others follow in his footsteps. In any season, Wolf Walking behind your Guide is an effective way to maintain your intention and learn Conscious Walking.
- **To renew your intention** when it wanes on the Trail. An empowering way to do so is to re-walk the Gateway Labyrinth. It works because the established Path takes you to the center, and knowing that fact helps focus and quiet the mind while walking.

Healing Nature Guides typically give their clients instruction in Conscious Walking. On the following page is a general description of the workshop that many Trail organizations offer.

Blindfold Trail Walking

In a metaphysical sense, deprivation can lead to Awakening. Sensory deprivation is a relatively safe and easy form of awakening. Fasting, meditation, retreats, rites of passage, near-death experiences, and Shamanic Journeying are forms of sensory deprivation

---

CONSCIOUS WALKING WORKSHOP

For improving Walking Meditation, Blindfold Walking, and sensory perception, and for training to guide the sight-impaired.

Imagine walking in a special way—with a sense of presence and with an intent that goes beyond merely reaching a destination. In this workshop, you learn how to feel with your feet, and how to use physical movement to create new movement in your mind and heart.

You begin by walking the Labyrinth, to wind down and get centered. You then get instruction in:

Deerstepping, *which is developing sensitivity by coming down gingerly on the ball of the foot rather than the heel.*

Wolf Walking, *which is creating a sense of presence through shadowing the person in front of you by stepping in his or her footprints.*

Blindfold Walking, *which suppresses sight to supercharge the other senses and stimulate psycho-emotional activity. Includes training for guides of blindfolded and sight-impaired Trail Walkers.*

Each of the three forms of walking can be practiced independently; yet they are taught in sequence, as one prepares for the next. Combining them has a synergistic effect.

The workshop culminates with putting everything to practice on a Healing Nature Trail Walk.

Some Trail organizations offer special Blindfold Walking Workshops for couples, which many find to be a unique and powerful bonding experience.

---

that most of you are likely familiar with. Several other shamanic sensory–deprivation techniques are covered in this book:

▶ **FIRE-INDUCED TRANCE**, found under *The Dance of Remembering and Forgetting* in chapter 24, *Reentry*.

▶ **FULL IMMERSION GROUNDING**, found under *Shamanic Grounding* in chapter 8, *Grounding in Nature*.

> **WATER GROUNDING (FULL IMMERSION)**, found under *The Role of Water* in chapter 8, *Grounding in Nature.*

> **THE LABYRINTHINE JOURNEY INTO DEATH AND REBIRTH**, as undertaken by shamans (found under *The Contemporary Use of Labyrinths* in chapter 9, *The Labyrinthine Experience*).

Along with those techniques, Blindfold Trail Walking can be an effective way to ply the body-mind connection. Eliminating sight, which accounts for an average of 85 percent of our sensory input,[4] gives a considerable amount of attention to the other senses. This is evidenced with blind people, who typically have enhanced auditory ability.[5, 6, 7] Many of them are able to literally hear solid objects in front of them,[8, 9] and a higher percentage of them display musical talent than does the general population.[10, 11]

These exceptional performances are likely due to neural plasticity, which is the mind's adaptive ability to rewire itself.[12, 13, 14, 15] Yet sighted people can benefit from reduced sensory input in much the same ways as blind people, even if not to the same degree.

Healing and Awakening-wise, the benefit comes from sensory receptors and processors being used atypically, which encourages atypical thought processes and expressions of feeling. As illustrated a number of times in this text, here again we see Nature's alchemy with the body-mind connection.

There are two ways to benefit: Blindfold Sitting and Blindfold Walking. The first is commonly practiced while meditating on the Cosmorinth (see chapter 18), Blindfold Rooting (see chapter 8), and in personal Comfort Spots and Trailside Havens (see chapter 22). Blindfold Sitting can be safely practiced by most people, as it carries little risk.

Blindfold Walking, on the other hand, can leave those not accustomed to it psychically vulnerable. There is the additional risk of physical injury from tripping, running into objects, and being poked by branches. Blindfold Walking is allowed on certified Trails only if the Walker is accompanied by a Healing Nature

Guide (all Guides are trained in the practice) or a partner who has taken the Conscious Walking Workshop with the Walker.

How to Blindfold Walk

The idea is not to get from point A to point B, but rather to be bathed in other-than-sight sensory stimulation. Walking while blindfolded catalyzes the process by forcing you to compensate with more attentive listening, feeling, and attuned presence.

Yet focusing too much on locomotion itself detracts from the concurrent psycho-emotional processes that are stimulated by this exercise. It's important to listen to the rate at which you are processing sensory input, and pace yourself accordingly. Let yourself *be*, rather than trying to *do*. After all, you've already arrived at Nature; the remainder of the Journey is inward.

Two Ways to Blindfold Walk

▶ **Independently,** by feeling your way with your feet. To assure your safety, a Healing Nature Guide or trained partner needs to accompany you.

▶ **Guided,** from behind or up-front.

   a. **With two reins** four- to six-feet long, attached to shoulders or hips.

   b. **By touch,** lightly on one shoulder or the other. Use a finger or a stick.

   c. **By voice,** with low-key commands, whistles, or clicks—the simpler, the better.

Preparatory Steps

1. **Attach and adjust reins** if you are using them.

2. **Practice being guided** by walking with your partner for a few minutes with your eyes open.

3. **Blindfold yourself.** Merely closing your eyes is not enough, as you are subconsciously aware of the fact that you

can open your eyes at any time, which reduces the efficacy of the sensory deprivation.

4. **Consciously breathe,** to center and sensitize yourself. Follow the *A Short Course in Conscious Breathing* guidelines in chapter 7, *The Gateway: Breathing in Nature.* Use *Slow Breathing,* as described in the same chapter.

5. **Begin walking.** Proceed slowly, stopping wherever and whenever you feel the impulse.

Blindfold Listening Guidance

More than any other sense, listening compensates for sight. Listen with every step, as a sound missed could mean a misstep—or missing a guiding voice. And you must listen closely, as guiding voices from Nature speak subtly, in the soft language beyond words.

Hear the reminders of our living relationship with the Trees: the swish of the branch and the creak of the trunk as they sway in the wind. Imagine that you are hearing them exhale the oxygen that you need to inhale, and listen to yourself exhaling the carbon dioxide that they need to inhale.

The sounds keep coming, from the soil underfoot, and from every winged, furred, and scaled being about you. The variety and complexity of sounds is a glimpse of the raw beauty of the natural world—a loveliness that is layered and nonlinear. You are Becoming One with the ever-present Primordial Chant.

By attuning yourself to sound in this way, you are engaging in one of the elemental tools of shamanic healing. First, it helps with overall sensitizing to the Trail experience. Second, it is a subconscious reminder of the Labyrinth within each of us. Anatomically, our inner ear is known as the *Labyrinth of the ear,* for its various cavities, canals, and ducts.[16] Listening, then, is negotiating another Labyrinth—one that engenders the body-mind connection in a very intimate way.

The connection is further encouraged by the inner ear's additional function of maintaining physical balance.[17, 18] Let this sense of balance—which works in unison with all of the surrounding trills and chatters and whispers—not only keep you balanced on the Trail, but also guide you toward mental and emotional balance.

> ## FOR MORE ON SENSORY DEPRIVATION
>
> *The therapeutic benefits of modulating sensory reception can be further explored with two techniques presented in chapter 6, Sensory Reduction Technique (SRT) and Sensory Receptor Modulation (SRM).*

When the Trail Is Distant

If you are not able to set foot on a Trail, you can still Walk it blindfolded, even if you can't go outside. It's done with a technique called *Envisioning,* which is described in chapter 25 under *Why Remote Walking Is Possible.*

CHAPTER SIXTEEN

Center and Trail Maps

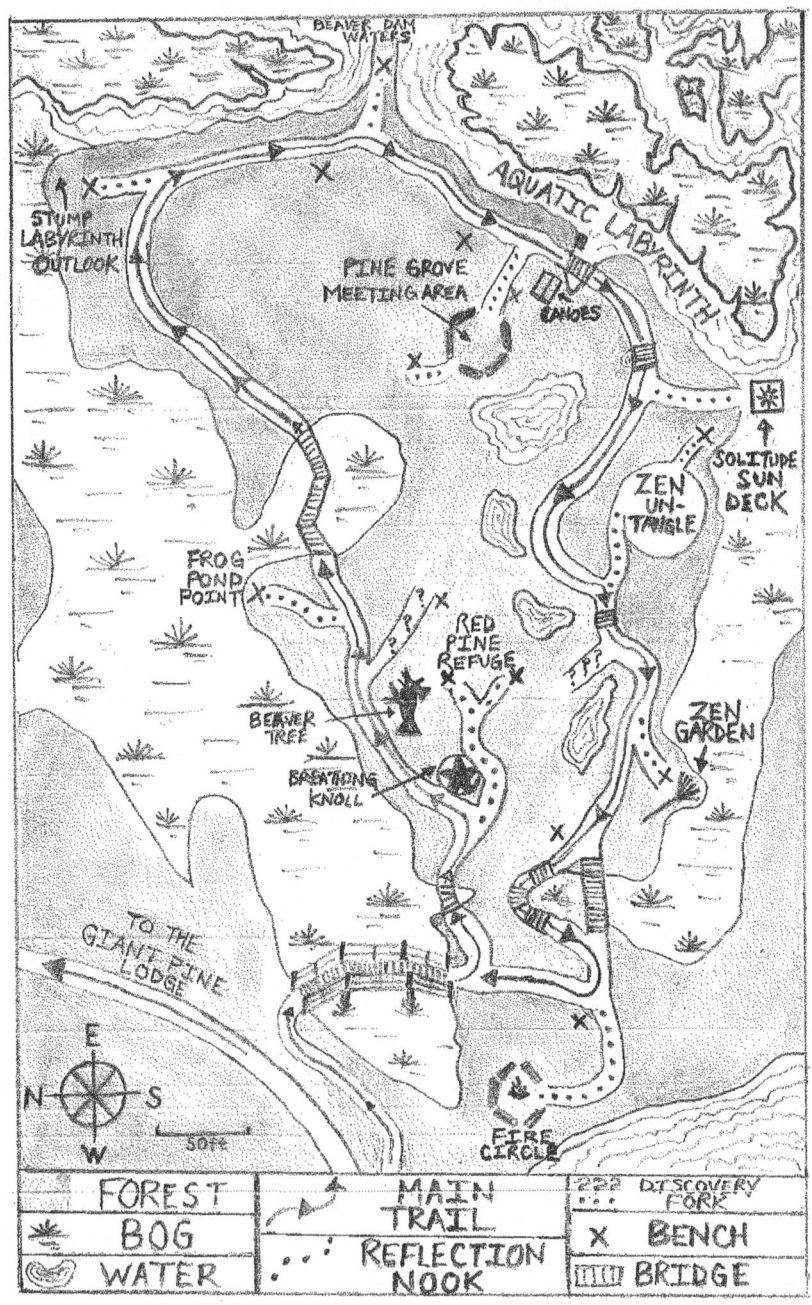

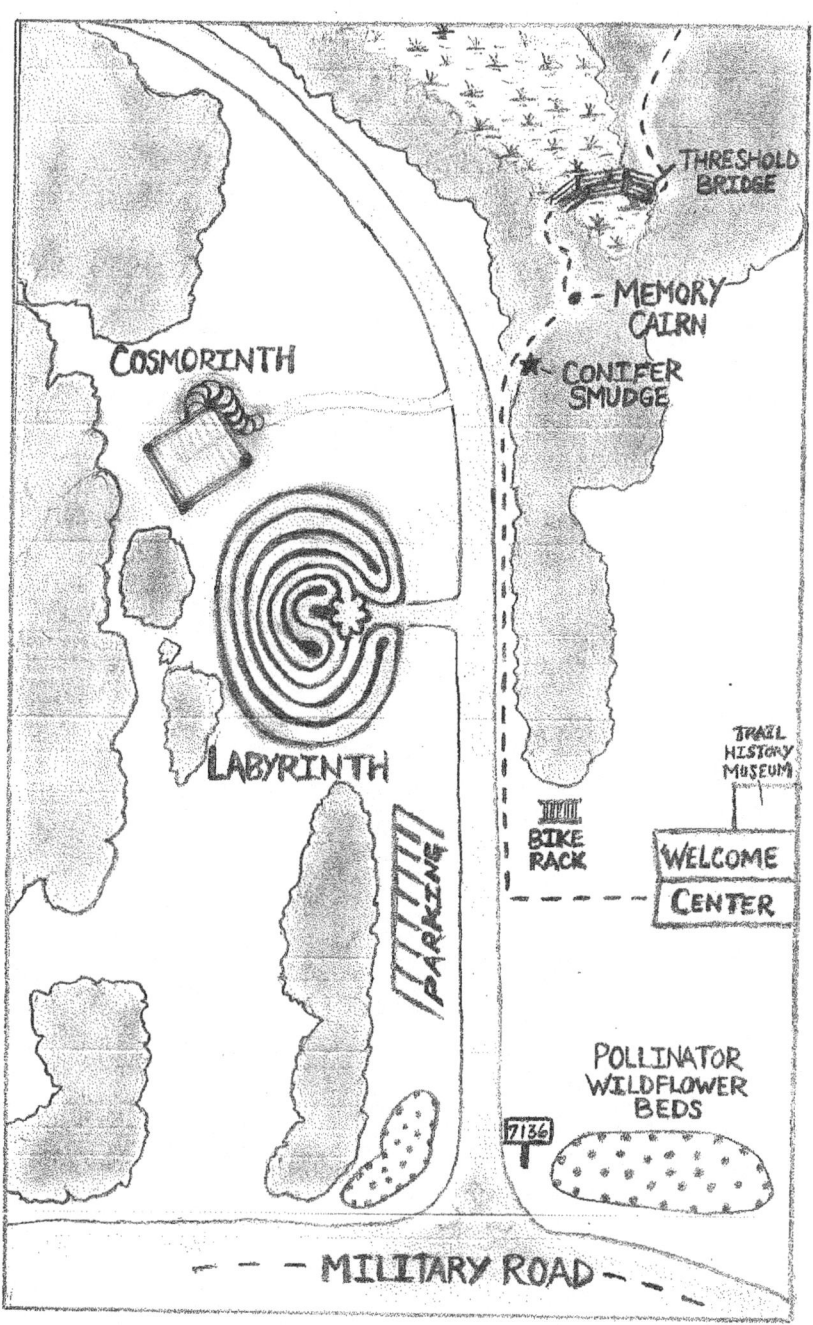

CHAPTER SEVENTEEN

Our Nature Guide and Sister Trail Legacies

Back in chapter 14 you met Sarah, your Guide for this, your virtual inaugural Walk of the Healing Nature Trail. Sarah, along with Tamarack and all the other Guides, follow in the footsteps of a continuum of revered Guides that goes back more than one hundred years. Today's Guides honor those Elders by carrying on their work. Here is Tamarack's story of how the spirits of those esteemed forebears are living on through their legacies and the gateway Trails they created.

Ernest Oberholtzer is one of the great unsung Nature Guides of the last century. The Pathways that drew him were the voyageur canoe routes through the North Country wilderness. He worked tirelessly to establish the Boundary Waters Canoe Area in northern Minnesota, which is now the most visited wilderness in the country, and he was one of the founding members of the Wilderness Society.

In Ernest's biography, *Keeper of the Wild*, author Joe Paddock states, "There are always two factors present in the childhood of significant environmentalists: first, they develop a strong early love bond with nature, and second, an admired adult mediates this relationship and teaches respect for the natural world."[1] Along with Ernest, I'd like to introduce you to the admired Elders of mine whose voices echo through these pages.

My Mothers in Nature

When I was a child, Nature was my sanctuary. I came from a troubled family, and my teachers struggled to keep a curious boy like me engaged at my desk. Nature became my refuge—she lifted my spirits and healed my woundedness. I would speak to her, and she would understand. And she would not only accept, but cherish, me, for who and how I was.

The same was true of my biological mother, Dorothy. My earliest memories are of Mom walking with me through the Meadow that surrounded our house and sharing my joy as I came to know the Wildflowers, Butterflies, and Bees. We would often come home with seasonal wild edibles: asparagus, strawberries, hickory nuts; and I always came home feeling everything was right with myself and the world.

Finding Resonant Voices

In my college years, I was swept away by Mahatma Gandhi and Aldo Leopold, two humanistic naturalists who died in the year I was born. Yet the way they touched my heart, it felt as though they never left. When I heard these words from Gandhi, "What we are doing to the forests of the world is but a mirror reflection of what we are doing to ourselves and to one another,"[2] my comfortable, private relationship with Nature expanded exponentially. Right then I realized that there can be no separation between my nature, the natural realm, and what we humans have made of Nature. As Gandhi was a unifying force for the people of India to find their identity, shuck colonialism, and end environmental exploitation, he helped me see that to achieve the same on a personal level, I had to "realize brotherhood [and] identity with all life."[3] Self-realization within the context of Nature was no longer enough for me. "The purpose of life is undoubtedly to know oneself," he said. "We cannot do it unless we learn to identify ourselves with all that lives."[4]

On the healing powers of Nature, Gandhi gave me equally concise guidance: "Nature has provided us with sufficient reserve of vitality,"[5] and "Men should seek out and be content to confine the means of cure to the five elements of which the body is composed, i.e, earth, water, akash [open spaces], sun, and air."[6]

Along with Ernest Oberholtzer, Aldo Leopold was one of the founders of the Wilderness Society. He is regarded as the father of ecology, and his book *A Sand County Almanac* (Ballantine, 1986) resonated so strongly with me when I first read it that I felt it was written for me. Living only an hour-plus drive from where I was born and raised, Leopold gave Gandhi's human-nature relationship guidance the regional rootedness that I needed. When Leopold said, "There are two things that interest me, the relation of people to each other, and the relation of people to land,"[7] and "Harmony with land is like harmony with a friend,"[8] I knew what he meant.

Between stints in college, I hitchhiked around the country to find American Indian Elders who could help me experience what it's like to live with other humans who have a strong land ethic. While I knew it only from a relationship with a Nature that was free of humans, this ethic was intrinsic to their culture.

Every Elder I spent time with oozed a land ethic that I could only call transcendent. Yet they didn't see it that way; to them, it was merely their intuitive modus operandi. The two Elders I'd like to honor here as Nature's Guides who made clear footsteps to follow are Makwa Giizis (whom I introduced in chapter 7) and Keewaydinoquay Pakawakuk Peschel. She was an Ojibwe medicine woman whose Healing Trail was bordered with Sweet Grass, St. John's wort, Cedar, and Mullein. For her, the plants were people. Whether human or plant, the people were literally Nature—there could be no separation. Makwa Giizis mirrored the same awareness, through breathing with the Trees and listening to the voices of the wind, the animals, and the Mountains. They, along with he and his people, all shared the same breath and spoke the same language, so how could all of life—including humans—not be intrinsically related?

Those Whose Shadows Grace Our Trail

One of the early locations of the Healing Nature Trail, about thirty years ago, was a tract adjacent to the Nicolet National Forest's Headwaters Wilderness, about three miles from the current Trail. Realizing that I was walking in the shadows of Nature Guides who were there before me, I began by getting to know them. I wanted to honor them for their work, learn what they knew, and adopt their approaches. In that way, I could contribute to their legacies and better function in balance with my new surroundings.

The area's first Nature Guides were the Indians, who I learned about by studying archival materials held by the local historical society and library. Those savvy Natives introduced the younger members of their clans and new arrivals to the surrounding Woods and Waters, and took them up the Lake Superior Trail, which is now known as Military Road, the route that brings people to the Healing Nature Trail.

Following in the footsteps of the local Indian Guides were three newcomers to the area: Sam Campbell, Carl Marty, and Walt Goldsworthy. They were each lured here by the mystique of the Northwoods, and they each found unique and effective ways to imbue others with that transformative magic. Only Walt was still guiding when I moved here. Sam had passed on twenty-five years earlier, and Carl was gone for nearly ten. Yet like Aldo Leopold and Mahatma Gandhi, their enduring presence was so strong that I could still hear their stories, and they answered when I asked for advice.

Walt Goldsworthy

Known as the *Thoreau of Three Lakes*,[9] Walt came to the area in 1946 to grow cranberries on the region's rich Peat Bogs. The experience brought him a deep awareness of the intricate interrelationship of all Nature, which included humankind.[10] His awareness was nurtured by living most of his adult life in small cabins on secluded Lakes.[11]

Early on, Walt made friends with the first Northwoods conservationists: Sigurd Olson, who with Ernest Oberholtzer established the Boundary Waters Canoe Area; and Carl Marty and Sam Campbell, whom I will introduce shortly. Walt was so inspired by these people that he devoted the rest of his life to preserving the local natural treasures and sharing them with others.[12]

"May there always be wilderness trails where man can go to find his way," said Walt.[13] Early on in our relationship, Walt taught me an important lesson: to be effective in reaching people, we need to meet them where they are at. He did that by becoming a prolific and visionary trail developer for people on their Journeys of Self-Discovery and Healing, and for hikers, boaters, snowmobilers, and motorists. Later in this chapter, I describe several of his trails.

In addition to trails, Walt was the moving force behind the establishment of the Thunder Lake Wildlife Refuge, the Sam Campbell Memorial Forest, and the Three Lakes Museum—all local treasures that enrich the lives of people who come from around the country.[14]

Walt found other innovative ways to meet people where they were at and offer them gateways to Nature. He represented the Northwoods at tourism trade shows in the big cities, and for twenty-two years, he wrote a newspaper column, "Lakes and Woods."[15] It was his book that inspired me to seek him out.

Yet with all of that, I think what Walt liked best was sharing the mysteries that lie in the sylvan shadows with a group of curious people. As the first interpretive Forest naturalist ever hired by the US Forest Service,[16] Walt worked for years as the resident naturalist on the Nicolet National Forest's Franklin Lake Interpretive Trail.

Walt moved people because he understood the healing powers of Nature, and he could convey it. In his book *Wilderness Reflections,* he said this about Primal Aromatherapy (see chapter 11): "I rested, to enjoy the fragrances of the North Country[17] . . . The fragrance of sun-warmed Pines . . . these and many more simple gifts of Nature are a most potent balm for mind and muscle."[18] In the book, he extolled the powers of Grounding (see chapter 8): "Only by an intimate association with the very soil itself could the human soul and spirit be motivated and inspired to fully exploit the creative talents of man."[19] He conveyed the intrinsic value of Nature-immersion experiences when he said that while the wilderness "may be more idyllic for practicing the basics of a good life, these basics are fundamental in their truth, hence, can be applied to life whatever fate may lead . . . and harmony in life will return regardless of locale."[20]

I believe Walt's legacy endures because he conveyed the double entendre of *healing Nature* in all he did, as expressed in this quote from his book: "[Nature] teaches that while man has rights to the fruit of the land, he has equal responsibility to maintain the health of the land and his own person."[21] What Walt has created and preserved will continue to enrich not only our lives, but the lives of many generations to come.

Carl Marty

At around the same time as Walt, Carl Marty succumbed to the spell of the tall Pines and sparkling Waters. He came to establish the luxurious Northernaire Hotel on the shores of Deer Lake, just two miles from the current Healing Nature Trail.[22] Ostensibly a mecca for vacationers, the Northernaire served even better as a platform for Carl's conservation proselytizing.

From the hotel, he launched daily boat and bus tours of the wilderness, with Walt serving as Interpretive Guide. "No one can be exposed to the wilderness without becoming aware," professed Carl.[23] He went on to say that "we have it in our power—and now within easier reach than ever—to so upset the balance of nature as to endanger and perhaps wipe out our own human family."[24] It's not hard to see why he took such advantage of the format the hotel gave him.

Soon Carl became known as *Mr. Conservation*. He took the title seriously, stating that "conservation is a sacred obligation of the living to those who have left us and to generations still unborn."[25] Along with that, his conservation ethic had a soft side. He took in orphaned wild animals and allowed them to meander around the hotel and grounds—and through the dining room—much to the delight of the patrons. In the process, he learned much about wild animal behavior,[26] which he delighted in sharing with his guests.

"There is no safer place in the world to bed down for a night's sleep than the very center of the forest," said Carl.[27] He had a knack for bringing that sense of Nature's comfort and security to his hotel guests—along with experiencing the comfort and security his posh accommodations provided them. Here again was a vital lesson for me in meeting people where they are at, which was punctuated by the seriousness with which Carl took his mission as a Guide on the unique trail to Nature that he crafted.

Sam Campbell

Of all my inspirations, Sam may have been the most like me. His mother, Kitty, raised him as mine did me. Kitty, a diligent student of Nature, instilled in Sam the passion to cherish and protect all that lives.[28] Like me, Sam was a poor student. When he was called upon for answers, he often had none. He could, however, expound eloquently on the plants and animals of Field, Forest, and Pond whenever such subject came up in class. At other times, he was either reading about natural history rather than world history; or he was looking out the window, dreaming about the nesting Sandhill Cranes or newborn fawns he knew so well.[29] Like me, he learned early on that, as he said, "Animals are not wild naturally, except as they are made wild by man."[30]

And like me, Sam used every tool at his disposal to sing the praises of Nature. He wrote twelve books, gave around 10,000 public lectures, produced nearly half a million feet of film, opened to seekers of solace his island cabin retreat (which still stands, just three miles north of the Healing Nature Trail), and developed a trail for them that presented Nature in all her raving beauty and healing might.[31]

Sam first came to the Northwoods in 1909, as a boy on a camping trip, just as I did. And as with me, the shadowed Forests, countless Lakes, and lush animal life made him feel as though he had, in his words, "someway slipped into Heaven[32] . . . Never could I forget the effect that vast forest had on my thought."[33] It left him "light of heart and free of care, knowing . . . in a way that passes the powers of reasoning."[34] As with Sam, I know the feeling well.

In an age when the natural world—and nearly everything else—was being objectified and divided into its simplest components for scientific scrutiny, Sam embraced creation as a living, breathing entity. A Squirrel's being included the Trees she lived in and the Hawks who hunted her. Viewing a sunset was a prayer, a doorway to the soul.

Following, in Sam's own words, is an abridged version of his vision for the Discovery Trail that he created with his writings and lectures, and with an actual Forest Trail on the mainland adjacent to his island retreat (which he called the *Sanctuary of Wegimind*, after the Ojibwe term for *mother*).[35] In his visualization, you can see the inspiration for many of the features of our Healing Nature Trail. And I think you'll see as well why Sam came to be called the *Philosopher of the Forest*.

I have a sense that down somewhere within my own erroneous thinking is all that which grieves me, and that it is my own creation.[36] I know, too, that man's true sanctuary is not a place, but a state of mind that can be attained anywhere. I have learned that the contemplation of natural beauty and grandeur is a tremendous aid in doing so.[37] Our quiet, meditative propensities, which flourish amidst Mountains, Forests, and Streams, are too important and beneficent in our evolution to be lost.[38]

Before us are grand things and unspeakable freedoms. It is all ours, but we need to work for it, by calling forth strength of mind and body that we never knew we possessed.[39] Nature can help, for it is a kind of X-ray, which looks one through and through, revealing true substance.[40] Then if we see things well, we shall understand them; and if we understand them, we shall appreciate them.[41] We will see that the storms of the Ocean take place on a very thin surface, and so it is with the thin scum of selfishness, fear, greed, and misunderstanding. In the depth of our true being, there resides an undisturbed harmony to which we may easily turn.[42]

As the peace of the Sanctuary settles upon us, our burdens become lightened. Here before the majesty and magnitude of creation, we are born anew. Who could walk intimately with Nature, noting the bird calls, kneeling to dainty Flowers, breathing the fragrance of the Balsam Firs, and still hold selfishness in thought?[43]

The purity of the scene erases from thought all memory of the aimless maelstrom of cities, and instead we hear voices which utter no sound, but tell of the depth of Life. Yet we do not catch these voices if our thoughts are in a whirlwind of our own making.[44, 45] Our hearing is handicapped by practical knowledge and a vague thing we call reality.[46] We must be good listeners to hear over them.[47]

All Nature is decorously quieted by the cloak of darkness. Voices are involuntarily softened, moves are gentle and slow, and thoughts are rendered tranquil.[48] Who could look on the vast canopy of starlit heavens, and not feel a grandeur which softens our grief?[49]

I would hasten the day that man awakens from his carnal dream to see in his brother creatures divine provision for the birth and expression of his better self.[50] There are life-sustaining Sanctuaries in our blessed woods—let there be more![51] It is to this end that I must direct all things.[52]

Mother Trails, Sister Trails

The Healing Nature Trail is not alone—it is nestled in a community of awe-inspiring sister trails that are all located within several miles of us. They each played valued roles as inspirations for our Trail, and they served as surrogate trails until our current trail was completed.

Most of the sister trails are associated with the Sam Campbells, Walt Goldsworthys, and Carl Martys who founded them. The trails in turn nurtured and weaned their founders to become the esteemed Nature Guides we have come to know. These trails are referred to as the Guides' *Mother Trails*.

Following is a description of the trails, which have welcomed many seekers and witnessed many transformations. All of them are still in existence and open to the public. Along with foot trails, there is one water trail and one paved trail for cars and bicycles. Many people who come to Walk the Healing Nature Trail like to take in other trails as well. Maps that give directions to those sister trails are available at our Welcome Center.

Not included here are descriptions of the direct progenitors to our Trail, the first one of which I developed in 1971. For that Trail history, please see the *Designed by Nature* section in chapter 2.

Military-Butternut Lake Road Scenic Byway

One day thirty years ago when exploring the upper Great Lakes region for a new Healing Nature Trail location, I came upon Military Road. Its many bends and rises, along with the tunnel effect created by the overhead tree canopy, made me feel like a gnome entering an Enchanted Forest. Right then I told myself that if I ended up choosing this area for the Trail, I would like to find a site for it on Military Road. And that is what came to be.

From an Indian Path called the Lake Superior Trail, to a military supply route in the War of 1812, to today's bicycle-motor vehicle route, Military Road has had a long and vibrant history. In the heyday of Carl Marty's Northernaire, tour buses left daily for chartered wilderness tours via Military Road, which began only a mile from the hotel.[53]

In 1992, the ten-mile section of the road that runs by the Healing Nature Trail was designated a Heritage Scenic Byway. Walt Goldsworthy, who guided many motor tours on Military Road, worked for thirty years to secure the designation.[54] Franklin Lake Road, which continues the Byway for four miles to the Franklin Lake Interpretive Trail (also discussed in this section), was designed specifically to enchant people the way I was on Military Road by highlighting the ancient Hemlock Forest and undulating glacial landscape the road winds its way through. With its stellar natural features, and being lightly traveled, the Byway has become a favorite biking route.

I'm particularly fond of the Scenic Byway because of its ability to meet people where they are at, then bring them into Nature. We are a car culture, and it's largely cars that take folks to the trails along the Byway that I am about to describe. The Healing Nature Trail also is accessed by the Byway.

Scott Lake Trail

Five miles southeast of us lies the Headwaters Wilderness. Just into the Wilderness, on the north of Scott Lake Road (Forest Road 2183), is Shelp Lake. A short trail winds from the parking area through a grove of ancient Hemlocks, then out on a boardwalk over the Bog surrounding the Lake. Here is a great opportunity to keep your feet dry while getting a close-up look at Bog plants and animals. Scott Lake, which is blanketed with wild rice, is found on the opposite side of the road. Adjacent to the Lake is a mile-plus long trail that circles through a stand of towering White and Red Pine, Hemlock, and Yellow Birch that are hundreds of years old. A Research Natural Area, it gives an authentic feel for what the Northwoods was like before the logging era.

Giant White Pine Trail

A half-mile farther east on Scott Lake Road, then a little over a mile north on Giant Pine Road (Forest Road 2414), you'll find a small parking area on the left-hand side of the road. A rustic two-mile long trail takes you from there through one of the best surviving examples of a mature Hemlock-Sugar Maple-Yellow Birch-Basswood Forest capped with a super-canopy of towering

White Pine. Understory shrubs include Mountain Maple, Beaked Hazelnut, and Fly Honeysuckle, with a groundcover of Oak Fern, Blue-Beaded Lily, and Bunchberry.

Sam Campbell Memorial Trail

Three-plus miles north of us on Military Road (Forest Road 2178), then left another mile on Old Military Road (Forest Road 2207), brings you to the Sam Campbell Memorial Forest and Hiking Trail Complex. It was dedicated in 1989, with Sam's old friend Walt Goldsworthy hosting the dedication program.[55] Sam had established a series of interconnected trails on the mainland just north of his island sanctuary, Wegimind, which he named Sunset Trail, Friendship Trail, Chapel Trail, and Vanishing Lake Trail.[56] They were the current Trail's predecessors. The self-guiding brochure available at the trailhead is based on Sam's writings. A section of the Trail leads to Wegimind Point and Vanishing Lake, which are featured in a number of Sam's writings. The entire Trail is three miles long and meanders through a Forest of Pine, Fir, Cedar, Spruce, and Hardwoods.

Franklin Lake Interpretive Trail and Adjacent Trails

At the northern terminus of the Military-Butternut Lake Road Scenic Byway is the Franklin Lake Campground and Interpretive Trail. The mile-long Pathway meanders through what has come to be known as the *Hemlock Cathedral*—a virgin stand of immense Hemlock and White Pine. For six years, beginning in 1963, Walt Goldsworthy was the resident naturalist at the campground and would guide Trail walks.[57] "Every day," Walt's wife Doris told me, "Walt and I would walk the Trail through the Hemlock Cathedral to give thanks and experience what Walt called *communion with nature*."[58]

From the Trail, one can continue on the thirteen-mile Hidden Lakes Trail, with its scenic vistas overlooking small Lakes and its section through a breathtaking stand of great Hemlocks. Another option is the six-mile trail to Anvil Lake.

The campground has magnificent stone and log cabins, pavilions, and fireplaces, all constructed by the Civilian Conservation Corps in the 1930s. The buildings are now on the National Register of Historic Places.

Crystal Creek Paddling Trail

Two miles southwest of our Trail, a bridge on Highway 32 crosses the channel that connects Deer Lake to the south with Big Stone Lake to the north. Just south of the bridge, on the west shore of Deer Lake, stood the Northernaire Hotel. North of the bridge, on Big Stone Lake was the Northernaire's beachside lounge, called the Showboat. Sixty years ago, a pontoon float called the *Wilderness Queen* left the Showboat dock three times an afternoon for two-hour excursions described by Walt Goldsworthy, the tour's Guide, thusly: "You enter this last bit of primeval wilderness through the scenic portals which guard the entrance of Crystal Creek, a sequestered stretch of wilderness antiquity that echoes the romance of past ages. Recently re-discovered, this long-forgotten Waterway which once felt the touch of the canoe paddle of the passing Indian and pioneer trapper, has caught the fancy of modern-day adventurers." [59]

Today, you can retrace the route by canoe or kayak. From the Highway 32 bridge, paddle south on Deer Lake one mile, to the confluence with Crystal Lake on the right. Although much of the shoreline is now developed, Nature's splendor is still there to behold. Two miles up Crystal Lake, you enter Crystal Creek by going under the Highway 45 bridge. From there, you can go upstream about a mile, to the railroad grade.

"No work begun ever pauses for death," wrote Robert Browning.[60] With the exception of my mother, all of our Trail's Elder Nature Guides have passed on. Yet for those of us who read their words and walk their Trails, their essential work to bring us back to the caring embrace of our Mother Nature continues with a new vitality.

CHAPTER EIGHTEEN

Unwinding at the Gateway Labyrinths

Here begins your guided Trail Walk. Whether you are being accompanied by a Certified Healing Nature Guide, your healthcare practitioner, or this text, we recommend that you begin your Walk at one of the Trail Gateway Labyrinths. By day, the gateway is our classic Labyrinth, inspired by the design found throughout ancient Babylon, Egypt, Persia, and Greece. The Labyrinth's Path is bordered by multicolored Wildflowers, to support declining Bee and Butterfly populations. In the evening, the Cosmorinth is the gateway to the Labyrinthine Journey amongst the planets and constellations.

Yet before walking either, let's start with a general description of the Labyrinth. It is a special type of maze that is designed to help unwind the body and quiet the mind. Comprised of a single Path that coils in from the perimeter starting point to its center, a Labyrinth guides you back out on the same Path.

As opposed to standard mazes, there are no forks in a Labyrinth's Path and no dead ends. With no decisions to make, you have the opportunity to give yourself completely over to the experience. All you have to do is follow the Path, and you are guaranteed to reach the center and return to where you started.

There is one more thing: you must be present. The Labyrinth gives no other choice, because its Path twists and turns to the right and left, doubling back upon itself numerous times as it takes you deeper and deeper toward the center. The return Path is the same, only in reverse.

The only choice you have to make is how present you want to be. The more you engage your senses of sight, smell, and hearing, the more present you will be, and the more you will gain from . the experience.

One beauty of the Labyrinthine experience is that being present is all you have to do—the Labyrinth does the rest.

As the Labyrinth guides you, a sense of trust and safety, of being cradled, is bound to permeate your being. The tensions and concerns that you brought with you, and the drama of the wild world you live in, seem to shed, as though they were a heavy overcoat on a hot day. A sense of peace then comes over you, leaving you in the state of conscious being, with uncluttered space for listening.

The Gateway by Day: A Classic Turf Labyrinth

Now let's walk the Labyrinth, which lies in the middle of a grassy Meadow at the beginning of the Healing Nature Trail. Bordered by a Pond and surrounded by towering Pines, the site itself is calming and inviting.

A short stone-lined Path across the driveway from the Welcome Center takes you to the threshold of the Labyrinth. At the beginning of the Path you notice a Cairn of many-spangled stones, with a sign beside it that reads:

> *One left for an Offering*
> *One to accompany your walk*
> *One to take for*
> *remembrance*

You caringly tuck the Crystal who asked to come along with you into your pocket as you slowly go down the Path. Ahead you take in the sheer majesty of the ancient-looking panorama laid out before you.

**The Gateway Labyrinth under
construction at the Healing Nature Center.**

The Journey Inward

You enter the Labyrinth from the South, the direction of nourishment and support. As you step over the threshold, you realize right away that you have entered a living organism. The Path is carpeted with soft grasses, and the Path's borders are festooned with Herbs and Flowers. You are infused with the life-energy—you can feel it, smell it, and hear it.

After only a few paces, you skirt the edge of the Labyrinth's heart: a small grotto in the shape of a six-petaled Flower. The center design is inspired by that of the Chartres Cathedral in France, where it is laid out in mosaic tile on the cathedral floor.

The design parallels the Seven Direction cosmology of the Algonquian people of eastern North America. Along with the four cardinal directions (South for nourishment, West for wisdom, North for introspection, and East for new beginnings), there is the Above, the Below, and the Within.

Yet the grotto has only six petals. The seventh is the stem of the Flower: the Path that leads into the grotto from the East. The Algonquians keep an opening on the eastern side of ceremonial circles, to allow for the easy entry of inspiration and fresh starts.

However, it is not yet your time to immerse in the Heart of the Journey. As close as you are, you are still separated from it by a hedge. The Labyrinth's intention is to inspire you by giving you only a taste of what is to come.

After briefly skirting the Heart, the Path veers off and loses itself in a web of its own making. From above, the pattern looks not so coincidentally like the folds of a brain.

The Path now takes you in a wide clockwise arc around the entire Labyrinth about midway between the Heart and the perimeter. You end up back near the entrance, to be reminded about where you began and what brought you here.

Only, you are not here to linger, as the Path doubles back upon itself and takes you all the way back around the Labyrinth, to the opposite side of the entrance. Here again, you are reminded about why you came and to whence you shall return. This is essential on the Labyrinthine Journey because it helps you maintain perspective and gives you the motivation to continue.

Again, you double back on yourself, this time skirting the very outer edge of the serpentine form. You are able to gaze out over the perimeter hedge and drink in the undulating waves of Meadow Herbs and Flowers, pristine and undisturbed. The serenity, the taste of what could be, accompanies you all the way around the Labyrinth's perimeter, until you come for the third time right up to the entryway.

However, this time the Path turns to take you deeply into the bowels of the Labyrinth: the dark recesses of your soul. On the way in, you again skirt the Heart, to be given another taste of what you may reach.

Yet you linger not long, as the Path turns your back to the Heart, only to spin you back around and have you come straight onto it and stare into its depths. There you linger, feeling the draw to your Journey's consummation.

No, it is not yet the time. Your Path whisks you off to the North, in the opposite direction of the heart, only to befuddle you by doubling back and taking you quickly right back to the Heart's edge. This time your sojourn with the Heart is *very* brief, and you again descend into the darkness of your undifferentiated inner landscape.

Back and forth you go, through tight, dizzying turns, until—as though it were a mirage appearing before you—the Heart-Center sits at your feet. You step into it and feel the flush of accomplishment, along with a sense of finality and release.

The heart is a place to linger, to drink the nectar that is beaded up on each petal, with its unique and empowering gifts for the Return Journey. Yes, you have arrived.

The Way Back

Enriched blood lingers not long in the heart. It is a vibrant organ, with a strong sense of ultimate purpose: to send you back on your Return Journey. To retrace your steps, imprinting in your memory all that you have gained on this quest, so that you take it back and transform your life.

On the way back, you erase what you have shed on the way in, like fresh blood scouring the plaque that has accumulated on artery walls. You have come in on this arterial Path from the extended limbs of your life, into your core—your Heart-of-Hearts—to regain what you have lost touch with.

Now you are sent back to those outer reaches of your personal universe. Cleansed and empowered, you feel lighter on the way out. Still, each step is conscious, as you remember what you have come here to forget. You do not want to lose a single teaching, a single reminder of what you brought with you and why you had to experience it. In this way, your travails become your teachings, your blockages become your open windows, and your blindness takes you to breathtaking vistas.

As you leave the Labyrinth, you may be overtaken by laughter or tears; or you could feel numb or overwhelmed by the experience. Whatever your state, it doesn't matter, as it is merely a passing cloud on these first steps of the new and unfolding Labyrinthian Path of your Life.

The Night and Day Gateway: The Cosmorinth

While walking the Labyrinth, you noticed the elevated platform with the spiral staircase off to the far right. Now you want to experience it, so you approach the serpentine, stone-lined Pathway leading up to its spiral staircase.

But before you set foot on the Path, you notice a Cairn similar to the one at the head of the Path to the Labyrinth. Only this one seems more bejeweled. You look closely, and you see Crystals of myriad shapes, forms, and hues. You read the little sign at the base of the Cairn and pick up a Crystal that feels warm to the touch.

> A Crystal in your hand
> Crystals in the sky
> Let the one you hold
> Help your spirit fly

The closer you get to the structure, the more it appears to have emerged from the surrounding Forest. The platform, which

looks to be eight- or ten-feet wide and deep, perches atop four weathered Tree trunks. Winding around one of the trunks is a staircase made from a massive log cut into roughly eight-inch thick discs, then stacked to form the steps. The railing, crafted from gnarled and twisted Tree branches, seems like it grew right there to meet the need.

Before ascending the staircase, you read the placard mounted off to one side:

Inspired by the shipbuilding tradition of placing a gold coin beneath the mast before it is raised, symbolic stones have been placed beneath the Cosmorinth's primary pillar: the one supporting this staircase. In shipbuilding, the gesture was done with the intention of making the ship's voyages safe and fruitful. The intention here is the same, for the cosmic voyage you are about to embark upon.

Here are the stones resting under the mast:

Meteorite is the remnant of an asteroid or comet that has survived the intense heat and speed of crashing through the Earth's atmosphere. The placement of a Meteorite under the foundational pillar gives cosmic presence to the viewing platform as well as serves as a reminder of the infinite possibilities of the universe.

Tektite, composed of silica, is formed when large comets or asteroids crash into the Earth. The tremendous force of impact causes terrestrial rock to melt and get thrown into the atmosphere. The lava-like spray falls back to Earth, transformed into Tektite. As offspring of both Earth and Sky, just as we are, Tektite symbolizes our Cosmorinthian Journey: coming from Earth, venturing into the Sky, transforming, then returning to Earth.

Moqui Stones, also known as Shaman's Marbles, are concretions of sandstone encased in iron oxide. In Hopi legend, the ancestors use these stones to play marble games. When finished, the ancestors let their marbles lay, to tell their living relations they are happy. The Moqui symbolizes our past-present-future connection, and it serves as a reminder that healing from yesterday, in order to experience a better tomorrow, begins today.

Daytime Use

In daytime, the view of the Labyrinth from this high vantage point is breathtaking. It takes you to a reflective place: you linger a few moments to gain perspective on what walking the Labyrinth brought you.

Then you notice the telescope, which is used at night for intimate Journeying amongst the celestial orbs. Yet right now, you're more drawn to the cushioned seating, which you arrange so that you can lay down comfortably and let your gaze drift into the infinite. Today, for you, there is a sky of broken clouds, bordered by ever-changing azure Pathways. You take several deep, relaxing breaths, then meld into the Labyrinthine skyscape with no boundaries and infinite possibilities.

Some people prefer to find meandering Pathways in the treetops, and others follow the paths taken by overhead Birds and Butterflies. Still others cherish cloudless days, where they lose themselves in the vast expanse of the blue, blue sky.

On your way down the spiral staircase, you notice another daytime user: the Bees who nest in the log's wormholes. With the nectar and pollen provided by the Wildflowers in the beds the Center has established, along with the nesting habitat the Center has provided, there has been a sizable increase in the Bee and Butterfly populations.

FOR MEDITATION

Day or night, several people are so enamored with meditating suspended between Earth and Sky that they come regularly to sit. Some incorporate conscious sky gazing into their practices, and others blindfold themselves.

Journey into the Night

As beautifully as the Cosmorinth serves by day, it takes on an entirely different persona by night. The world below disappears, and the world above comes alive. All is cool and quiet, and there are no distractions. Sensory input is cut to a minimum. You can hear your breathing; you can hear your heart pounding.

For those reasons, many people prefer coming in the evening rather than the daytime. If you are one of them, we encourage you to arrive early enough to partake in a Sunset Smudge atop the Cosmorinth. Being cleansed by the last of the sun's golden rays, you are now uplifted by cosmic energy and ready for your upcoming amble through the Celestial Maze.

There is no lighting on the Path to the Cosmorinth, or on its steps or viewing platform. Those who arrive after dark are given a small red-lens flashlight to find their way. Red light barely disrupts the nighttime calm, as most animals cannot see red light, and the dull hue is only minimally disturbing to humans. Guests are asked to turn their lights off as soon as they get situated on the platform.

A DARK SKY OASIS

Night light pollution, which is caused by excessive or improperly shielded outdoor lighting, reduces the visibility of celestial bodies; contributes to the incidence of obesity, diabetes, and attention deficit disorder;[1] and is deleterious to wildlife.[2] The Healing Nature Center, a member of the International Dark-Sky Association (IDA), follows IDA guidelines to eliminate glare (light that shines into the eyes) and skyglow (light shining into the night sky), to assure that Cosmorinth users have an unparalleled cosmic experience.

In the Celtic Druid tradition, the night sky is seen as a Crystal Cavern. It is entered on a Solo Journey, to discover what treasures for the psyche lie amongst the countless Crystals bejeweling the Cavern.

Dusk is the Threshold Bridge you cross, from the brightness and busyness of your everyday life to the indefinable realm of the boundless interior. You pass over from the sure to the unsure, from the tenuous comfort of your distractions and escapes to the uneasy awareness that soon there will be nowhere to turn but inward. There is nothing left to grasp onto other than your shaky grip on what you thought you had.

Without form or direction, you drift aimlessly around the Great Cosmic Maze. You try to gain some footing on the undulating Pathways of the Northern Lights, but they defy your intention and keep dancing to some different drum.

Other nights, it could be the skeletons of Trees silhouetted by the rising Moon; or the ever-unfolding patterns of clouds across the Moon and Stars; or the craters, ridges, and plains of the lunar landscape, expanded across the sky by the Cosmorinth's telescope.

Any of these Labyrinths embedded within the Cosmic Cavern can fling us into the void of Outer-Inner Space. Once there, you come to know what baggage you took with you, because you cannot shake free of its grasp. If it burns to the touch, you know without a doubt that it is something you need to heal through. The real beginning of the Healing Journey is when you have no choice but to take full responsibility for what you hold in your grasp. It can only be yours, because you drift alone with it through the Cosmos. There is no one around to blame, and nobody to rescue you.

This is the gift of the night. This is what you came for: just you and the ultimate Labyrinth—the Cosmos. Here you have the quintessential, all-encompassing yin and yang: the Cosmic Inferno. And within that, Cosmic Harmony.

Some people like to think that when crossing the threshold of dusk and being swallowed into the night, they leave everything they know behind. The stark reality is just the opposite, as is often the case with what we *think* we know. All that gets shed is what we assume to know, or what we hope to someday know, or what we're told is important to know but we were never quite able to grasp.

What we truly know is what remains in the deep, dark silence when all else is stripped away. This is all we take with us—this is all we *can* take with us—when we tumble into the galactic freefall known as the Cosmorinthian Journey.

You've now fully prepared yourself: you are centered, stripped of excess baggage, and you have a vision to fulfill on your upcoming Walk. The Forest looms ahead, and you are filled with anticipation. Yet you know from hard experience that the joy of discovery carries with it the agony of knowing. If ignorance was not always bliss, at least it made few demands.

PART IV

A WALK ON THE WILD SIDE

This book section serves four purposes:

1. ***A trail guide*** *for those not accompanied by a Healing Nature Guide or healthcare practitioner.*
2. ***An envisioning tool*** *for those who live too distant or are physically incapable of Walking the Trail.*
3. ***A guideline for healing and Walking Meditation features*** *to look for on trails not designated as Healing Nature Trails.*
4. ***An example and inspiration*** *for individuals and organizations establishing Healing Nature Trails.*

So as not to create expectations, and to keep your first Walk from being a sight-seeing tour, we recommend that you read just chapters 19 and 23 of this book section before your Walk. You will then be better able to have an intrinsically organic and intuitive Nature-immersion experience.

CHAPTER NINETEEN

The First Steps on the Trail

Y ou are about to enter the maze called the Healing Nature
Trail. A maze is a complex of Pathways without a clear route
to the center—not to mention what it might be like to attempt
coming back out. There are going to be false starts and dead ends,
and you may have to retrace your steps here and there to get back
on track. Or at least what you hope is on track.

Yet two things are certain: you'll have to take personal responsibility for your venture, and you'll have to risk going out on your
edge. Even then, there is no guarantee that you'll make it through
the maze. Nor is there the clarity that you have to make it through
in order to reach your goal.

Nowhere is *nothing ventured, nothing gained* more true than here.
With the maze, the courage to venture forth is the courage to
heal. That means extending trust—not in any particular person
or belief or healing modality, but rather in the process. When
there is movement, there is the potential for change. And when
the movement is conscious, the maze becomes a passageway to the
mysteries of the mind and the knowing of the heart.

With that thought, your optimism wanes. The Labyrinth just
took you on a journey to the center of your mind, where you
found a morsel of inner peace and self-knowing—a moment of
hope. Yet now you feel defeated before you start. Time and again,
you've struggled mightily to make it through that maze to the
treasures of the mind and heart. Only every time, you ended up
on your knees, whimpering. With every passageway you tried,

you kept hitting dead ends made up of the boundaries between your heart and mind. You know that the longest walk before you today is not the Trail itself, but rather the distance between your heart and mind—that's the Wolf in your belly.

You drag your feet to the trailhead, which is directly across from the Labyrinth. Right as you step foot on the Trail, you look up, and your eyes meet this sign:

The image sends a chill up your spine. "That's why I'm here!" you exclaim. In that instant, it comes clear that your appointment was not with the Center, but with your destiny.

Then you read the words below the image: *Welcome home,* and a tear finds its way down your cheek.

The small sign on the wall in the Welcome Center that read *Leave your baggage here* now makes sense to you. Thanks to the Labyrinth, you've been able to release your grip on much of what would otherwise have kept your mind someplace else, even though you are physically here. Another sign on the wall: *The lighter your load, the easier your walk* suddenly takes on another meaning.

Under the trailhead sign is a log bench, which reminds you of one more thing you wanted to do to lighten your load and ease your Journey: you sit down and remove your shoes and socks, so that you can take full advantage of the restorative benefits of Grounding (see chapter 8). You could have borrowed a pair of light moccasins from the Welcoming Center—which you were tempted to do because you are not accustomed to walking barefoot—but you read that the maintenance crew walks the Trail barefoot every morning to make sure it's comfortable, and you trust in that.

The Trailhead Smudge

No glance ahead can give you a clue for what is coming, as the Trail quickly disappears into the Pines. You set foot on the Path, and you notice that with every step it gets narrower and narrower. The grove of young conifers that the Trail cuts through is closing in on either side, to the point that boughs are brushing your clothing and bare skin.

Shouldn't the vegetation have been trimmed back? you wonder. Is the whole Trail going to be like this?

Then you smell the piney fragrance the boughs are emitting. It's pleasant, and it lifts your spirits. *Ah,* you say to yourself, *this is the Conifer Smudge I read about. No wonder I'm feeling good!*

The essence causes you to remember that here and there throughout the Trail, branches, Ferns, and Sedges would be sweeping you; and that they get cut back only when absolutely necessary, to maintain the Smudge effect. A warm smile graces your face.

Smudging is a traditional practice akin to burning incense, anointing with holy water or essential oil, or the washing of feet or hands that often precedes ceremonies. Here in the Forest, the cleansing essences come raw from the plants—a living Smudge— rather than being released by burning or extraction. Yet the effect is the same: the feeling of being cleansed and refreshed, and the pheromone-like properties that transpose you to another state of consciousness. Some psychic-sensitive people can be sent into a trance state from a Smudge alone.

Potawatomi Elder and college professor Robin Wall Kimmerer states that "a ceremonial smudge . . . washes the recipient in kindness and compassion to heal the body and spirit."[1] So prepared, you venture onward.

THE BRUSH-DOWN SMUDGE

For people who are suffering a high state of anxiety or heavily traumatized, a vigorous Smudge is often necessary. Your therapist or Trail Guide will take a fan of boughs in each hand, have you take off your hat and glasses, and brush you down all around, from head to foot.

First Stop: The Remembering Cairn

A few steps beyond the Conifer Smudge, you come to a small, neatly stacked pile of multicolored stones and unique pieces of driftwood. You brought a stone along—a special one given to you by a lover who left you in pain. You've never been able to come to peace with that relationship, and now you want to release your attachment.

You gently place the stone on the backside of the Cairn, so that you don't have to look at it again. That should make it easier, you think, but still tears flow.

To fill the void, you choose another stone, of a shape and color different than your lover's gift. But then you put it back, realizing that a substitution alone will not erase the pain.

Instead, you choose to Walk the Trail alone. You want to come alive again: you want to feel the pain because you know that if you don't allow it, you won't be able to feel yourself.

You've come to find out who you are, and you are now ready to venture forth, afraid and alone. Maybe on the way back you will stop here and see if you are ready to take another stone home with you, to mark the memory of your newfound relationship with your rediscovered self.

Crossing the Threshold Bridge

Back on the Trail, you immediately enter a grove of tall Balsam Firs. Just as quickly, you take a left turn, then a right, and find yourself at the foot of a rustic wooden bridge. It's a long span, and it arches over an expanse of Wetland.

You can't make out what's on the other side, and you know you're not supposed to. You trust that the Shadowy Forest will accept and guide you when you are ready. But first you know that you must face your threshold—this bridge between things you have trouble letting go of and things you may have trouble hearing.

This is your last opportunity to either turn back or commit yourself fully to your Healing Journey. There is nothing in between but the all-consuming Bog. She does not discriminate: whoever lingers indecisively breaks through the floating mat of vegetation and becomes hopelessly mired in regret and defeatism.

The lure to cross the Bog is there: the song of Birds and tall Pines swaying lazily in the breeze beckon you. Yet the stronger the draw, the tighter your chest constricts.

One reason is that you can still pick up on the subtle sights and sounds of civilization behind you. Even though you read in the

Trail literature that a last reminder of what you are leaving behind could help give you clarity on why you are here, you still wish that distraction wasn't here at this critical moment.

Taking a deep, clearing breath, you tell yourself it's now or never. You place one foot on the first wooden slat.

Your courage builds, and your other foot follows. It has now become the Bridge of No Return.

The slope is steep. You grab the handrail to help you along. Yes, I will need help, you remind yourself. I need help now. I know the Caring Mother awaits, and I know her plant and animal children are there to support and guide me. I just have to release myself—at least for this day—from the made-up beliefs that have been blinding me and the numbing crutches I have been leaning on.

You grasp the Token in your pocket and take a couple of deep, centering breaths. A new strength courses through you, and you let go of the railing.

The Bridge has built-in design features for catalyzing the threshold experience. Employing the body-mind connection, these features create physical responses that open pathways for parallel responses in the mind. Here is each design feature and what it can potentially cause:

- **Abrupt Changes of Direction before the Bridge.** Activates new neural pathways, which creates an opening for new possibilities.

- **The Bridge Itself.** As a transition zone between two landmasses, it instills a level of uncertainty and begs curiosity.

- **Wooden Plank Walkway.** A level of trust is needed for stepping out into thin air, supported by only a slat of wood.

- **Steep Entry Incline.** Along with activating new neural pathways, looking upward and the extra exertion hint at the effort needed for this quest.

- **Railing.** The dance between self-reliance and support—and the sense of safety—are going to play roles.

- **Level Center, Suspended over Water.** A glance downward says that the feeling of relaxation at the apex of the arch is tenuous. A journey is movement, and movement means risk and change.

- **Panoramic View between Two Worlds.** The vista instills a sense of comfort and spaciousness, which relaxes and opens the mind—broaden the view, broaden your perspective.

- **Steep Exit Decline.** Less regularly used neural pathways come into play, along with the sense of descending into something new.

THE SHADOW SIDE OF THINGS

On first impression, the Bridge spans a Wetland. Yet it is much wetter than appearance would have it. The vegetation forms of floating mat mask two to three feet of water underneath. Here is the first of Nature's many trailside lessons that things aren't always as they appear.

As you step off the Bridge and onto the Trail, you have to turn either right or left. Tacked to a Tree in front of you is a rustic arrow made of White Birch sticks. It points to the left. You realize you'd have gone that way anyway, because it would take you around the Trail in a clockwise direction. That, according to the Trail Guide, would heighten your sensory awareness and magnify Nature's healing energies, because you would be flowing in harmony with them.

The regional Ojibwe call doing things in a clockwise fashion *Walking the Sun Trail*. Both Sun and Moon travel clockwise (which they call *sunwise*) across the sky. They say the *Path of Life* follows the Sun Trail by starting at birth in the East, the direction of new beginnings, then ending in the West, where we ultimately go to join the Ancestors when we pass over from this life. The Ojibwe and many other indigenous people enter ceremonial circles—and conduct their lives in general—in a sunwise fashion.

You take your first tentative steps on the Trail, feeling uplifted by the thought that you could be following the tradition of your ancestors and others who lived in balance with Earth energies.

CHAPTER TWENTY

Plying the Body-Mind Connection

N apoleon said that men are ruled by toys,[1] which in psycho-therapeutic parlance means that physical metaphors are important to our well-being. And so it is with the Healing Nature Trail, which is one of many bridges, bends, and benches. If you weren't previously aware of that, you will be shortly. Immediately after stepping off of the bridge, you take an abrupt left turn. Then after a very short stroll under the Forest canopy, you suddenly find yourself in a small opening. At your feet is a short bridge spanning a canal, which the Beaver have dug to float logs out to their dam.

Transitions from one habitat type to another, such as the one you just experienced, are common on the Trail. So are small foot-bridges without railings, which—even though they're only a step or two above ground level—can create a slight sense of uneasiness and have you crossing with caution.

The entire Trail, in fact, keeps you on your toes. There are numerous sharp turns, small changes in elevation, variations in topography, and forks in the Trail. The walking surface varies as well, going from sod to Pine needles to boardwalk to wood shavings.

The same is true of the Labyrinths. The Gateway Labyrinth has fourteen switchbacks, and there are endless potential turns in the Zen Untangle, Cosmorinth, and Aquarinth. Add the several styles of Finger Labyrinth and the Zen Garden to the mix, and you have a total experience designed to keep you present, attuned, and challenged.

One rejuvenating feature that can be easily overlooked is the Trailside Benches. You'll notice a number of them spread throughout the Trail system. Ostensibly for rest and reflection, they serve another purpose as well, which has to do with their construction. They are comprised of large-diameter log sections lying directly on the ground. Their mass and substance make them effective conveyances for the Earth's Grounding energy (see chapter 8). Even if you are not able to sit or lie directly on the Forest floor, you will still be able to gain the benefits of Grounding by spending time on the benches.

Where many people would believe that Grounding is comforting, in practice it fuels the state of centeredness and sensory acuity needed to respond to the Trail's ever-changing environmental conditions.

Yet the question remains: Why has the Trail been designed to keep you present, attuned, and challenged?

As Goes the Body, so Goes the Mind

Fires can't be made with dead embers, nor can enthusiasm be stirred by spiritless men, said equal rights activist James Baldwin.[2] The Trail and its environs fan the embers of the spirit with their abrupt changes, which necessitate physiological readjustments to the landscape. You need to refocus your eyes and alter your stride. You might have to watch where you step or decide which Trail fork to take. With every twist and turn, you have to readjust your bearings.

The body-mind connection is so strong that each of the functional readjustments you make creates a parallel shift in your mind.[3, 4, 5, 6] When you change direction on the Trail, you open up the possibility for a mental change of direction. When you step off the main Path to take a side fork, you make it all the more likely that you'll be able to explore other possibilities for your life.

In addition, suppressed thoughts and feelings find the opportunity to emerge and be cleared. Outmoded patterns of behavior that we were previously blind to can be recognized. The ego is encouraged to follow suit and relax self-protective boundaries, which increases your state of presence. Feeling more yourself, you have the wherewithal to abandon your conventional relational modus operandi and open to new possibilities.

With virtually every feature of the Trail, the designers took its potential effect on the body-mind connection into consideration. They knew that there is no easier or more effective way to create avenues for psycho-emotional change than by creating literal avenues for changing up the physical self. Altogether, these Trail features create a continual-movement change-up, with the cumulative effect building in the mind the further you progress on the Trail. Along with that, your ego's efforts to resist change progressively weaken.

Eventually, the old saying, *As goes the body, so goes the mind*, proves itself out. If you are like most people, at some point on your Trail Walk you will start to experience a surprising sense of mind-expanding openness, along with a flood of considerations and feelings that you didn't know you were capable of. A little further down the Trail, fresh perspectives might take shape around old experiences, and new possibilities could come to light. If you are here because of trauma, the newfound sense of self you gain can make your Healing Journey look not quite so scary.

Two Highly Effective Techniques

Along with body-mind connection features intrinsic to Healing Nature Trails, here are two exercises you can use to accelerate the process:

1. The Nose Knows

"Learn to practice breathing in order to regain control of body and mind," says Buddhist monk Thich Nhat Hanh.[7] He goes on to explain why: "Breath is the bridge that connects life to consciousness, which unites your body to your thoughts."[8] The breath-bridge between body and mind is strengthened by breathing through the nose, which is commonly known as *Nasal Breathing*. It opens up channels to our feelings and deep-seated memories,[9] emotion circuits in the brain,[10] and the medial temporal lobe and recognition memory.[11] It improves perception, learning, and reasoning.[12] Find more on Nasal Breathing in chapter 7.

2. Finger Walking

Most Healing Nature Trails have Finger Labyrinths (see chapter 9) available for use. They provide a unique opportunity for plying the body-mind connection. Finger movements and hand gestures give cognition and retention a helping hand, so to speak, as the hand–mind connection is strong. When abstract concepts are presented to the accompaniment of complementary finger and hand motions, the concepts become easier to grasp than without the motions. Finger-tracing the Finger Labyrinth, then, makes the Labyrinthine Mind Journey considerably more effective than if taking the Pathway was just envisioned, or if it was only visually traced.[13, 14, 15, 16, 17, 18]

CHAPTER TWENTY-ONE

Sensitizing on the Breathing Knoll

I inhale, she exhales
She exhales, I inhale
She breathes into me,
I breathe into her
Her breath is my life,
my breath is her life
We need each other,
the Tree and me
We are one breath,
we are one body

You have crossed the little bridge over the Beaver Canal and immediately the Trail takes you atop a knoll crowned with Elder Pines. The view of the dappled Forest floor rolling down the knoll to the south and the Blue Iris-bejeweled Bog to the north takes your breath away, then tempts you to take in one of theirs.

"Drink it all in," whispers your Guide, Sarah, so as not to break the spell. You and Sarah had agreed to meet on the Breathing Knoll, and you're glad she's there to share the moment with you. "Alfred Hitchcock said drama is life with the dull bits cut out,"[1] adds Sarah. "That's what you're doing here: leaving the audience and getting up here on Nature's stage to engage in the dramatic performance which is your life."

The Original Aromatherapy

Although Sarah's role is to help you personalize your relationship with Nature, she remains as transparent as possible so she doesn't get in the way of your experience. She suggests, "Take a few more breaths. Go slow and deep, all the way down into your gut and up into your sinuses."

Next, Sarah instructs, "Now, breathe your next breath down through your pelvis, down your legs and into your feet. Feel it flowing through the soles of your feet and into the ground. You are now Rooted (see *Rooting* in chapter 8). You can take in the nourishment of the Earth, just like the Trees. You can stand strong in a storm, just like the Trees.

"And like the Trees, you can exhale into the sky. Start deep in your gut, bringing up all that stale air, those toxic memories, and those hurtful behaviors. Bring them up through your chest, your throat, and out the top of your head. Let the cleansing breeze blow them away!"

After a few more cleansing breaths, Sarah asks what you smell. You describe the piney essence given off by the surrounding Trees being baked in the midday sun. Every now and then, you catch a whiff of the cool, moss-freshened air wafting up from the Bog below. You take another deep, conscious breath, and a smile spreads across your face as you bask in olfactory bliss.

"This is the original Aromatherapy," whispers Sarah. "Nature's special blend. Aromatherapy overlays the whole Trail experience. Here, breathing is healing—the air is dripping with body-mind medicine! Whether you're conscious of that or not, healing happens."

The Timeless Breath

Sarah motions for you to come over and sit with her under the great Red Pine (*Pinus resinosa*) that towers above everything else atop the knoll. Even if your eyes were closed, you're sure you could still feel the Tree's stately presence.

"We're here to become fluent in silence," Sarah softly states. "There is a language that the Trees and the animals and the Earth speak, that we hear when we listen with our nose and eyes and ancestral mind. We call it *Naturespeak*. The Ojibwe people of the area call it *Sisiquat*.[2] Linear time disappears. Objects take on new forms. We can then see this great Tree as the Earth breathing. The Tree reaches up and expands as the Earth inhales, then contracts back to the soil as she exhales. One breath can take hundreds of years, so recognizing it as a breath falls beyond our normal grasp. On this Walk, let us listen with our whole beings, and we will begin to hear the whole story of life."

You stare in awe, realizing that you will never look at a Tree— or perhaps anything else—in the same way again. The awareness makes you wonder what this could mean for your healing.

After a moment, Sarah continues, "If you can embrace this perspective right off the bat, it could change your entire Trail experience. We typically see things not as *they* are, but as *we* are. With a Naturespeak mind-set, we can see not only new possibilities, but a new world. We'll come to realize that our old world was largely a construct of our conditioning and that it disguised so much of what we could have been seeing and experiencing."

Breathing in Earth and Trees

After another respectful moment's pause, Sarah motions for you to part the Pine needle carpet and scoop up a small handful of the dark, moist earth beneath. Following her example, you hold it to your nose, breathing moist, warm air into it. Inhaling the musty-yet-sweet fragrance the soil gives back, you repeat it several times, wanting to make sure you carry the aroma-memory with you.

The two of you circle around to the sunny side of the trunk, where Sarah has you breathe into the bark while cupping your hands around your nose. "That's so you can capture and inhale what the Tree gives back," she says. "It's healing balm like no other—it enriches body, mind, and spirit.

"When you need stronger support," she adds, "pick a few needles and crush them between your palms. Then take in the essence with a slow, full, deep-belly breath, always through the nose."

> **If you have allergies or a sinus condition** *and struggle to breathe through your nose, take a decongestant or neti pot sinus rinse before your Walk. If that does not help, you can still benefit from Aromatherapy, though at a slower rate than if you could breathe normally.*

Conscious Breathing Intentions

"Let's take what we've opened up to here along with us," says Sarah. "But before we go, I invite you to breathe along with me, to energize our intentions. 'Small is the number . . . that see with their own eyes and feel with their own hearts,' said Albert Einstein.[3] By consciously breathing into these desires, we will better see and feel what we are each here for.

"Breathe in awareness; breathe out numbness.

"Breathe in initiative; breathe out indifference.

"Breathe in joy; breathe out despair.

"Breathe in healing essences; breathe out toxins.

"Breathe in nurturing relationships; breathe out exploitation.

"Breathe in Nature; breathe out separation.

"Breathe in love; breathe out love."

Tree Canopy Aromatherapy

You continue on the trail. As you walk, Sarah tells you about an adaptation of a traditional healing-breath practice that is available at select Healing Nature Trails, including this one. A licensed Recreational Rope Tree Climbing Instructor takes you up into the treetops, where the Trees' healing essences are particularly potent.

"It's called *Tree Canopy Aromatherapy,*" she says, "and you don't have to have prior training in order to do it. However, it does take scheduling well in advance, and it is weather dependent."

Your heart skips a beat as you imagine being cradled high in the upper branches of an immense Elder Pine. What must it be like, you wonder, to be in the treetops with the Birds, gently swaying in the breeze as you become intoxicated with essences coming straight off of the boughs all around you?

Reading your feelings, Sarah asks if you ever climbed Trees as a child.

You nod.

"This isn't a whole lot different, except that you do it with ropes, harnesses, helmets, and pulleys. The focus is on safety, for both the climber and the Trees.

"Once you're harnessed and clipped on your rope, you can ascend at your own pace, and you're able to move around the Tree more than you might imagine. You might want to just sit and enjoy the view, or you can swing, stand on a limb, or go up into the canopy.

"Whatever you choose to do, the moment your feet leave the ground, you are moving in a new, exhilarating way that creates new, exhilarating possibilities for your inner processes. It's a phenomenal way to take advantage of the body-mind connection.

"Even with that, most people say that watching a Tree rock back and forth in the breeze is one thing, but rocking with it is another-worldly experience!"

Walking the Medicine Stick

"You may not be floating in the treetops this time," says Sarah, "yet you can take some of that energy with you on your Walk. These sticks here on the ground hold the memories of many dances in the sunshine, and of being whipped around by many a violent storm. Their buds have held the promise of new life through cold, cold winters, and their lush leaves have nurtured Caterpillars and shaded nestling Birds.

"In the autumn, they released their leaves to the Forest floor, knowing the protective carpet was needed to protect their Forest kin who slept beneath until spring. The twigs stood bare to the Arctic blasts and bitter-cold nights, trusting that warm breezes and sweet sap would again come to swell their buds and renew the Dance of Life.

"There is an ancient healing tradition called *Walking the Medicine Stick.* Lying under an Elder Tree you find a dead stick—one who wishes to guide you with her stories of what she's seen and done. One who is weathered and porous enough to absorb your pain and take on the memories you wish to release. You start your Healing Trail carrying the stick in your left hand, which is your giving hand, as it is the one closest to your heart.

"As you walk, you might feel your tortured history, with all its misery, flowing out of your body and into the stick. And even if you don't feel it, it still happens. The stick is glad and honored to serve in this way, as it is her purpose to take the stories of the storms and the Caterpillars and the nestlings—and your stories— back to Mother Earth to be composted. Once they are broken down, their elements will be taken up as nourishment to support new life and new stories, based on the strength and wisdom of the old.

"The traditional ritual way to be involved in the process is to break the Stick in half at the end of your Walk, then reverently lay the Stick in the fire. The breaking and burning is an act of empowerment that releases you from the clutches of victimization. You are then free to walk on, cleansed, refreshed, and rebirthed into your new life."

You have no question on what to do. A Medicine Stick, whose furrowed surface says she has seen many turns of the seasons atop the Tree, calls out to you, and you firmly grasp her in your left hand.

The Trail's Healing Breath

Trail Walkers have the opportunity to bathe in the healing breath of numerous aromatic Herbs and Trees. Already you have spotted Monarda Mint (*Monarda fistulosa*), Evening Primrose (*Oenothera biennis*),[4] and Sweet Fern (*Comptonia peregrina*)[5] in the pollinator flowerbeds at the entrance and in the Gateway Labyrinth Path dividers. Now that you're in the Forest, you come across the red berries and shiny perennial leaves of Wintergreen (*Gaultheria procumbens*).[6]

While Sarah describes the growth characteristics and healing properties of these Herbs, she reminds you about the Elder Red Pine you met atop Breathing Knoll. "Look up," she says, "and see how many other kinds of Trees you notice. Most of them have healing properties, and we're benefiting from them right now. There's Yellow Birch (*Betula alleghaniensis*), White Pine (*Pinus strobus*), Tamarack (*Larix laricina*), Black Spruce (*Picea mariana*), and—as you can see all around us—the abundant Balsam Fir (*Abies balsamea*)."[7]

It's a warm afternoon, so Sarah encourages you to go barefoot, or to slip on a pair of moccasins. "Heavy footwear insulates us from the full Grounding effect of the Earth's electromagnetic energy," she says. "Grounding can amplify the peaceful, euphoric feeling you are already experiencing from the pheromones given off by the Trees. Adding to it are the negative ions being generated by the Trees and flowing water.[8] And let's not forget the added bonus: your immune system is being boosted.

"Now, if it was getting toward evening," Sarah continues, "or even if it was a cloudy day, we could stop to watch this Evening Primrose opening her flowers in slow motion—a natural movie. The chemical compounds you could smell in the blossom were used by the local Ojibwe to help heal wounds and bruises. Today, the blossom extract is used to ease the symptoms of premenstrual syndrome.[9]

"Over here are some Sweet Fern Bushes. Go ahead and bruise a leaf, but be prepared to be inundated with a delightful, spicy aroma. It makes a great invigorating tea, which many people find to be delicious. Traditionally, Sweet Fern was used to line berry-gathering baskets, to repel the Bees and other Insects that were attracted by the sweet berries.[10]

"Right at your feet is Wintergreen, and I can see by your reaction that you're already familiar with it. Most people know the refreshing essence—it's *methyl salicylate*, which has long been used to treat muscle pain. It's essentially the same compound found in aspirin.[11]

"This Yellow Birch[12] over here has similar properties. Just scratch a twig with your fingernail, and the Tree will release a fragrance that is nearly identical to Wintergreen's. In days past, Yellow Birch was commonly tapped for her syrup, which was used for medicine,[13] and as a flavoring."

Sarah smiles at you. "I bet you already know that the needles of most conifers are high in vitamin C. The White Pine, which you see towering above us here, was best known in the old days for keeping scurvy at bay. A vitamin C power tea is made from steeping the crushed needles of Pine or Cedar in warm water."[14, 15, 16, 17]

Bad Breath for Biting Bugs

A few Mosquitoes are buzzing around your head, so you apply some of the natural Insect repellent you brought along. Sarah takes note and says, "If you take a look at the ingredients, I bet you'll see that they come from plants like those we're getting to know here along the Trail. You might be surprised to hear that most of this vegetation produces Insect-repelling substances. If you didn't bring any repellent with you, you could just go directly to the source. Nearly all strongly aromatic plant essences repulse Insects. All you have to do is the same thing we did for Aromatherapy: Crush the leaves or needles between the palms of your hands. Then rub the oils you extracted directly on your skin, rather than inhaling them."

"What about the Balsam Fir?" you ask. "It sure would be handy if they worked as a repellent, because they're everywhere."

"It's almost as though we saved the best for last," she replies. "It's true: here in the North Country, it seems as though you're never more than a few steps away from a Fir Tree. She has many secrets to share with us—secret to most of us, anyway. The Ojibwe rely heavily on this Tree, whom they refer to as *Elder Sister*. Her sap, which is antibacterial and antiseptic, can be used to treat cuts, scrapes, and lesions. It's easy to obtain: just pop one of these resin-filled boils on the bark, which as you can see are numerous.

"The sap also makes a good cold and headache treatment. Put a dab on your upper lip, so that you can continually inhale the essence. The Ojibwe inhale the steam-extracted essence from the needles, and many others treat colds with a tea made from either the needles or the sap."[18]

"But what about Balsam Fir's Insect repellent properties?" you ask. "That's what I'm most interested in right now."

"And I can understand why: I could use some of her help myself! Fortunately, there are several options to choose from, to fit the situation. The volatile oils in the needles make a good Insect repellent, which can be either rubbed directly on the skin from the crushed needles, or you can use the essential oil that is available for purchase. If Mosquitoes are biting through your hair and clothing, you can let them absorb the heavy smoke produced from placing Fir boughs on a smoldering fire. Or, for a fragrantly fashionable look, tuck a few fresh boughs under your hat brim, so that they drape loosely over your face."

Sarah takes the last option, and you're surprised at how well it works.

CHAPTER TWENTY-TWO

Exploring Trailside Haunts

"**B**y the way," says Sarah, "take note of any special places along the Trail where you feel naturally relaxed, and that appeal to your sense of aesthetic. It might be where we sat on the soft needles under that great Pine, or out on one of the points that have beautiful overviews. Or it could be a quiet nook. Some people find a *Power Spot*—a place with healing or revitalizing energy. Others find a place that they think sits on a *Ley Line*,[1] which is an alignment of landforms or places of spiritual significance. It just has to be a place that speaks especially to you."

Comfort Spots

"We generally refer to these special places as *Comfort Spots*. For many who've been here on the Trail, their Comfort Spots have become valuable partners in their healing processes."

"How so?" you ask.

"For some, it's a familiar place to return to, where they know they can find the solace or inspiration they need. Yet for many others, they don't have to be physically present to benefit. Imagine you're meditating and you want to visualize a peaceful place to help bring you to a state of mindfulness. Your Comfort Spot could do the trick."

"Are there any ways to use a Comfort Spot remotely for healing?"

"You bet! I have a client who envisions being at her Comfort Spot when she gets stressed at work. She says it calms her right down. And Comfort Spots can be a big help for people working through trauma. When traumatic memories surface, they close their eyes and go to their Comfort Spots. Over time, this helps them let go of their stories, as their special place on the Mother's Bosom helps them to realize that it's possible to feel safe and supported."[2]

"It sounds like these people are creating a Comfort Spot within," you muse. "What a beautiful way to return to Nature, by having Nature return to you!"

TO VISUALIZE YOUR COMFORT SPOT REMOTELY

Close your eyes and take several deep, slow breaths. If you can, either go outside or listen to a recording of Nature sounds. Let the images and sensations of your Comfort Spot drift into your consciousness. Look around and notice particular objects, such as a fallen log or patch of blueberries. Smell the pregnant air and feel the soft breeze in your face. Stay there until your heart is calmed. For more on this technique, see Remote Walking in chapter 25.

Regarding the Beaver Tree

On the north side of the island, the Trail dips low and skirts the Spruce Bog. Sarah stops and encourages you to look inland from the Bog toward a large, dead Tree. You wonder why the Tree died, as other than having no leaves, she looks to be in her prime.

Then you notice it: about a foot and a half off the ground, her truck is girdled about two-thirds of the way through. I'm surprised she's still standing, you think to yourself.

"Who did this?" you ask.

"Beaver."

"How do you know that?"

"We Trail Guides all have naturalist training, so that we can use Nature's metaphors with our clients."

"Neat. So maybe you know the answer to my next question: Why didn't they finish the job?"

"That's a good question. Do you have any unfinished business in your life?"

That hit you right between the eyes. You realize that it's so easy for you to see other people's inadequacies and failings. Just as it's so easy to make excuses for your own.

"Let's sit down here for a while," you tell Sarah. "I've got some work to do."

"Before you start," replies Sarah, "see that Hemlock sapling over there that's a little shorter than you? How old do you think she is?"

"I would guess eight or ten years. But the way you asked the question, I'm prepared to be surprised—like with the invisible three-foot-deep water under the Threshold Bridge."

"You're right. Here's another example of things not only in Nature, but in life, being more—or other—than they initially appear. That little Hemlock, that's no more than the diameter of your little finger, is probably one hundred years old. If she were growing in the open, she'd be so big that you couldn't get your arms around her. Instead, she's biding her time while she grows in wisdom and resilience. Then, when an overhead Tree topples and creates an opening, she'll have the wherewithal to shoot up into the light."

"Now that's a potent metaphor! My unfinished business, my failings and inadequacies—I wonder what's under them, waiting for the light of day . . ."

A Trail Divided

After you process the metaphor of the Tree, you feel as though you've done a day's work. Yet you know you've just begun—that the Beaver Tree just gave you a doorway to the real work. You know from past counseling work that you would just be going through the motions if you continued on the Trail. You remind yourself that the first step on any Healing Journey has to be taking personal responsibility for your state of being.

Right away this realization is put to the test, as the Trail forks. Now what? You don't want to risk getting lost or missing anything, so you consult the map. It shows the left-hand fork, which is the main Trail, going straight ahead and taking you to Trail features you have read about—features you look forward to taking advantage of.

The map, however, just shows the beginning of the right-hand fork—the Discovery Fork. How long it is, where it will ultimately take you, and what you might or might not experience are all a mystery.

"I get it," you tell yourself. Sometimes the straight and narrow, the known entity, is the way to go. However, that's not why you came. Familiarity may bring comfort, but not anymore—not for you. The same old, same old has grown thin.

A line of Joseph Campbell's comes to mind: "We must be willing to get rid of the life we've planned, so as to have the life that is waiting for us."[3] You came to step into the Void: that place where all that you know dissolves into a formless, shapeless mélange. You want to strip down to the essence and question everything. It's no longer good enough to just get by; you want what works.

Even though you have apprehension, you want to "follow your bliss," as Campbell would put it—you want to feel your feet solidly under you and your heart dancing for the sheer joy of being alive! Alone, you take the Discovery Fork.

The Havens

When the Discovery Fork brings you back to the main Trail, Sarah tells you that the Trail has its shadow side. While the Trail facilitates movement and direction, she says, the Trailside Havens offer places to withdraw and slow down. While the Trail is a venue for external exploration, the Havens foster the Inner Journey. "'Here in solitude and peace my soul was nurst, amid the loveliest scenes of unpolluted nature,' said Robert Southey, who was a nineteenth-century poet laureate of England.[4] Rather than being the movement, you have the opportunity in the Havens to reflect on the movement within and around you.

Sarah goes on to say that all five Havens offer beautiful settings, Grounding benches, and gated privacy. The gates are unobtrusive—they're just dead branches placed across the entryway Paths. Four of the Havens open to panoramic vistas. Experiencing the expansiveness of the view plies upon the body-mind connection, which helps open mind and heart to new possibilities. One of those possibilities is the avenue provided for the release of pent-up stress and emotional baggage.

"Yet it's not just a vista," says Sarah, "it's the sense of awe that comes with it. The view alone doesn't work—especially if you see it regularly. You have to be drawn into it and swept away by it."

"What if I'm just too self-absorbed or too numb to get into it?"

"What can help is a dynamic meditation called *Coming to Oneness* that Tamarack taught us Guides. He learned it from the Seneca people, and it instills that sense of awe by taking you out of yourself—beyond your ego—and projecting you into the Circle of Life. It's also a good stress release and a Way to relax around troubles and open to new possibilities. Coming to Oneness works particularly well with panoramic vistas because they're a part of the meditation. Together they instill a sense of awe that becomes transcendent."

"Hmm, can you teach it to me?"

"Sure—it's easy. All you do is focus on something small that catches your attention, like that Caterpillar there. Before long, you notice the Oxeye Daisy she's perched on, then the whole bed of Daisies. Now you see that Butterfly visiting the Flowers, and the Bees. Look at that Bee taking off, maybe for the Flowers over on the rise to the south. Now I see you're looking east, at the three White Trumpeter Swans who just landed on the Beaver Pond. See how before you know it, you get taken in by the wonder of it all? By consciously narrowing down your focus, you created the dynamic tension to expand into the Oneness."

"You're right, it's easy—it just happens. But it seems to be the opposite of meditation—instead of turning inward, you expand outward."

"From Zen perspective," replies Sarah, "the distinction between the two is only a construct of the mind. When we use one as an avenue to the other, we reunite them into their original oneness."

Going back to describing the Havens, Sarah says they are typically used for:

▶ Reflection and Sitting Meditation

▶ Therapist–client work

▶ Lunch and a short rest

▶ Half-day or day-long retreats

Each Haven has its distinctive features, which contribute to the unique experience it has to offer. Here are descriptions of each, in the order in which they appear along the Trail:

1. **Red Pine Refuge.** Tucked into the deep Forest behind the Breathing Knoll, this special place features two benches nestled between Elder Pines.

2. **Frog Pond Point.** Being right down at Bog level, you can commune with this most unique and mysterious of Northwoods habitats by being able to see, smell, and touch it.

3. **Stump Labyrinth Outlook.** Perched atop the base of a fallen Tree is a Finger Labyrinth weathered by the seasons and the touch of many hands. The healing energy is strong here, with much support from the Otters, Swans, and other wildlings in the Waters that lap the point.

4. **Beaver Dam Waters.** Tumbling over the dam from the Beaver Pond into the channels of the Aquarinth below, water healing energy is strong here. Sit next to the spillway and bathe in negative ions, or immerse yourself in the Pond for Water Grounding (see chapter 8).

5. **Solitude Sundeck.** On a quiet peninsula between the Aquarinth and Zen Untangle is a private pier with a Mosquito net canopy. It is ideal for therapeutic sunbathing, meditation, and reflective reading, and it is a favorite place for therapists to bring their clients.

Frog Pond, Red Pine, and Solitude Sundeck can be reserved for therapist sessions and retreats.

With this being your first time on the Trail, you tell Sarah that you want to see and experience all the Havens. She understands your curiosity and enthusiasm, but at the same time she reminds you that you are here for a reason. "Getting to know all five of the Havens could take a day in itself," she says. "I suggest you choose one now that you think would best serve your work. Then after your Walk, you might have time to get to know some of the others."

Gathering at the Pine Grove Circle

Just before the canoe livery for the Aquarinth, you notice a side Path leading into a Virgin Pine Grove. You are entranced—you can't help but follow your impulse and enter.

It turns out to be a very short path, ending in a circle of log benches. What an idyllic place for small-group meetings, you

realize, as your feet sink into the thick carpet of golden Pine needles underfoot.

Then you look up.

Your eyes follow the bark's craggy creases upward, upward, upward, until your gaze gets lost in the ferny branchlets wafting in the breeze far above. The only sky you see is what manages to peek through the cracks in the ever-moving canopy. The scene is framed by a circle of russet columns that must be what the creators of Stonehenge were trying to equal. It steals your breath.

You feel dizzy and lightheaded, and you have to sit down. "You can see why this is a popular destination," says Sarah, after allowing you a short while to soak in the ambience. "Sometimes Trail Walkers will get together here and share with each other what they are experiencing. More often than not, they learn from each other's experiences. And they inspire and support each other.

"But the main users of this Circle are healthcare practitioners with their groups, workshop presenters, and sanghas. Families like coming here also, sometimes to reconnect, and sometimes with their therapists to work on issues. Yet whoever it is and whatever their purpose, nearly everyone comes because they find that the steadfast and wisdom-rooted Elder Energy does wonders in facilitating their process.

"And speaking of Elder Energy, now's a good time to mention again that things aren't always as they appear. Sure, a grove of giant Pines like this is great. But what if there's nothing like it around? Remember that hundred-year-old Hemlock that was shorter than you? See those pint-size Spruce and Tamaracks out there on the Bog? Some of them are just as old as these Pines; and if you were to sit next to them, you'd feel the same sense of presence and calming energy as with these big Trees."

"I get it," you reply. "I remember hearing somewhere that Mother Earth provides for her children, no matter where they're at. There's an old Oak Tree in the park down from my apartment. And my mother has a Bonsai Tree in a little pot that's way older than me. And think how ancient rocks and hills are. . . . Yeah, I hear what you're saying."

CHAPTER TWENTY-THREE

The Zen Trilogy

"We're now two-thirds of the way through our Journey," announces Sarah as we step back on the main Trail. "I see you're still struggling for a breakthrough. I wonder if you might be trying too hard. Listening takes relaxing, and making sense of new information often takes new pathways to process it. The ancient sages of the Far East knew this, and they came up with the method of *inquiry through noninquiry* that cuts to the quick."

"Tell me more," you say. "I meditate, and I've been a casual student of Zen, but I have a hunch that from what I've seen so far, the folks who designed this Trail have come up with a unique way to use Zen to crack open Nature."

"There's no reason for that," Sarah replies, "because Nature is already Zen—essential Zen, that is—before it took on some of the characteristics of the established spiritual practices of the time."

She goes on to explain the way of essential Zen, which is "to release yourself to the Void: the realm that is neither within nor without, neither above nor below. There is no form or shape, no light or dark, and nothing to hang onto. To enter the Void is to freefall, with no expectations and no safety net. Nothing matters: belief, desire—even strength of will—can gain no foothold. There is no past or future, and everything that anchors you in the present has been rendered null and void.

"With the final three Labyrinthine experiences: the Aquarinth, the Zen Untangle, and the Zen Garden (which we collectively refer to as the *Zen Trilogy*), there is no set form or shape. As Indian mystic Kabir said, 'Wherever you are is the entry point.' That's one of the beauties of these three experiences—you can't *not* be ready.[1] Wherever you jump off, they can take you into the Void, where anything is possible. You are no longer bound by your past, nor are you enslaved to your future. True change is now possible, and these three Labyrinths can help you craft it."

Part 1: Paddling the Meanders of the Aquarinth

Almost immediately, you come upon a thatch-roofed gazebo off to the side of the Trail. It reminds you of something you'd see in a tropical Native village. Inside are four canoes: two solo boats, a small tandem, and a wooden dugout, which you can't take your eyes off of.

Sarah notices. "It was hewn out of the trunk of an old, old White Pine who was laid down by a storm. The paddle was carved from the same Tree. One of the staff here at the Center crafted them—they're replicas of what the Natives here used to make."

"With such a heritage," you muse, "that boat must have some stories to tell—especially with how ancient the Tree must've been that she came from."

"Yeah, people who've been out on the Water with her say she has quite the wisdom to share."

On the opposite side of the Trail is a canoe launch. You've been waiting for this, as you are a water person, and you were hoping that some connection with water would help you make a breakthrough.

"First, some background," says Sarah. "Awareness is the first step in healing: it's what makes it possible for us to be consciously engaged in the process. Water, as I'm sure you know, is the universal solvent. It likes to absorb and diffuse whatever comes its way. Variable in its form, water seeks a common level. It adapts easily to new surroundings and changes easily to fit its surroundings. All things immersed in water are equally embraced, and all things floating upon its surface are equally supported. Could there be any better metaphor for the Healing Journey?

"When we submerge in water, glide over it, or merely dangle our feet in it, we intuitively know that we are being unconditionally accepted. There is no judgment or expectation; we are embraced and cherished for just who and how we are. She is there for us, giving a format for our quest, amplifying our every effort, and clarifying the voices we hear."

Sarah tells you that the canoe launch takes you directly out to the Aquarinth, which is comprised of a network of meandering Waterways that fork, rejoin, and dead end. The Waterscape is sprinkled with floating islands of Sedges, Lilies, and Cranberries.

"Our Aquarinth appears to be the only one in the state," she says, "and perhaps the country. We couldn't find another one anywhere."

Back to the description, she tells you that the way of the Aquarinth is a slow and sinuous paddle around the murky backwaters of the mind. There is no marked route, and there is no center to reach, as with the Gateway Labyrinth. Instead, this one is for listening. There is nothing to fix, nothing to heal, and nowhere in particular to go. The experience is completely open to where you need to go in order to find those lost parts of yourself.

This unique experience is best suited for those who are ready to relax their boundaries and listen to the quiet murmurings of their souls. The expansiveness of the Wetland, the quiet depths of the Waters, the free flight of the Birds, the wind singing in the shoreline Trees . . . all encourage openness, inquisitiveness, and a sense of reverence.

"Yet not everybody is a water person," Sarah explains. "And some need perspective more than introspection. For them, you'll see up in that Tree the equivalent of the Cosmorinth, only this one overlooks the Aquarinth. We call it the *Osprey Nest.*"

She points to a ladder leading up to a small observation deck that reminds you of the lookouts that were called *crow's nests* on the old wooden sailing ships. You can't resist: you climb up to get a view, which makes you feel like you could spread your wings and rise above the tangle you find yourself in.

Yet you know it's not what you're here for—you must go down and immerse yourself in the riverine mind-maze. The boat slips quietly into the Water, and you let it take you wherever you need to go.

Part 2: Breaking Through in the Zen Untangle

Your time on the Water left you feeling more comfortable in your own skin than you've been in a long time. Yet it wasn't enough. Shaming voices keep spinning around in your consciousness. *You should be at work. Why didn't you finish your degree? If you didn't keep that secret, you might not have had a falling-out with your best friend.* You tell Sarah what's haunting you, and that you're ready to give up.

"Come with me," she says. You pass the turnoff to the Solitude Sundeck, and you soon come to another side Path. Sarah steps aside and motions for you to go first.

The Path ascends several feet to a flat-topped rise that is about thirty feet in diameter. In its center stands a middle-aged White

Pine; and the ground around it is strewn with an array of boulders, driftwood, and Tree stumps. The circle is neatly bordered with birch logs.

"This is what my head feels like," you tell Sarah.

"You're not the first one who sees this as a metaphor for their knotted-up mind and bottled-up emotions. When people come to the Trail to reach a state of deep and undefended consciousness, and they haven't achieved it by this point, they're often ready to pack out, just like you. Some of them lament about how they're still stuck in old thought patterns, or how they're unable to break through self-imposed psycho-emotional boundaries. This place, the Zen Untangle, is able to help most of them break through.

"It's got such a reputation that some folks come just for the Untangle. A few people find it so helpful for clearing their minds that they return weekly or monthly. For them, it's a pilgrimage."

How It Works

"Why?" you ask. "What makes this experience so special?"

"Some folks feel a concentration of energy here. They call it a Power Spot or a confluence of Ley Lines, similar to some people's Comfort Spots, which we talked about a little farther back on the Trail. The founders of the Trail first saw something special in this site because they were drawn by all the animal signs. They found an observation platform about twenty feet up in this Tree in the middle of the Untangle, so one of the previous owners must've been drawn to this spot also. And they noticed that the Path leading up to the rise came from the north, which in Ojibwe tradition is the direction of introspection and guidance."

"That all sounds great," you reply, "but I still don't get how this tangle of sticks and stones is going to help *me* untangle."

"I'm not surprised that you'd be scratching your head at this point. Again, it's all about the body-mind connection, which— as you now know—is so strong that the body's movements and rhythms are mirrored in the mind, and vice versa. This makes it possible to use the body as a doorway to the mind. So when we are muddled in confusion, we can use physical movement to help unravel the tangle.

"It's done by meandering around and between the boulders and stumps in random fashion. Avoid stepping in the same place twice, and continually look for new pathways. Once you get the hang of it, quit thinking about where you shouldn't go, and just allow yourself to move free-form, without rhyme or reason.

"In essence, what makes the exercise work is that we are using random movement to relax the mental patterns that keep us trapped in the same thought and feeling loops. A feeling on its own lasts only a minute or two, then it dissipates. However, when we have a troublesome thought on our mind, it keeps triggering the feeling. That's why it seems as though the feeling never goes away.

"The Untangle breaks the loop, which allows for greater emotional expression and the ability to visualize new possibilities. Repressed feelings and forgotten memories often surface. The avoidance patterns and boundaries that keep us from being fully conscious begin to dissolve. Along with that, sensory acuity and mental sharpness increase.

"Even if the nagging thought persists, we now understand the thought-feeling connection, and the fact that we can do something about it, rather than being victimized by a situation beyond our understanding or control."

Sarah stresses the fact that the key is *aimless meandering*, which means *with no pattern and no goal in mind*. "Goal orientation keeps us emotionally numb and married to our past," she says. "Fortunately, this unique Labyrinth makes aimlessness pretty easy to achieve. With the stumps and boulders placed in no particular order, you'd have to try hard to go the same way twice in a row."

Why It Works

You ask how much time she recommends meandering around in the Untangle in order to get your mind untangled.

Sarah replies with an explanation of the science behind the Untangle. "Let's start with the relationship between short-term and long-term memory. What we think and perceive is first held in our short-term memory. For it to be converted to long-term memory, it has to have either made a lasting impression on us, or we have to give it attention. That has to happen within fifteen minutes; otherwise, it gets swept away, and it's gone forever.

"By having to be constantly engaged in where you place your next step, lest you stumble and fall on a rock, it's impossible to keep focused on those same old crippling thoughts and draining feelings that have been haunting you. So after fifteen minutes, your short-term memory is filled with only vague impressions of countless random movements.

"The neural synapses that govern your patterned psycho-emotional responses—that nagging mental clutter—have now had time to relax. This allows for a broader range of thought and feeling than you've been experiencing. There is space for repressed memories to surface, and for old stories to be given a new interpretation.

"And what some folks—especially therapists—find most liberating is the opportunity to escape entrenched thought-conclusion loops.

"Another important factor is that it can take some time for the body-mind connection to fully activate. For many people, it takes only a few minutes; yet there are some so wounded and defended that they need to spend two or three days here on the Trail before they start breaking through. The Zen Untangle speeds up the process for nearly everybody.

"Even those who are doing well by the time they get to this point on the Trail enjoy the Untangle because they say it helps them feel even freer, and more relaxed and engaged, than they already were. For some people, the Untangle turns out to be a threshold experience: having gained perspective and realized things that previously escaped them, they go on with new hope."

Have Untangle—Will Travel

While you're walking the Untangle, Sarah waits for you back on the main Trail. Twenty minutes or so later, you come back to join her.

"I can tell by your serene look that the magic worked," she says. Your soft smile is all she needs for confirmation. "One reason you're feeling the way you do is that you're leaving the Untangle through the Northern Gateway, which from native perspective empowers the Inner Journey and brings new awarenesses. This is possible because, in contemporary terms, you have recentered by shifting from your rational mind-based memory to your limbic mind, which is the home of your intuition, emotions, and deep-seated memories."

"Yeah, I wouldn't have believed it if I hadn't experienced it," you say. "But what about when I'm back home? I can't have a Zen Untangle in my backyard; my landlord wouldn't allow it. Yet I know there'll be times when I could use it."

"Same here," says Sarah. "Only I don't even have a yard. What I do is scatter pillows, the vacuum cleaner, pots and pans . . . anything I can grab, around my living room, and voila, I have a Zen Untangle! Outside, I find a Field or a corner in the park where there are tufts of Grass, sticks, or whatever, lying around, and I just go at it."

"That helps," you say. "Thank you for the ideas—they give me options for helping myself *when* I need it."

"I have another one for you. I learned this in my Healing Nature Guide training. It's a portable Untangle that you can use anywhere—your breath. With a little practice, it can be just as effective as this Untangle. The goal is the same: to take our mind off of our troubles, which breaks the endless thought-feeling spiral. We do it by breathing differently than normal, which keeps us focused on our breath rather than our worries. Here's what to do: breathe about half again faster than normal, and through your mouth. If you can, add sound to your exhale. Keep it up for fifteen minutes or so, even while you're doing something else, and that should do the trick."

A New Beginning

"Now, with a fresh slate and limbered-up mental processes, you should be ready for Nature's guidance and healing embrace. At this point, I sometimes suggest that people go back to the *Welcome Home* sign at the beginning of the Trail and start over. It's usually those who are struggling with addictions or have been trapped in extremely codependent relationships. Occasionally, someone is blocked just because she isn't accustomed to being deep in Nature. However, I think you can continue from here, as you've been able to engage yourself pretty well up to this point.

"Remember, though, that this is still a new beginning for you," she cautions as we start walking. "New awareness is just hot air if it can't be acted upon. Just remember that every step is a new step—a fresh start."

Here again you see that the Trail is designed to facilitate what is needed. And when it is needed. Right away you're crossing another one of the Trail's short bridges, which supports leaving those old and all-too-familiar ways behind—or just passing over something that's best left alone—and transitioning to new heights and directions.

In fact, it's inevitable. The next few steps after the bridge take you up a short, steep incline, followed by a T-intersection. For the first time, you can't just lumber forward on the Trail. You have to choose going either left, to stay on the main Trail, or right, to take the Discovery Fork.

You recall the words of philanthropist Margaret Shepard: "Sometimes the only available transportation is a leap of faith." Yet this time, you stay on the main Trail. You have clarity and direction, and you want to stick with it.

THE HEALING NATURE TRAIL

Part 3: Tending a Zen Garden

A tight curve takes you through a grove of small-diameter stumps, which are all that remain of saplings harvested by the resident Beaver colony. The coarse chew marks and decomposing condition of the stumps remind you of what has come and gone in your life, yet rough-edged memories persist. Like those fading reminders of what could have been, you want those old regrets and dashed dreams to transform into something fresh and fertile as well. You whisper a few words of gratitude for the breath of hope.

Again there is a quick change of direction, followed immediately by a short section of Trail that hugs a slope. You thought you were so present since leaving the Untangle, so you're surprised that you have to re-center yourself and watch your step in order to keep from sliding off the Trail. Even so, you are thankful for this visceral reminder to not revert to your accustomed pattern of unconsciously plodding along in your mind.

"You might want to slow up here," says Sarah. "Out on the tip of this little peninsula on our left is a form of garden from the Far East that is commonly known as a *Zen Garden*. If you're not familiar with the term, Zen Gardens are also called *Dry Landscape Gardens, Japanese Rock or Sand Gardens, Meditation Gardens, Healing Gardens* and *Restorative Gardens*.

"The Zen Garden here is the wrap-up of the Zen Trilogy, and it is the seventh and final Trail Labyrinth. It's another progression in the Labyrinthine experience, which some people see as its ultimate expression."

You tell her that you've seen pictures of Zen Gardens, and maybe one in a movie, but never one in real life.

"They have quite the history," she continues. "Classical Shinto, Hindi, Daoist, and Buddhist traditions are represented here, amongst others. This type of Labyrinth evolved as a site for reflection and inspiration, and as a place to go on retreat. On occasion, a Zen Garden has served as a sanctuary.

"Think of such a garden as a piece of Nature that has been isolated *from* Nature, yet it is still embraced *by* Nature. I know that sounds paradoxical, especially when you can see that this little garden in front of us sits on a lush peninsula surrounded by a vibrant Marsh, which is bordered by a dense Conifer Forest.

"Yet isn't that the paradox in which many of us live? Even though our urbanized existence seems so differentiated from the rhythms and beauties of Nature, she is still our ultimate mother. And in essence we are nothing *but* Nature—and nothing *without* Nature.

"The Garden, then, meets us where we are at: children who have gotten lost, yet our mother was there all the time."

The Unpacking

"What you say resonates strongly with me," you reply. "I'd like to spend some time here—I think I need it. But first I really need some clarity. This looks more like a wannabe Garden to me: all I see is a glorified sandbox, with a little pail, a couple of garden tools, and a pile of sticks and stones. How is this stuff going to help me reconnect?"

"You're right: this is a wannabe Garden. And you're at a gotta-do point in your life. The idea here is to bring wannabe and gotta-do together to bridge the gap between you and Nature. Which isn't so hard, really, because you already *are* Nature."

"Wow, I get it!" you exclaim. "My essential self is in attunement with Nature because it *is* Nature. I'm here to bring my conscious self into attunement with my essential self."

"That's a good way to put it," states your Guide. "But still, there's more to this sandbox. There's a German term, *Auspacken*, that means to *unpack*, as in emptying your suitcase. It also has a slang definition: to *unpack what's bothering you or what you're hiding.* When we say, *Speak your mind!* or *Come clean!* a German speaker might say *Auspacken!*

"I'm afraid you're losing me. I don't see why a Zen Garden is needed for that."

"The beauty of the Garden is that the unpacking is nonverbal. Sometimes people can't admit things to themselves, much less to others. Or they don't have words for it. Here is a way to express it by creating a landscape. It's a lot like art therapy: you just give your thoughts and feelings free reign to create what's going on inside."

"Ah, here's the body-mind connection again!" you state.

"Exactly. You have a blank slate here for graphic expression. Once you get going, a synergy develops: you move some sand, and it shuffles something around in your mind, which dislodges a feeling, which gives you the impulse to grab that dark stone and place it over there to the right, and so on. What you're doing is working with the core expressive archetypes of space, form, and intention."

"Are you saying, then, that this piece of raw Earth is like an artist's canvas, and my paints are the pebbles, sticks, pinecones, leaves, bones, and whatever else is at hand, and this rake and trowel are my brushes?"

"You've got it. And your intention is to manifest the landscape of your mind. You'll see that a maze of sorts emerges, which gives pathways for the mind and heart to wander and explore."

"But what if I get artist's block, so to speak?"

"Usually all it takes is touching the sand to start bringing form to the story. Just remember that the story is already there. Some envision the story to start with, and some just let the process flow."

Etching a Trauma Story

"Now that you've grasped the concept," says Sarah, "I'd like to tell you how a Zen Garden can be used in trauma recovery. As you may know, some people remember their traumatization stories, and some don't. Those who do are sometimes either too ashamed or too afraid of a Trauma Memory Response [a traumatic reaction brought on by a trauma-related trigger; see chapter 34] to retell their stories. Those who don't remember may have been very young when they were traumatized, or they blotted out the conscious memory as a survival strategy.

"Whatever the case, it's an important step in many people's Healing Journeys to be able to recall and acknowledge their stories. Here is where the magic and mystique of the Zen Garden comes in—especially for those so drained by their traumatization that they can't shed another tear. Sometimes someone has retreated so far into herself that she can't take a full breath. Or a therapist comes with a client who has sunk into deep depression, or who is contemplating suicide. I often bring them directly here, because there's something about a Zen Garden that encourages *Auspacken*.

"If *Auspacken* is possible, it could give them enough wherewithal to begin letting go of their stories. That, for so many, is the critical next step in getting on with their recovery.

"It doesn't seem to matter whether their stories are right at the tips of their tongues or deeply buried in their somatic memories. What does matter is the opportunity to give form to the wordless—or to that which is too frightful to verbalize."

You ponder this. "So how do they give form to something they can't recall?"

"It may just be intuitive impressions guiding their hands," Sarah replies. "I typically start with Conscious Breathing, to help them relax into themselves and gain a sense of place. Then I'll use Aromatherapy, to enliven their senses and bring them fully into the now. I might have them take a handful of ground from the Garden, breathe into it, then inhale the fertile, musty essence that the earth returns. Or I'll suggest that they pick a few needles from a nearby conifer and inhale the fragrance they exude. That tends to stimulate the body-mind connection, and the storyteller's hand then begins the silent process of speaking the unspeakable. Their story takes shape before them, in a way that is both safe and recognizable.

"I can't begin to tell you what it's like to witness the miracle of someone expelling the story that has been haunting him for so long. There it is, laid out before him—it's no longer trapped in his head; it's no longer wracking his body. Sometimes my tears of relief flow right along with his, and sometimes I can't help but join him in dancing ecstatically around the Garden!"

225

"It must be an immensely rewarding experience for you as a Guide," you say. "Yet it seems as though there is still some unfinished business. There he is, just him and his story. Then what?"

Ritual Release

"Then comes the most empowering part," replies your Guide. "He is standing literally at his story's graveside, and he might need some time for mourning. Even though that story has stalked him mercilessly, it has also—for better or worse—helped form his identity. Walking away from that story could leave a void in his life. It's one of the reasons people stay in abusive relationships. So to see himself through the pain and uprootedness of separation, he needs some time to reconnect with his reason for leaving the story, along with renewing the courage to do so.

"Once he's done that, he can walk on. He knows that Mother Earth will then play another role in his healing, by washing away the story he left behind. There's a high chance that this approach will work for him, because he is walking away from something tangible, rather than just trying to escape the memory.

"Or he can erase the story himself, by whooshing it away with a bucket of water or—even more engaging—obliterating it with his bare hands. This is the approach used by Navajo healers with their sand paintings. A healer creates a symbolic painting from colored sand, then helps his or her patient imbue the painting with the essence of the sickness. The painting is then wiped away, and the strength of the sickness with it.[2]

"The therapists I guide often recommend this active ritual release for their clients, because (as with so much of Nature's healing way) the hands-on component energizes the ritual and makes it more effective by bringing the body-mind connection into play.

"Therapists also tend to suggest the story-destruction approach to those who have been extremely victimized by their traumatizations. For those who have been so overpowered, this could be the most significant level of control over their situations that they've had.

"That's pretty much the overview. Is there anything else I can do before I leave you with your story?"

"You've already given me far more than I could have imagined," you reply. "I have a lot to reflect on. Thank you for this time you took with me. Being here on this spot with you has made your words all the more meaningful than if I had just read them."

CHAPTER TWENTY-FOUR

Reentry

Y ou have returned to the Trail from the Zen Garden. However, you haven't gone more than a few steps and you're faced with a choice—a fork in the Trail. After the intensity of the *Auspacken*, you thought you'd be able to automatically relax into the comfort of the tried-and-true.

But you still have decisions to make, only it's not the same type of decision as with past Discovery Forks. Here you can see some distance ahead on both Trails. The Main Trail would take you under the biggest White Pine you've ever seen, then across three short bridges as you wrap around a marshy bay. The Discovery Fork, on the other hand, crosses a long, low bridge that cuts across to the far shore of the bay.

Something inside nags at you, causing you to feel edgy. You fully expected to be walking on with a sense of accomplishment, only now you wrestle with some dark urge to reenter the Void and continue the open-discover-release process.

A Bridge over Troubled Water

As you approach the long Bridge, you realize why you felt edgy when you looked down upon it from the fork in the Trail: the Bridge has no railing.

But wait—you can't blame your edginess on the Bridge. After all, one of the reasons you came here is to learn how to take more personal responsibility for your life, and externalizing on the Bridge would just feed the all-too-familiar feelings of helplessness.

Ha! Here's the body-mind connection at work again, you realize. The Trail designers probably placed this edgy-looking Bridge here right after the Zen Garden to keep people like me from sinking into complacency. It could well be that I have more work to do. Okay, here I go. Like John Burroughs said, "Leap, and the net will appear."

It doesn't take you more than a couple of steps on the Bridge to realize that it's not just edgy looking. It has a bounce to it that makes you feel insecure. I'm sure it's safe, you tell yourself; yet all the same, you slow down. Every step becomes more deliberate, and you realize the Bridge is helping to re-center you.

You look over the edge, which entices you to get down on your hands and knees and gaze into the Water. How deep is it? Are there any Fish or Turtles swimming around down there? What about Leeches?

With some apprehension, you dangle your feet in the water, which feels refreshingly cool. There you sit, for what seems like a long time, even though you have no particular reason for doing so. It just feels good to relax and let your mind wander along with your gaze.

The Last Sojourn: Healing by Fire

Your Guide awaits as you come off of the Bridge. "While you were sitting there," she said, "you reminded me of a quote I heard somewhere: *Get lost in Nature and find yourself.*"

"That's especially true considering where I'm coming from," you reply. "I now see how important it was to let go and trust in Nature."

Sarah nods, with a reassuring smile.

"You've now come full circle," she continues. "Up ahead, the Trail takes a sharp right and brings you back to the Threshold Bridge. But first, I'd like to take you to a place where you can sit in council with Earth, Air, Fire, and Water. There Nature speaks loud and clear; and with that, you'll be able to see and hear in the distance reminders of the modern life you'll be going back to. There is where you'll have an opportunity to bring it all together: your past, your experience here, and the life you'll be walking back into. It is a great place to review your Trail experience, to imprint it in your long-term memory."

Taking a short side path, the two of you round a bend and step into an opening overlooking a Tree-ringed Pond. Off to the west, you can see a couple of buildings. Before you is a fire ring, surrounded by log benches. You sit down and wonder how many individuals like you, and how many groups with their therapist guides, have sat here before you, staring into the flames while reflecting on their Trail experiences.

"The voices that have spoken to you will go on speaking, wherever you are," says Sarah. "All you have to do is keep listening to them."

"Easier said than done," you say. "In just my short time here, I can see where immersion in Nature helps get to the essence of communication. But what about after I leave?"

"The essence of communication is what many Native people call Truthspeaking. You've experienced the essence here—you've Truthspoken—as it's all about spontaneity and listening. How you speak your Truth is just as important. I think it was Franklin Delano Roosevelt who said, 'Be sincere; be brief; be seated.' If you can do that, you're halfway there. The other half, of course, is listening. You can be spontaneous and listen—i.e., Truthspeak—anywhere."

"Maybe *you* can."

"And so can you. Buddha said that three things cannot be long hidden: the sun, the moon, and the Truth. I'll give you a clue for how you can find hidden Truth anywhere: Enter the stillness. Then just embrace the naked Truth for what it is. Any words we try to put to Truth end up being only a bad translation. That's why Roosevelt said, 'Be brief.'"

"Again," you reply with more than a hint of frustration, "I'm not in Nature all the time like you are. Let's be real; I need something that works for me back in the city. Otherwise, I'm afraid I'll end up right back where I started from."

"It is said that *the only sin is separation*," says Sarah. "The only thing that separates you from Nature is the illusion of separation that your mind creates. Remember: You are Nature's child wherever you go; and Nature is everywhere, even though we may have cleverly disguised it. This includes us. No matter what we do, say, think, or feel, our inner nature is still Nature."

"I get it: it's my state of mind, not my state of place, that separates me from Nature."

"That's it! One reason it's so important to have a clear state of mind is so that you can listen to the stillness. Nature can then bring you to the layer of honesty you thrive best at in any given moment. There are times when it's vital to recognize that love and hate are the same core emotion, and that there is no difference between praise and criticism. In the stillness, there are no words or beliefs to distinguish between them."

Taken aback by the profundity of your sharing with Sarah, you turn to the Token that you've been carrying with you in your breast pocket. Gently and reverently, you take him out and hold him before you in cupped hands. Tears come to your eyes as you realize how much strength and support he has contributed to your healing mission.

The Dance of Remembering and Forgetting

After a few minutes, Sarah sits beside you and says in a voice barely above a whisper, "Hippocrates once said that Nature cures—not the physician.[1] Yet for Nature to cure, we need to not only listen, but remember.

"However, we need a way to remember that is lasting and not subject to the whims of our fickle thoughts and feelings. To understand how to accomplish that, we need to look at the three parts of our brain: the *reptilian*, which manages reproduction and basic body functions; the *mammalian*, which is the seat of our emotions and long-term memories; and the *primate*, which is responsible for our rational processes. It's the mammalian brain's long-term memory that we want to access, which we can do with the shamanic technique of fire-induced trance."

"Why fire?" you ask, "and why trance?"

"Because fire is what made us human. Around a half-million years ago, our distant ancestors tamed fire, which allowed them to prepare the high-energy foods needed to support our evolving brains. You'll notice that all other animals fear fire, yet we are drawn to it. This special relationship we have with fire is the doorway to the deeper reaches of our minds, which is why shamans have been using it as a healing tool for time immemorial. Trance is simply the state of consciousness we dwell in when we are centered in our mammalian minds. To enter trance, you just have to sit before a fire and let your ancestral memories guide you."

The Dragon's Breath

"This is called becoming the *Dragon's Breath*," says Sarah as she helps you start a fire. "As I'm sure you know, Dragons are formidable symbols in our folklore. Since ancient times, they've been one of shamans' most potent spirit helpers. In the East, they're known to bring growth and good fortune; and in the European tradition, they help with clarity and the ability to overcome adversity. That's the Dragon's Breath."

"Hmm, interesting. But how does that help my healing?"

"Fire is the Dragon's Breath, and Fire transforms. It's one of the most potent vehicles for change. A fallen Tree branch takes years—maybe decades—to break down into soil, yet Fire does it in a matter of minutes. Think of a decomposing branch as burning slowly. The same by-products: carbon dioxide, water, and minerals are produced as when a Tree burns, only at a much slower rate. It's the same with healing, and that's why Fire—the

Dragon's Breath—is such a powerful and favored transformational tool for shamans."

"That makes sense," you say, "but I don't get the connection between sitting in front of a Fire and becoming the Dragon's Breath."

"When you breathe," explains Sarah, "you engage in the same slow-burning process as the decomposing branch—you're breaking down food into carbon dioxide, water, and minerals. The same thing happens on a healing level when you use Conscious Breathing. Now imagine what breathing Fire could do to rev it up!

"Here's how it's done: when the fire flares up, inhale; then exhale between flareups. Take a deep breath when the fire surges, and breathe shallow when the Fire wanes. Let the Fire's rhythm tell you how fast or slow to breathe. Before you know it, the Fire will have you naturally breathing in sync with it—you'll have become the Dragon's Breath."

Sarah then steps back to let you gaze into the flames. Before long, their leaping and swaying have seduced you into a trance state. Everything you heard, saw, and felt on the Trail comes back to you, and it merges with everything you brought here with you. In that instant, there is no more separation. You are no longer the victim of your past, nor are you above what happened then. You accept, and you embrace.

Letting-Go Rituals

As the fire fades to embers, you come back to the iridescent Dragonflies darting over the Pond and the soft breeze twitching the Pine needles on the nearby branches. You let out a long, satisfied sigh as you realize that you have just imprinted what you gained here into your long-term memory.

Taking a pencil and a piece of paper from a box beside your bench, you write down what you'd like to release, fold the paper, then thoughtfully lay the paper on the embers.

As your old fears, regrets, and judgments take flame, you watch the smoke rise into the ethers. I have released myself of my burden, you tell yourself, and I have done it in a way that will not contaminate others. You feel good as you watch the golden flames transform your woundedness into bright energy and clean ash that the Flowers and Trees will convert to fresh aromatic essences, which will support the healing of others.

You then hold the Medicine Stick in front of you that Sarah early on suggested you carry with you on the Trail. The Stick has become a repository for your grief. All the relationships that you lost came flooding over you as the Trail took you back to them and helped you see that those people left because of your woundedness, not because of their failings. You start sobbing uncontrollably, and Sarah rubs your back to comfort you.

After you've caught your breath, she leads you in taking several deeper, clearing breaths, which help relax you. Then she suggests that you break the stick in two, as a symbol of breaking the grief.

You reverently place the pieces on the coals and watch them smolder. You're glad they don't burst right into flame, as the thick, ropey smoke that rises from them draws forth those old memories one more time. You take the opportunity to express your gratitude for each of those beautiful people who graced your life and taught you about yourself.

Bringing It Home

You feel complete as you cross the Threshold Bridge. It's been a long time since you've felt so good about returning home. With what you've gained here—and with what you've left behind—you know your life can be different from here on.

"You've done some tremendous work today," says Sarah.

You can't help but smile and feel good about that. At the same time, you know that it's going to take a lot of work. "What can I do to keep on track?" you ask.

"Let's stop at the Cairn on the way out," she replies. "There might be a Crystal or a Burl that speaks to you there. If so, take it along home and place it where it'll be a regular reminder of what Nature gifted you here. You can take your Token home with you also.

"But mostly, it's what you carry inside, and how you keep it alive. Have you heard the saying that *there's nobody like an old fool, because there's no substitute for experience*? Fortunately, experience works both ways. If I could give you only one piece of advice, I'd ask you to remember that we become what we surround ourselves with. It's the easiest way to change and stay on the Healing Path: just hang out with the people you want to emulate.

"And you can do what many others find helpful: come back and Walk the Trail again. For some, it's a renewal of what they gained; some call it a retreat or pilgrimage. Some folks who live in the area stop by often, even if it's to just walk one of the Labyrinths. Others come annually, sometimes on the anniversary of their first Walk.

"I know you live some distance away, but we have people who even come from overseas. You can take a Remote Walk [covered in the next chapter] whenever you like. Some people put on a recording of Nature sounds, then envision they are Walking the Trail, or that they are sitting in their Comfort Spots.

"Yet there's one more thing we can do right now to send you off on the right foot."

For Gratitude: The Trail's End Feast

"There is one more thing you can do to keep your Walk alive in your heart. Did you know that every culture, in every era, civilized or aboriginal, typically marks the conclusion of rites of passage, rituals, and healings with a Feast? It's the same in our society. Have you ever been to a wedding, funeral, anniversary, graduation, or just about any other significant event, without a formal meal being offered?"

"I never thought of it that way," you say, "but you're right. There's something about a banquet, or even the main meal at Grandma's house when we have a family reunion, that brings us all together. Everybody seems to be in a good mood, and lots of stories and memories are shared."

"Believe it or not," says Sarah, "here's the body-mind connection again. Sharing food is Grounding: it fosters relaxation and goodwill, and it strengthens relationship. And as you noted, recalling old memories helps connect past with present."

"I know it was suggested on the packing list that I bring food, and bring enough to share if I had a Guide. Is that the reason?"

"Yes, that and more. It started for you at home already. The whole ritual of procuring, preparing, and packing the food is a metaphor for preparing to have the healing gifts of Nature feed your inner hunger for healing.

"With our healing ritual completed, you and I can now have our Feast of Gratitude, for all that you have been gifted, and for the honor it has been for me to serve you. In the tradition we follow here, which has been passed down to us from the Native Elders, we begin the Feast by placing a bit of each food in the fire, in remembrance of those who have come before us. This includes our ancestors, and those whose footsteps we followed on this Trail.

"As we take our first bite, let's think of the enrichment we gained from the Journey we just completed. Think of Mother Nature, who has given us the food that nourishes both our bodies and our hearts. Then let us follow Rumi's advice, when I think he said something like, *Gratitude is the wine of the soul. Go ahead, get drunk!*"

For Renewal: The Commemorative Feast

"What you say doesn't just make sense," you say, "I can *feel* it. I wish there was some way I could take this Trail's End Feast home with me—I know it would help me stay on track with my healing."

"Do you know how birthdays and wedding anniversaries help in renewing vows and resolutions? You can do the same thing, by holding Commemorative Feasts of your Trail Walk. Invite your friends or family to the Feast, and share the story of your Walk with them.

"It might seem strange to have a Commemorative Feast with people who didn't share the experience with you. Yet your Healing Journey is the Healing Journey of those close to you, whether or not they realize it. Here's the law of attraction that we mentioned a bit back: your wellness becomes their wellness.

"The same is true for those who follow in your footsteps, both literally on this Trail and in your life. For that reason, some people see the Commemorative Feast as not only support for them, but a responsibility to others."

The Healing Camp Deep in Nature

While you and Sarah break bread together, she tells you the story of another enchanted health-giving refuge. "It's down a spur off the far end of the Healing Nature Trail. You'd only notice it if it was pointed out to you. The Path takes you off of the island and into the wilds beyond.

"After a half mile, the Path ends at a camp that harkens back to the time when bark, thatch, and rawhide were the preferred building materials. Two wigwams, an arbor, and a lean-to perch on a ridge overlooking a pond teeming with Waterlilies, Chorus Frogs, and Waterfowl. Kamgabwequay, one of our Ojibwe Elders, named the camp Mashkodens, which means *Little Prairie*, after the Blueberry Meadow that rolls down from the ridge.

"It's there at Mashkodens that therapists bring groups for in-depth Nature-based therapy. The camp is also available for group Breathwork sessions, yoga, and other therapies. And when the camp isn't reserved for other purposes, it's available for individual and group retreats."

Sarah says that practitioners and retreat participants are drawn to Mashkodens for the feeling of intimacy with Nature that it offers. There's the smell of a wood fire, the essence of Pine from the bough mat around the hearth, the chortle of Ravens overhead, and the serenading of Frogs just a few paces away.

If you're quiet, she says, Deer venture out on the Meadow in plain sight. In the evening, Coyotes and Owls give concerts. Wolves, Bears, and Bobcats sometimes venture close to camp, yet it's the rare person who sees one. They're shy and typically disappear at the first sign of humans. What you do see, though, is an array of Wildflowers, Birds, and Butterflies, with Chipmunks scampering at your feet and wild berries tempting you in their season.

"It sounds like a fairytale place," you say. "I can only imagine that, in such an openly inviting setting, just being there has to be healing."

"You're right; that's what nearly everybody tells us. And that's why I'd like to suggest that you or your group book your stay at Mashkodens well in advance, to be sure you get your preferred date."

Find Healing Nature Anywhere

"There's one more thing I'd like to leave with you," says Sarah. "Now that you've Walked the Trail, you know that the magic is not in the Trail per se, but rather in who the Trail introduces you to. And you can find her everywhere—now that you know what to look for. A walk in any city park, along any Waterway, or through any patch of Trees, Grass, or Scrub can be turned into a Healing Nature Walk. Even though it doesn't have all the features of a certified Healing Nature Trail, you'll still be caressed in her caring embrace. Her essence is there—her Aromatherapy, her Grounding energy, her guiding voices.

"Other features you're looking for are likely there as well, though they may not be as obvious as on a Healing Nature Trail.

Let's say you want a Reflective Haven or a Panoramic Vista. Reflect on what it brings you, then look around you for the place that will do it. Be careful not to get hung up on envisioning an actual Haven or Vista. Instead, focus on reliving the *experience* you had there. Then you might notice that what you're looking for is already there before you, only in a form that you aren't familiar with.

"Another way to help a healing feature materialize is to read about it in the Trail Guide. Take note of its basic characteristics, rather than its visual description, and you might then watch it take shape in front of you. Like all mothers, Nature usually finds a way to give us what we need."

Farewell

It's time to leave. You give your Guide a long hug—it's the only way you can say *good-bye*. Though it's not like you to be at a loss for something to say, you realize that the world Sarah opened up for you goes beyond words.

"I understand," says Sarah softly. "Please feel free to contact me after you've had some time to sit with all of this. Otherwise, I'll be in touch with you anyway, to check in on how you're doing and to work with you on integrating what you've awakened to here today.

"Right now, why don't you just take some time for yourself. The gate swings both ways, by the way; so you might want to walk the Labyrinth again before you hit the road. Or you could go up on the Cosmorinth, find a comfortable place, and let everything percolate for a bit. On the other hand, you might just want to relax at one of the picnic tables near the parking area. Whichever option you choose, it's a good way to transition back into the world out there."

First, you head for the Welcome Center to check out and leave a donation. And you want to get a book or two that caught your eye on the way in. Sarah suggested that you pick up some Balsam Fir essential oil, so that you can continue Aromatherapy and body–mind connectedness on your own.

That's all fine and good, you say to yourself, *but the main reason I want to take some of that Northwoodsy smelling oil home with me is to bring back memories of this dreamy day I just spent in another world.*

While in the Welcome Center, you notice a large print of the Threshold Bridge that speaks to you. A copy goes home with you, to hang in your living room—but not only for its beauty. You want it to remind you of the span there once was between your life and the serenity of Nature, and of how you bridged that span to bring the two together.

Before leaving, you would like to do one more thing: leave a few words in the guestbook for those who come here after you. Here is what the cover reads:

Dear Journeyer,

*We hope you had a rich and rewarding time
here at the Healing Nature Center.
We invite you to share something of your experience
in this notebook—a new awareness,
a special moment, or anything else you like.*

*Along with us, other guests
would like to hear about your time here.
What you leave of yourself on these pages
may inspire others, and maybe help someone
surmount a hurdle.*

*We are deeply grateful for the time
you spent with us here in the Cradle of Nature,
and we want you to know that you have a place here—
you are always welcome back.*

*We wish you safe travels
and an ever-enriching Healing Journey.*[2]

PART V
ADDITIONAL TRAIL FEATURES

As our mother, Nature is there for us. Along with that, we need to be there for each other, as some of us are not able to immerse ourselves in Nature as easily as others. Chapters in this section give guidance for customizing Trails to accommodate those with special needs. This section also provides reflective and inspirational material for enriching the Trail experience.

Every Trail needs support and sponsorship. The last two chapters in this section give examples for how to accomplish that.

CHAPTER TWENTY-FIVE

For Those with Special Needs

One word captures the focus of all Healing Nature Trail staff—accessibility. They dedicate themselves to making Nature's healing powers accessible. This poses unique challenges for the staff; first, because the chasm between Nature and modern humans is already extreme, and, second, because it can be even more extreme for people with certain physical or psycho-emotional conditions.

Yet, thanks to dedicated individuals and the wonders of human ingenuity, nearly everyone's needs for healing Nature immersion can be met on most Healing Nature Trails. If you have special needs, or if you know or care for someone who does, please do not hesitate to contact a Trail office and see what is possible.

From a Nature-immersion perspective, special needs people fall into three categories:

▶ Those with physical or psycho-emotional conditions that require specific adaptations.

▶ Those with unique abilities for communing with Nature.

▶ Those who do not have direct access to a Trail, or who are not able to travel.

Let's take a close look at each of these categories through the lens of how the parent Healing Nature Trail in Wisconsin meets these needs.

Physical and Psycho-Emotional Conditions

This category covers by far the greatest number of people who need special services. In terms of physical conditions, Healing Nature Guides are trained to guide people with limited-mobility, who are wheelchair-mobile, and who have sight impairments. Following are the general groupings of people in this category, along with how their Nature-immersion needs can be met.

Limited Mobility

This grouping includes individuals who are able to walk but have limited ability to do so. The typical reasons for such are cardiovascular conditions, diabetes, obesity, congenital conditions, amputations, age, disease, or being in recovery from medical procedures. Accommodating Trail features are listed in chapter 30, *Trail Design*. Standard accommodations provided by the Trail staff at the Welcome Center include:

▶ Portable fold-up chairs.

▶ Canes and crutches with wide pads, to prevent sinking into the ground. They must be used on the Wheelchair Trail (described under next grouping), due to the narrowness of the Main Trail.

Wheelchair and Crutch-Mobile

The main Healing Nature Trail is too narrow and rugged, and in many sections the gradient is too steep, to accommodate wheelchairs. For these reasons, the Healing Nature Center has developed a separate trail system that meets the criteria for wheelchair accessibility.

The *Rolling Wheel Healing Nature Trail* can accommodate most light to medium-weight wheelchairs of standard width. The Center Director makes the final determination regarding the suitability of a particular wheelchair for the Trail.

Some Healing Nature Trails have all-terrain wheelchairs for use. They can negotiate steeper gradients and obstacles better than typical wheelchairs, and they are less prone to tipping.

Due to the Trail variables, the proximity to water, and fire exposure, Trail users in wheelchairs and on crutches must be accompanied by specially trained staff, which includes Healing Nature Guides.

Rolling Wheel Trail features:

- A wheelchair- and crutch-accessible Labyrinth.
- Smudging by being brushed with Balsam Fir boughs.
- A wheelchair- and crutch-level Cairn.
- A low-gradient Threshold Bridge.
- A private Trailside Haven.
- A specially equipped canoe for the Aquarinth.
- A Fire-reflection circle and adjacent Pond.

Sight-Impaired

This grouping includes functionally blind individuals as well as those vision-compromised to the point that they need a Guide to safely negotiate the Trail and have a quality Trail experience. In partnership with the sight-impaired individual, the Center Director helps determine whether or not the individual needs trained assistance for the Trail. Healing Nature Guides are trained to act as guides for the blind.

From a Nature-healing perspective, *sight-impaired* is a misnomer. Most of us rely on sight for 85 percent of our sensory input. Consequentially, we miss much of what our other senses could be providing us if we lived in an environmental context where sensory input was more evenly balanced.

Sight-impaired people, on the other hand, benefit from the reverse situation. The acuity of their senses of hearing, smell, taste, and touch is magnified beyond that of sighted people. The same is true of their spatial and movement sensitivities. One could say that they are gifted in these areas.

This giftedness gives people who are blind and vision-compromised a unique opportunity to benefit maximally from a number of Trail features and Nature's healing gifts, such as:

- Aromatherapy.
- Grounding.
- Nature's guiding voices.
- Conscious Breathing.
- The body-mind connection, catalyzed by changes in elevation and direction.
- Bridge sway, particularly on the Bridge over Troubled Water.
- Panoramic vistas, experienced by stereoscopic sound, the feel of the breeze, and the touch of the sun.
- The Labyrinth of Sound, comprised of the variety and complexity of Nature's voices.
- Finger Labyrinths.
- The Zen Garden.
- The sound of the Drum, Rattle, and Rainstick (available at the Welcome Center for Trail use).
- The feel of a Token (also available at the Welcome Center).

Psycho-Emotional Conditions

Healing Nature Guides are trained to work with the therapists or guardians of many individuals with psycho-emotional conditions that inhibit their ability to independently Walk the Trail. The Center Director has the ultimate authority to determine an individual's capability for negotiating the Trail, whether or not that individual is accompanied by a healthcare practitioner, guardian, or Guide. The Center Director works in collaboration with the individual Walker and his or her therapist to make that decision.

Unique Abilities

As with the sight-impaired, many individuals diagnosed with conditions such as autism, hypersensitivity, ADD/ADHD, and depression, or who are symptomatic of such conditions, find that some of their symptoms become assets on the Trail. Some autistic people have a knack for understanding the language of animals, hypersensitive individuals sometimes respond quickly to Aromatherapy, and those with attention-deficit traits often notice more than others.

Some individuals in this grouping are best served by Trail Walks modified to meet their particular needs and abilities. These determinations are made by the individual's therapist in consultation with the Trail Guide working with them, or with the Center Director.

Another grouping under this banner includes those with unique or exceptional physical abilities, such as Tree climbing, swimming, running, or tracking. These abilities can serve as catalysts for a heightened Trail experience. Trail Guides are trained to help design Walks that incorporate these aptitudes, in order to take full advantage of the healing and Awakening opportunities a Trail Walk affords.

For example, a Walk for Tree climbers might include Treetop Breathing in Nature, Aromatherapy, Panoramic Vistas, and Labyrinthine Envisioning. These climbing experiences are facilitated by Healing Nature Guides who are Certified Recreational Tree Climbing Instructors.

Inability to Access Trail

Some physical and psychological conditions keep people either bedbound or housebound. For various reasons, a number of others are unable to travel to a Healing Nature Trail. Fortunately, this book and related online resources can bring the Trail to them, by way of a process called *Remote Walking*.

The founders and directors devoted considerable energy toward making Remote Walking a key feature of the Healing Nature

Trail concept. They wanted the restorative properties of Nature to be available to everyone, including people who are immobile.

Remote Walking also benefits those who are physically challenged and cannot traverse the complete Trail or take advantage of all the Trail has to offer. Someone with impaired breathing can then still be helped by Aromatherapy, and someone who cannot negotiate the Zen Untangle or Aquarinth can yet experience them and gain from them.

Why Remote Walking Is Possible

In chapter 5, we covered how immersion in Nature quickens and strengthens the healing process. Recent research shows that many of the same benefits can be attained by merely viewing Nature through a window. Even more remarkably, a similar effect can be gained by gazing at a mural of a Nature scene.

The reason a view or image of Nature works is that they help us imagine we are immersed in Nature. The ability to do so is called *Envisioning*.

Animals generally relate to their environment through their senses. They rely on smell, sight, hearing, and touch to find food and shelter, and to navigate. We humans do the same.

In addition, we can Envision, and we are the only animals capable of doing so. Here's how Envisioning works: If we were hunting an animal, we could create a mental picture of where to find her, based on our knowledge of the animal's habits and habitat. This saves us the laborious—and often unsuccessful—task of directly following the footprints or scent of our prey over long distances in order to catch up with it, as other animals have to do.

Envisioning, then, gives us the ability to perform beyond the capabilities of our physical senses. We are able to mentally create what does not exist, and what exists beyond the reach of our senses. *Once we create it, we can experience and gain from it.*

Our sense of empathy is based on our Envisioning ability. When someone is sad, we can envision her state of being and cry along with her. Even more, we can envision her existence from a verbal description or video footage, to the same effect.

How Remote Walking Is Accomplished

In her ultimate wisdom, Mother Nature provided us with the quintessential place for our minds to open and our spirits to soar. The Trail's developers are the first to admit that it was not them, but Nature, who designed the Trail. They merely listened to her guidance. We can do the same through Remote Walking: We can close our eyes and Envision, and the Trail will appear in the landscape of our minds. We can then set foot upon it.

Here's how it is done:

1. Find a quiet place, free of distractions.
2. Center yourself by taking several slow, deep breaths.
3. Invite your personal guide to join you by opening this book to Part IV, *A Walk on the Wild Side,* and playing a recording of Northwoods Nature sounds.

   or

   By watching *A Walk on the Wild Side,* a video-recorded Trail Walk.

4. Envision being there: the wind swaying the Trees, Chipmunks scampering about, an Eagle soaring overhead, and people like you on the Labyrinth and Trail.
5. Take your shoes off, step on a soft rug, and imagine you're feeling the mossy ground underfoot.
6. Walk your fingertip along the Path of a Finger Labyrinth (or paper image of a Labyrinth) while reading or viewing the Labyrinthine Walk.
7. Smell the Pine-scented air by placing a few of drops of Aromatherapy Oil on a napkin or in a diffuser.
8. Bathe in a Panoramic Vista by opening your window to let the sun and breeze splash your face.

Guided Remote Walking

There is one more key component of a Trail Walk that you can incorporate into your Remote Walking: a Healing Nature Guide. The experience and personal stories that a Guide can contribute would bring a Remote Trail Walk all the more to life. Guides have dedicated their lives to doing all they can for Nature-assisted healing, so many of them would not only be willing to travel to a client's home or recovery room, but they would consider it an honor to do so. They can also guide Remote Walkings by telephone and Skype.

As trained storytellers, Guides can take clients on Remote Trail Walks in three different ways:

▶ **Reading** a story of a Trail Walk, with pictures, based on Part IV of this book.

▶ **Narration** accompanying the *A Walk on the Wild Side* video.

▶ **Customized Guided Visualization,** to meet a client's personal needs.

To help bring Remote Walks to life, Guides bring a photo album, a Finger Labyrinth, smudging boughs, Aromatherapy Oil, some Forest soil, and water from the Aquarinth along with them.

Experience shows that a Guide can contribute significantly to the quality and effectiveness of a Remote Walk. For those who are going to be immobilized for extended periods of time, it is advantageous for a Guide to facilitate at least the first Remote Walking. The Guide can then train the client to maximize his subsequent self-guided Remote Walks.

BRINGING THE ACTUAL TRAIL TO THE CLIENT

Some Healing Nature Guides have filmed Trail Walks with head cameras, which allows immobile people to visually take actual Trail Walks, conducted by their personal Guides. Other Guides have the capacity to livestream Walks, which gives Guides and clients the ability to have interactive Trail experiences in real time.

Self-Guided Remote Walking

Here is a simplified Envisioned Trail Walk that you can take on your own anytime, anyplace, with no audio-visual aids needed. Use it when traveling, lying awake at night, or taking a break at work.

Start with Conscious Breathing (see chapter 7), to bring yourself into the moment and relax into the experience. Then slowly read the following visualization (or you can have it read to you).

I imagine that I am heading toward the Threshold Bridge to enter the Maze known as the Healing Nature Trail. Just before the Bridge, I calm and center myself by walking the Labyrinth. I also brush by the Pine boughs that hang over the Trail; the aromatic essences they release give me a cleansing, uplifting Smudge.

Right after that, I come upon the Cairn, where I place the special stone I brought to commemorate the experience.

Now I am about to step off of the archway between two worlds—I am leaving my travails behind and entering the rejuvenating realm of Nature. Already I feel lighter as I take a deep breath of the clean, Pine-laced Forest air. The comfortingly soft ground beneath my feet makes me feel welcomed as the Trail takes me into a grove of towering Pines.

There I feel safe under the protective canopy.

A Tree calls to me, and I sit back-to-back with her. I feel her energy, coming up from the ground and running along my spine. Closing my eyes, I breathe with the Tree. She exhales, and I inhale her breath. I exhale, and she inhales my breath. We are one breath, one life.

Now I hear the wind whistling through the high branches. The Tree responds, listing ever so slightly one way, then the other. Yet I feel it, and I raise my arms to catch the breeze and join in the leisurely dance.

As I sway, my breathing falls in sync with the waves of wind and the swaying Tree.

A sigh springs forth spontaneously from me, and then a humming sound that harmonizes with the whistle of the wind and the titter of the Birds.

I get caught up in the chorus and I want to keep dancing. Yet the Trail beckons. I feel so light that it's as though I'm drifting over the Pathway on the wings of a Butterfly. Am I just high on the fresh, oxygenated air? Or maybe it's the negative ions and endorphins from the Trees?

Whatever the case, I feel more alive than I have in a long time. I'm stepping light as a child, and I'm starting to see through the haze. What a beautiful day it is!

CHAPTER TWENTY-SIX

Trail Meditations

There are two general types of Healing Nature Trail Walks: those that are intentional, structured, and guided; and those that are unintentional, free-form, and self-guided. People whose relationships are in turmoil, have health crises, or are tormented by inner demons come to Nature with clear intention. Their sense of purpose supports their Walk in these essential ways:

> Energizes them physically and psychically.

> Keeps them attuned to the Trail experience.

> Helps them choose which Trail features would best serve them.

> Gives their Guide clear direction.

> Makes their overall Walk maximally effective.

As valuable as intention can be, it can also blind—especially when one focuses too hard on it. There is the risk of overstimulation and losing perspective. As contradictory and confusing as it might sound, there is a point on the Walk where intention needs to become unintentional.

When we hold onto intention too tightly, it becomes our only fuel. We trust in it rather than the process. We filter out what does not seem to fit with our intention. Crossing the Threshold Bridge is the time to hand our intention over to Mother Nature and place our trust in her caring hands. Author Thomas Wolfe said that Nature is the one place where miracles not only happen, but they happen all the time.[1] We need to relax into that awareness—and trust in it—in order to be fully open and present to the Trail experience.

Intention-Softening Meditations

Here are two meditations that can be practiced at any time on the Trail when intention starts to take over. For the first meditation, repeat the words slowly, with a pause between each phrase. For the second meditation, inhale and exhale slowly and fully. Do the meditations while walking, to engage body, mind, and spirit. Some people like to have their Guide recite the meditations, which helps the Walker fully relax into it.

> There is nothing to do
> nothing to change
> nothing to fix
> nothing to heal.[2]

> (On the inhale) I have arrived.
> (On the exhale) I am home.[3]

When Intention Escapes You

Sometimes a person feels troubled, and she's not sure why. Nothing seems to be going right. Her life seems to be no more than a series of dead-end jobs and unfulfilling relationships. A cloud of depression hangs over her. Her spirit screams for change, but she doesn't know what to ask for.

She's gone to a couple of therapists, and she's worked through a number of self-help books. They did prove helpful, but each time the effect eventually wore off.

So here she stands, at the start of the Trail. What can she do to find clarity of intention?

Fortunately for her, clarity of intention does not necessarily mean having a clear intention, but rather being clear that here is the place—and now is the time—to walk her Healing Journey. Following are two time-proven ways, one verbal and one nonverbal, to distill our clarity of intention.

An Affirmation

When we verbally state something that we are going to do, we empower and clarify the action. The result then usually meets our need better than if we had not verbalized it. Affirmations serve the purpose well, and here is a favorite that Guides share with their clients:

1. Now is my time to awaken and heal, and I know that Nature's way is my way to do it.

2. I believe in my ability to come together with Nature and co-create joy and healing for myself.

3. I allow myself to believe that I deserve Nature's healing gifts.

4. I give my whole being—body, mind, and spirit—to becoming a vessel for Nature's healing gifts.

5. With Mother Nature's support, I have the ability to recognize, process, and release all repressed feelings, old stories, and harmful behaviors.

Walking to Intention

There are times when words don't seem to fit. The Birds are singing, the breeze is playing in the branches, and we came here to listen. Besides, we don't want to break the personal silence we worked to achieve.

Yet we are losing our clarity of intention. Or maybe we were fooling ourselves by thinking we had it.

We can bring it back with a form of Walking Meditation called *Conscious Walking*. Also known as *Deer Stepping, Fox Walking, Ice Walking,* and *Native Walking,* it is the way Native people move through natural environments in order to keep centered and consciously engaged with their surroundings. You can learn about Conscious Walking in chapter 15, and you can take a Conscious Walking Workshop at most Healing Nature Trails.

Meditations for No-Intention Walks

From a Zen perspective, the idea of setting specific intentions is a grand illusion. How can we know what we need if we have never had it? Or if we think we once did, is it possible that we lost it because we needed something other than that? Perhaps something deeper? Or perhaps we already had it and couldn't recognize it?

The more present we are, the less we feel the need to seek. Following are Walking Meditations with no other intention than to be fully present. They were chosen for their simplicity, and for the comfortable doorways they open to the self. Rather than choosing a meditation, let it choose you.

Awakening the Senses

Start by Walking Consciously for fifteen to twenty minutes, then become one of your senses for an equal amount of time. Either continue walking or sit/stand in a place that calls to you. The important thing is to fully immerse yourself in the sense you choose, then breathe the experience into your being.

Here is your menu of choices:

Breathe.
Touch.
Listen.
Smell.
Taste.
Look.

Rewilding

Who we are is who we forgot we were. Here is a way to remember.

Slow down.

Breathe in your surroundings.
Breathe out your thoughts and watch them vaporize.
Lift your wings to the wind.
Slow down again.
Become your impulses.
Let your mind dance.
Flow with the wind and water.
Feel the lacy treetops.
Slow down some more.

Zen Meditations

Make a random choice of one of these individual meditations, then Consciously Walk with it until it melts away. (See chapter 15 for guidance on Conscious Walking.)

In one falling leaf lives the whole of autumn.

A baby acts without knowing why and moves without knowing where.

Speak rather than answer.

A heavy snowfall disappears into the sea.

I cannot be angry or argumentative with you. It can only be with my illusion of you.

We see things not as they are, but as we are.

If I think something rings true, the opposite also rings true.

By inhaling, I show that I am capable of taking in life.

Only from nothing can something arise.

Peace can be found only in death.

The Path becomes the obstacle.

All fear amounts to fear of death.

Truth cannot be written or spoken; it can only be lived.

To assert something is to miss it altogether.

A Flower has no meaning unless it blooms.

To admit I am a fool is to find trust in who I am.

Wants and needs are the same.

If I try to keep it, I am already mistaken.

Every moment, I create something.

Cursed rain brings the beautiful mist that filters through the treetops.

CHAPTER TWENTY-SEVEN

Supporting the Trail

The best way to provide and care for the Trail is to use it. The sole reason for its being is to be there for you, so come whenever you feel called. You are always welcome.

You also can bring the Trail to others like you by envisioning them Walking the Trail. So many people have lost connection with the Earth and their Path in life. Many more struggle physically and psycho-emotionally. Picture them on the Trail reconnecting with Nature and being bathed in her healing support; your envisioning will help it happen.

Other ways to support the Trail's reason for being are to **bring a friend** with you on your next Walk, **give a gift certificate** for a Walk, and **spread the word** to people you know and work with, including healthcare professionals. You could post on social media and write letters to the editors of papers and magazines.

The Healing Nature Welcome Center has several possibilities for spreading the word. You can acquire additional copies of *The Healing Nature Trail* to give to others who you think would like to know about the Trail. Wearing a Trail T-shirt or hoodie can give a lot of exposure. And if you take a Finger Labyrinth home with you, it is bound to be a conversation piece that leads to your Trail story.

It's All about Relationship

From Zen perspective, life is relationship, and that's the essence of the Trail experience. Whether it's with Nature, our inner selves, or our fellow Trail lovers, seeking fulfillment in relationship may well be our prime motivator. In this sense, your presence means more than anything when it comes to supporting the Trail.

Following are three special ways your presence can be felt—special because they engender relationship:

Volunteer

There is a wide variety of opportunities for helping to take care of a Healing Nature Trail, both directly and indirectly. Hands-on opportunities include Trail and Labyrinth maintenance, Wildflower gardening, and Bridge and Center repairs (which could include general labor, carpentry, electrical, or plumbing work). Sometimes assistance can be used at workshops and other events.

THE LABYRINTHIANS

One volunteering example at the original Healing Nature Trail is a group who call themselves The Labyrinthians. They support the Trail by caring for the Gateway Labyrinth's Wildflower beds and trimming the grass.

There always seems to be room for more outreach, whether it's distributing handouts and posters, updating the website, or writing/editing. Help is often welcomed for fundraisers and grant writing. With any other talent or interest you have, please contact the director to see how you can be of service.

Join Friends of the Trail

The camaraderie is contagious in the Friends of the Trail group. Its members share a love of Nature and a dedication to making the Healing Nature Trail the best possible gateway to Nature's healing gifts. Regular volunteers, stakeholders, and contributors are invited to join the Friends. Benefits include:

> ▶ Unlimited usage of the Trail for members and their families.

- Invitation to special events held just for the Friends, including an annual banquet.

- Discounts on Healing Nature Center workshops, courses, trainings, and goods.

Be a Trail Development Ambassador

One Healing Nature Trail can serve only so many people; and practically speaking, it is a regional resource. The goal of the Healing Nature Center is to help establish regional Trails across America, Europe, Australia, and wherever else Nature can reach out to her lost and besieged children. This includes Trails giving us access to all of Nature's many spangled forms: Prairie, Wetland, Beach, Mountain, Desert, Rain Forest, and Taiga.

If you know of an individual or organization that might like to establish a Healing Nature Trail, please ask them to go to www.healingnaturecenter.org, or give them a copy of this book. Part VI of the book gives detailed guidance on how to organize, design, and conduct outreach for a Healing Nature Trail.

Ways to Contribute

This chapter section serves as a guide for financial supporters of the original Healing Nature Trail, and a template for other Trails to develop contribution formats.

Trail usage donations and tuition cover most of the day-to-day Trail and Center overhead. Special services such as the wheelchair-accessible Trail are supported largely by grants. Yet funding is needed on a sustainable basis for Trail development, workshop presentations, expansion of services, outreach, maintenance, wages, and property taxes.

The Trail staff and Friends of the Trail respectfully ask if you would consider making a one-time or periodic contribution to support and assure the future of the Trail. This could take the form of donating to the Trail Maintenance Fund, establishing a memorial, contributing to the Legacy Fund, remembering the

Trail in your will, or a monthly contribution charged to your credit card. You may also donate a used vehicle, real estate, artwork, or collectibles. All contributions, monetary or otherwise, are 100 percent tax-deductible.

Following are the various ways you can contribute:

Trail Maintenance Fund

Any amount is accepted. The fund supports the upkeep of the Trail, Labyrinths, and adjacent grounds.

Tokens of appreciation for Trail Maintenance Fund contributions are awarded as follows:

▶ For all donors of $25 or more—A copy of *The Healing Nature Trail*.

▶ For donors of $100—A copy of *Becoming Nature* or *Wild Sounds of the Northwoods*.

▶ For donors of $300—Copies of *Zen Rising* and *Song of Trusting the Heart*.

▶ For donors of $500—A one-year pass to the Healing Nature Trail.

▶ For donors of $1,000—A Finger Labyrinth (choose from three classic designs) and a one-year Trail pass.

▶ For donors of $5,000—A custom-crafted Finger Labyrinth replica of the Gateway Labyrinth.

In addition, all donors of $1,000 or more are recognized with a brass nameplate on a permanent Birchwood Plaque in the Welcome Center. Donors of $5,000 or more are specially recognized on the Plaque.

Memorial/Dedication Plaques

$500 for the Trail Bench or Bicycle Rack Plaque.

$750 for the Stump Labyrinth Plaque.

$1,000 for the Pollinator Wildflower Bed Plaque.

$2,000 for the Hermitage Cabin Plaque.

$3,000 for the Zen Untangle or Zen Garden Plaque.

$4,000 for the Welcome Center Plaque.

$5,000 for the Trance Dance Studio Plaque.

$7,500 for the Cosmorinth Plaque.

$10,000 for the Gateway Labyrinth Plaque.

$15,000 for the Threshold Bridge
or Trail History Museum Plaque.

The Legacy Fund

The ability of the Healing Nature Center to continue its healing mission well into the future is secured by sustaining contributions from individuals, families, trust funds, and organizations. These contributors provide a support base that makes it possible for the Center to offer the best possible Trail and workshop experiences, along with making the Trail and other Center offerings available to everyone seeking Nature's solace and healing touch, regardless of financial state. Contributions in the form of currency, real estate, bequeathals, stocks, bonds, and annuities are accepted.

- A $25,000 bequest is honored by a Board of Directors proclamation to install a commemorative sign at the head of the Healing Nature Trail, dedicating it to the memory of whomever the bequester desires.

- A $50,000 bequest is honored by a Board proclamation to mount a commemorative tile beside the door of the Healing Nature Center, dedicating it to the memory of whomever the bequester desires.

A $100,000 bequest is honored by a Board proclamation to mount a commemorative tile beside the door of the Giant Pine Meeting Lodge, dedicating it to the memory of whomever the bequester desires.

CHAPTER TWENTY-EIGHT

Meet the Trail's Mothership: The Healing Nature Center and Preserve

Comprised of a Nature preserve adjacent to the Chequamegon-Nicolet National Forest, and a complex of footpaths, Labyrinths, and workshop-retreat spaces, the Healing Nature Center and Preserve is organized as a 501(c)(3) nonprofit organization. It is charged with the mission to make the therapeutic properties of Nature accessible to individuals, groups, healthcare practitioners, and their clients.

The Healing Nature Preserve's roots go back to 1971, with the founding of the Coldfoot Creek Natural Area, a 520-acre wilderness reserve eighty miles east of the Healing Nature Preserve. In 1987, the founders of Coldfoot Creek moved on to found the Healing Nature Center and Preserve.

The Center's approach is to create a synergistic format by incorporating shamanic and Zen practices, along with techniques based on contemporary neuroscience research. Primary areas of focus are trauma, stress and anxiety, relationship, self-discovery, reconnecting with Nature, and physical healing support.

As mentioned in the previous chapter, the Center is dedicated to supporting the establishment of regional Healing Nature Trails wherever they can serve people who could benefit from Nature's healing embrace.

The Center's flagship tool is the Healing Nature Trail, a first-of-its-kind Nature-immersion experience that enhances the body-mind connection with somatic sensitizing exercises,

Aromatherapy, plant and animal communication, and the shamanic use of Breath, Earth, Fire, and Water.

Brother Wolf Foundation

Along with the Trail, the Center sponsors the Brother Wolf
Foundation, a long-term project to establish a sanctuary for
unwanted domesticated Wolves who cannot be reintroduced
into the wilds. In conjunction with the sanctuary, an educational center is planned, to renew awareness of the ancient Wolf–
Human relationship. According to the legends of the Ojibwe
people of the Upper Great Lakes region, this kinship has existed
since the dawn of creation. It is so close that the destinies of
both species are inextricably intertwined. "As goes the fate and
fortune of Wolf, so goes the fate and fortune of Man," says one
of the Ojibwe legends. This profound relationship is a metaphor
for our kinship with all of life.[1]

Environmental Stewardship

The Center runs on the reduce-reuse-recycle philosophy. As
much as possible, the Center refrains from buying anything new
and sources materials and supplies locally. Old buildings are
restored with local, salvaged materials, rather than being demol-
ished and replaced.

The Healing Nature Trail features were constructed entirely
from salvaged materials: old docks for walkways, rescued utility
poles for bridge pilings, sawmill sawdust for Trail paving, and
castaway quarry stone for path borders.

Center staff members are active in regional environmental activities, from chairing the Natural Resources Committee to working
with local agencies and citizens to eradicate invasive plant species.
The staff helps individuals and organizations establish pollinator
flower gardens and backyard wildlife habitat through such projects as the National Wildlife Federation's *Garden for Wildlife* (www.

nwf.org/Garden-for-Wildlife) and San Francisco State University's *Great Sunflower Project* (www.greatsunflower.org).

The Campus

Two buildings stand on campus: the Center, which houses the office, bookstore, Trail History Museum, and workshop space; and the Giant Pine Lodge, which offers additional workshop space, along with rooming and eating facilities for Trail Walkers, workshop participants, and presenters.

Rounding out the campus are a Turf Labyrinth and a wheelchair-accessible Labyrinth, two Healing Nature Trails (one is wheelchair accessible), and Wildflower beds designed to support dwindling populations of pollinator species such as Bees and Butterflies.

Campus facilities are available for lease to therapists, workshop presenters, and educational and environmental organizations in alignment with the Center's mission.

Center facilities are available for:

▶ Individuals, groups, and Healing Nature Guides and therapists with their clients, using the Healing Nature Trail.

▶ Labyrinth walkers.

▶ Meditators (walking, sitting, and paddling).

▶ Personal and group retreats.

▶ Trainings, courses, and workshops presented by Center faculty and visiting instructors.

The Healing Nature Center is a sister organization to Snow Wolf Publishing and Teaching Drum Outdoor School.

The Programs

Consulting

▶ **Healing Nature Trail Development,** from site selection and design to organization and outreach.

▶ **Environmental Restoration.** Landscaping and recovery designs for Northwoods habitats, focusing on ecosystem integrity and endangered/invasive species.

Certification and Diploma Programs

▶ **Healing Nature Trail** certification.

▶ **Associate, Senior, and Off-Trail Healing Nature Guide** diploma courses.

▶ **Suicide Prevention** training and certification.

Therapy

▶ **Trauma Therapy** and management workshops.

▶ **Shamanic Therapy** and training.

▶ **Therapeutic Breathwork** sessions and training.

▶ **Trance Dance** for stress release and deep trauma work.

Personal Growth

▶ **Solo and Group Retreats.**

▶ **Zen Retreats**.

▶ **Wild Childrearing Training.**

▶ **Animal Guide Workshops.**

▶ **Dreamwork.**

Environmental

▶ **For the Birds, Bees, and Butterflies.** Workshops and tours for school groups, clubs, educators, farmers, and the general public, on establishing high nectar-producing Wildflower beds.

▶ **Wetland Restoration.** The Center is engaged in a model project to restore back to their natural state nine Ponds and a Stream in the preserve on which the Center is located.

PART VI
DEVELOPING A HEALING NATURE TRAIL

This book section is intended to be a guide for individuals and organizations wishing to establish Healing Nature Trails. It also is intended for Trail Walkers and other readers who know of someone who might be interested in developing or sponsoring a Trail.

Some of the following information will prove helpful for those of you who have private land and would like to develop your own personal or group-use Trail. Consultation services are available to you, and it is possible to have your Trail certified.

Or you may wish to create only a feature or two, such as a Labyrinth, Threshold Bridge, or Trailside Haven, in your backyard or on other private or institutional property. Consultation services are available to you as well; please feel free to contact a consultant even if you'd just like some advice.

CHAPTER TWENTY-NINE

Organization and Governance

This chapter is dedicated to getting you off on the right foot. Here you'll find nearly all the protocols and options you need to consider for establishing a Healing Nature Trail, from organizational, managerial, and governing structures to assuaging growing pains.

As concise and informative as you might find the following guidance, it is still no substitute for professional consultation and spending time at another Healing Nature Trail or similar organization. There are nuances and stylistic approaches that are better conveyed by example than words.

Numerous questions are bound to come up as you progress, so it's highly recommended that you develop a supportive relationship with a mentor or consultant—or both—right at the onset.

Where to Begin

Following are the three steps that will get you off to a solid start. If you are establishing a Trail under the guise of an already-existing organization, this section does not apply to you. Skip to *Growing Pains* in this chapter.

First: Establish an Organizational Umbrella

The best way to begin is by determining your organizational status. It's typically easier to do so at the onset than to backtrack and retrofit what you've already established. The primary reason for doing so is for governmental and liability reasons. To apply for grants, work with professional organizations, protect from personal indemnity, and secure insurance coverage (to name the major reasons), do establish your organizational structure before proceeding any further.

The easiest approach is typically to associate with an already-existing organization that would like to sponsor the Trail. It is oftentimes still possible to have your own internal structure and governing board.

If that option is neither possible nor desirable, you are looking at seemingly endless possibilities: private enterprise, sole proprietorship, general partnership, limited partnership, regular corporation, professional corporation, LLC (limited liability corporation), professional LLC, and LLP (limited liability partnership).

There is also the possibility of incorporating as a nonprofit, which carries a number of advantages over the prior list of possibilities: favored tax status, exemption from state sales tax, qualification for certain grants, donor incentive, and liability protection for staff and board members. The articles of incorporation, bylaws, and ethics and grievance policies intrinsic to such organizations can play helpful roles in your overall governing plan.

If you do not have someone in your organization with the expertise to help choose and establish a governing structure, consult an experienced CPA or corporation attorney.

Second: Develop an Internal Governing Architecture

Here you consider how you would like to have your day-to-day operations managed and accounted for. To establish a structure that will work best for you, use this seven-step process as your guideline:

1. **Reflect on who you are.** What are the values and relationship protocols that you would like to incorporate in your operating structure?

2. **Establish accountability.** With any organization involving three or more individuals, it works best to have one

focal point for overall accountability. For large organizations, this could be a board or committee; however, the vast majority of Trails are going to have a staff that is best served by having one person at the accountability helm. That person assumes whatever title is most appropriate for your organization, whether it is *manager, director, coordinator,* or some other option.

3. **Encourage close collaboration with all aspects of the organization.** Trails often have a sponsoring body, a governing organization, a manager, an operating staff, volunteers, and affiliated outside organizations. Coordinating amongst all of those entities can be achieved with periodic meetings, an online bulletin board, Skype or telephone conferencing, or any other method that keeps you connected and coordinated on a regular basis.

4. **Separate strategy-related topics from operational topics.** Operations need to function efficiently and in a timely manner, so they typically operate on a different timeline than the broader and more far-reaching considerations around growth, outreach, and directional strategies. For these reasons, and because operations and strategy meetings often involve at least some different people, operations meetings and strategy meetings should be held separately.

5. **Keep it simple.** No matter what your governing architecture, and no matter who your staff are, this is the precept that could make the most difference in terms of how well you function and serve the people who come to you. Simplicity in structure and/or operating procedures encourages clear communication; improves operating efficiency; and saves time, energy, and resources.

6. **Keep your operations centered under one organizational umbrella.** Too many chefs in the kitchen results in chaos—or worse. This warning is not to be confused with multiple organizations being involved with your Trail; it's

just that they need to be members of an umbrella entity or structure, so that they can all function as supportive organs within a single organism.

7. **Give exemplary leadership highest priority.** Top down, this helps assure steps 2 and 3 above as well as provides example and inspiration for everyone associated with the organization. From the bottom up, competent and trusted leadership allows the staff to give themselves the permission to become fully immersed in performing their roles without having to worry about managerial and operational considerations. Remember: *power destroys virtue.* Choose leaders who are team players and make everyone feel engaged.

Third: Seat a Governing Board

Commonly referred to as the board of directors, this body is responsible for the overall guidance and direction of your organization. Together with your governing architecture, which covers day-to-day operations, the governing board completes your organizational structure.

It is important to maintain the distinction between day-to-day operations and the guidance, direction, and overall decision-making authority of your board. Too many organizations, both young and old, fall into the trap of either an overzealous board of directors trying to micromanage, or a board so detached from the realities of an organization's operation that it leaves the staff trying to navigate a ship without a rudder. The following guidelines will help you avoid either extreme, by establishing a board of directors that will naturally steer you on a middle course.

First and foremost, give attention to the composition of your board. The ideal Healing Nature Trail board is comprised of mature, experienced, and dedicated representatives of:

- Stakeholders in the Trail.
- The communities served by the Trail.
- The skill sets needed for the Trail's health and maintenance.

You need an active board comprised of individuals who are engaged beyond just showing up for board meetings. When members visit the Trail and interact with the staff, they have a finger on the pulse of your organization.

Here are some suggestions for areas of expertise to have represented on your board when considering whom to invite to serve:

- Relevant healing professions.
- Legal/accounting knowledge.
- Administrative skills.
- Fundraising savvy.
- Connections with supportive and complementary organizations.
- Outreach and design skills.
- A Trail staff member, to represent operations.

There is no ideal number of board members, yet have no less than five, to help assure a broad spectrum of talent, representation, and input. More than nine members can get cumbersome when it comes to conducting meetings and making decisions. To eliminate the potential for tie votes, most sources recommend an odd number of board members. However, some people who have served on even-number boards have found that the specter of tie votes forces them to consider topics more thoroughly, in order to find common ground.

Board of directors meetings are the crossroads of your Trail organization's overall management, short- and long-range planning, and policy making. In your start-up phase, we suggest that you hold board meetings as needed, then settle into a four meetings-per-year routine. This works best for most organizations of this type, as they occur often enough to keep the board current in serving the needs of the Trail, but not so often as to risk board member burnout or micromanagement.

Conduct board meetings according to Robert's Rules of Order. For those not familiar with them, they often come across as redundant and excessive at first; yet nearly everybody eventually sees how they ultimately save time—and nerves—by contributing to efficiency, organization, and smooth decision making.

Simplified versions of the Rules of Order are all you should need, and they can be found online.

Ask your consultant or mentor for board meeting and agenda outlines that you can adopt for your usage. Depending on how you are legally organized or incorporated, there may be statutory provisions governing when and where to post meeting time and location, agenda, and minutes prior to your meeting.

Spend time on your agenda, both on the items you want to cover and preparing materials for each item. The agenda is the framework upon which you build the mechanisms to meet your operating needs and create your future.

Your First Order of Business

For a solid start, first place *Establish ethical and grievance guidelines* on the agenda of your inaugural board meeting. Having these protocols in place is invaluable for establishing a feeling of safe space for Trail Walkers and staff and providing a sense of integrity for healthcare professionals using your Trail. The guidelines address insurance and liability concerns as well. Along with seeking professional help to craft your guidelines, you can pattern them after those used by the Healing Nature Center, which you can find at www.healingnaturecenter.org.

Next, place *Establish a statement of province* on your agenda. Whenever there is instruction or services provided, there is the risk of inadequately trained or irresponsible individuals assuming roles as teachers or practitioners. There is the further risk of such individuals practicing without proper supportive context, or inappropriately to the situation. A statement of province is intended to reduce the occurrence of such abuses, by:

- Distinguishing responsible and properly trained instructors and practitioners from those who are not.

▶ Protecting the public from improperly executed or applied practices or modalities.

▶ Indemnifying responsible organizations and individuals from the uninformed, negligent, or unscrupulous actions of others.

Following is the statement of province used by the Healing Nature Center.

It is expressly forbidden to formally or informally teach, use, or present in media format, any and all practices or modalities learned at the Healing Nature Center/Trail, or from any of its publications or other media venues, or from any of its present or former staff, without specific written authorization from the Center.

It is further expressly forbidden to use the name "Healing Nature Center/Trail," "Tamarack Song," "Lety Seibel," or other present or former staff affiliated with the afore named Center/Trail or individuals, or any language specific to the afore named Center/Trail, individuals, or related practices or modalities, in association with any formal or informal teaching, healing, or other venue, without specific written authorization from the Center.

Conduct Effective Meetings[1]

In addition to board meetings, you will likely have periodic staff, project, volunteer, and fundraising meetings. Depending on how they are held, you could end up either tolerating them as a necessary evil or looking forward to them as a valuable contribution to fulfilling your mission. To assure the latter type of meeting, give attention to three components: size, who participates, and how it is conducted.

Size

Productive and pleasant meetings are comprised of five to eight participants. With more than that:

▶ Not everyone gets to contribute.

279

- Relevant exchange is reduced to surface remarks.
- Less informed people distract by requesting background information.
- Tough and involved topics end up being dealt with outside of meetings.
- People lose respect for meetings, which leads to poor participation, preparation, and results.

In small-group meetings, a sense of camaraderie tends to develop, which leads to clear, open, and focused dialogue. There is time for everyone to speak and be heard, which encourages resonance and leads to results.

Participation

Before inviting anyone, first create a clear agenda and plan enough time for each agenda item. Then use the following criteria for deciding who to invite to participate:

- Who has the most pertinent knowledge?
- Who are the primary stakeholders?
- Who can best implement meeting results?
- Who will gain most from the experience?

To avoid hurting the feelings of those who are not invited to attend, and to honor their contributions by giving them the opportunity to present their cases, send them the minutes, and involve them in meeting-related activities.

Conducting

Here is where all of your preparatory work comes together. Start your meetings by reviewing these guidelines and you are likely to have a successful meeting:

- Start by defining meeting goals and participant responsibilities.
- Encourage unique and personal input.

- Ask that contributions be clear, concise, and relevant.

- Request presence, patience, and respect for all perspectives.

- Give permission for participants to request the information they need.

- Suggest that everyone consider the perspectives of those not in attendance.

Modify these guidelines to best fit your organization's needs. Once you feel confident in conducting effective and pleasant meetings, you should be able to run successful meetings with two or three times the usual number of participants. Still, keep large meetings as the exception rather than the rule. Increase the number of attendees only when they can either make a valuable contribution or gain personally from the experience.

Growing Pains

Imagine that you are now a dynamic and well-established organization—you continue to grow in fulfilling your mission to make Nature's healing and consciousness-raising gifts accessible for a broad range of people. Yet along with the beauty of your blooming, a sluggishness sets in that makes nearly everything you do move in slow motion. It's as though a fog has descended over your organization and there's nothing you can say or do to make it lift.

Here are the common symptoms:

- You have more staff than you used to, yet you accomplish less.

- Sometimes you have more staff serving clients than you have clients.

- Your staff is fragmented—some do not know what others are doing.

- It takes so long to make decisions.

- A committee is now needed to handle what competent individuals once did.

- Essential steps get overlooked, along with a slow response to timely matters.

- Sometimes there is no one to take direct responsibility for a task.

- You regularly need to regroup in order to coordinate efforts.

- Your organization has become more task oriented than relationship oriented.

If you are experiencing a number of these symptoms, you are probably suffering the inefficiency, overbearing protocols, and impersonalization that comes from top-heavy management. This syndrome, common to most maturing organizations, goes under various names: *committee-itis, runaway bureaucracy, Parkinson's law,*[2] *the rebound effect,* and *Jevons paradox.*[3]

The bugaboo of this syndrome is that it self-perpetuates—and it worsens as the organization grows. The primary reason is that people tend to assume that more top-level management, committees, and meetings are needed to keep pace with growth. This belief is commonly espoused by the management teams of young, growing organizations.

However, what typically results is the dysfunctions listed above, along with a conservative approach to innovation and outreach. The effect on the staff is that many of them sink to a base level of efficiency and become entrenched in their positions. There's never enough time, and there are always too many tasks. There is committee meeting burnout and constant coordinating headaches. Some staff look for ways to avoid meetings. Paper shuffling and policy generation become major focuses, and projects get whittled down and given extended deadlines.

How to Fix It

The good news is that once you know what's going on, it's not that difficult to turn the situation around. It does, however, take the commitment of key staff members and solid, consistent follow-through, along with the support of your board of directors. Here's what to do:

First: Weed Out the Bad Apples

Have you noticed how one person can put in a full day of solid work and feel good about it, while the next person plugs along for half a day and complains about not having enough time? Do you see one person chipping in to get things done, while you don't see another person all day? How about the individual who quietly produces, while someone else talks the talk and has little to show for it? And what about the one who is supportive and encouraging, as opposed to the one who drains your staff's energy with emotional turmoil, criticism, and gossip?

If any of your staff fit one or more of the above scenarios, you have identified your problem. It turns out that the saying that *one bad apple spoils the bushel* is true with staff as well. To put it bluntly, *bad staff person* is a contagious and incurable virus.

When your staff are exposed to someone who is engaging in poor practices, 40 percent of them will begin to engage in poor practices themselves.[4] Another way to look at it is that each case of misconduct produces an additional .6 cases of misconduct.[5] This peer-influence effect is doubled when the people involved are of the same ethnicity or interest group.[6]

Unfortunately, this situation doesn't work in reverse: errant individuals seldom take on the ethical values of the forthright staff people around them.[7] For some reason, it appears to be easier to learn bad behavior than good.

Much of the responsibility for maintaining an ethical, pleasing, and efficient work environment rests on the shoulders of directors and others who are involved in staff procurement. They need to be careful of justifying the addition of an individual with sketchy character traits, on the grounds that he or she has a skill set the organization could really use. *I can manage the person,* the director might say. However, the hard truth is that there is no way to prevent the inevitable contamination that will persist long after the infected staff person leaves.[8]

The golden rule for directors: *Make no exceptions*. Choose your staff wisely, and assess them intelligently. Do thorough background checks, which includes court records and honest conversations with the past three employers. Have a minimum sixty-day trial period before offering a permanent position. Remember that if someone gives herself an hour to finish a task, it will take an hour; or if she gives herself a day, it will take a day. And remember that integrity is a matter of action—consistent action—not words.

And lastly, don't make exceptions for volunteers. Even though they may not be as intimately involved with your organization as regular staff, their level of integrity and performance does have a significant effect.

Yet directors cannot shoulder all of the responsibility, as it is impossible for them alone to turn an organization around. It all starts—and ends—with each individual staff member. The personal responsibility they assume, and their level of integrity, are the flesh and spirit of your organization.

Second: Get Un-Committeed

We create our own realities. So if you think you need committees in order to function, you will need committees. However, there is no way to un-create the reality that with the committee system, you can generally expect tasks to take longer, involve more people-hours, and generate more stress, than if competent individuals or task-specific teams organized and completed tasks directly.

Along with compromised competency and efficiency, committees are notoriously slow to respond to the unexpected, and they tend to maintain the status quo. Individuals who do not have the level of expertise to fully understand or contribute to a project, or who lack in group process skills, can bog committees down.

Yet committees have their place under certain circumstances. Here are some guidelines to help you avoid the pitfalls and benefit from the strengths of committees:

▶ Avoid standing committees.

- Call a committee only when it would be clearly beneficial.

- Keep committee membership small, yet large enough to create synergy and momentum.

- Select committee members with expertise and competency in the area to be addressed.

- Have the person with the most topical expertise chair the committee.

- Disband a committee immediately after it has served its function.

When the Founder's Role Is Fulfilled

There is a saying that organization founders can do anything, but not everything. Founders deserve recognition because of their remarkable ability to transform a vision into functioning reality, for the good of their community.

Yet there is a shadow side to founder flair and fortitude: it often invites fear and criticism. Some see their founders as grandiose, unable to delegate, doggedly dedicated to the original vision, and unable to transition to new leadership. Others judge founders unfavorably for their leadership style or use of their privileged position to influence board decisions, management, and staff functioning,[9] all of which the critics perceive as hurting the organization. The phenomenon, known as *Founder's Syndrome,* can be succinctly defined as *the power, influence, and privilege that a founder exercises, or that others attribute to a founder.*[10]

Aside from the concern over Founder's Syndrome, the use of the term itself is subject to controversy. Some see it as a pejorative label, which muddies the addressing of personnel, governance, and directional issues.[11] Others see use of the term as a self-fulfilling prophecy—it helps to create the "syndrome."

It would be surprising for a founder not to use his or her position of influence, power, and privilege to start an organization with a vision to realize. After all, the founder has a personal investment and a commitment to community. Yet at some point, the boards and staff of many organizations expect their founders to scale down their dynamism and influence,[12] to allow for the transition to a less heady and more steady entity.

In shifting out of the founding stage, organizations tend toward acquiring executive directors who focus on management.[13] Though there are exceptions, founders' skills are typically more entrepreneurial than managerial. Founders can birth ideas and give them a kickstart, then it takes others to nurture them to maturity. That takes administrative, fundraising, and growth-oriented abilities, which is the skillset the board or hiring committee should look for in a person to complement or follow the founder.[14]

As your Trail organization grows, take the challenge to have it continue serving the Earth and her children in the best possible way—by keeping it lean, focused, and highly functional. Then, rather than expending energy on trying to stay in existence, you'll be able to devote it to your reason for existence.

CHAPTER THIRTY

Trail Design

For something to serve its purpose and last, it needs to be built on a solid foundation. For a Healing Nature Trail, this foundation consists of site selection, design, and construction. Even though Trails can be established in habitats as diverse as Forest, Prairie, Wetland, and Desert, they all sport the same characteristics that are conducive to mindfulness, healing, and self-discovery. For this reason, the same development guidelines can be used for all Trail sites.

Following is the five-step process for developing the Trail proper. For specific design features that are recommended—and required for Trail certification—please refer to chapter 33, *Trail Certification,* and chapter 34, *Trail Certification for Trauma Healing.*

First: Contract with a Consulting Service

There is a saying that *experience is your best teacher.* A consultant can help you get the most from the financial resources and human energy available to you by first making sure you have the organizational structure in place to develop and sustain a Trail. Next, the consultant will aid with selection of a site and a Trail design suitable for the site and capable of handling the projected number of people who will be using the Trail. Finally, the consultant will help assure your success with solid networking and outreach plans. At every step along the way, the consultant keeps an eye out so that you don't make costly mistakes.

Second: Choose a Suitable Site

In the real estate business, you may have heard that it's all about *location, location, location*. The same is true with Healing Nature Trails. Although there are site requirements for having your Trail certified (see chapter 33, *Trail Certification*), certain requirements can be modified or waived. Most important are the overall ambience the Trail creates, the access it provides to Nature's key healing properties, and safety for Walkers. Before committing yourself to a site, consult the Trail certifying agency or your consultant, to make sure your prospective site has the potential for meeting certification requirements.

Third: Mark and Develop the Main Trail

There is no one-design-fits-all for Healing Nature Trails. Nature expresses herself in many different ways, and she is the one who ultimately designs the Trail. Here is where your consultant or an experienced Healing Nature Guide can play a valuable role, as it takes someone who can intuitively read Nature's guidance for the Trail layout and who has an intrinsic sense for the lay of a Trail that is going to meet the needs of its users.

Once your proposed Trail is temporarily marked, have a Healing Nature Guide take at least six people on a guided Walk to get their feedback on what does and doesn't work with your proposed layout. In addition, your consultant will gain input on where to recommend placement of Trail features (see next step).

Fourth: Develop Required Features

What most distinguishes Healing Nature Trails from regular hiking trails are the Labyrinths, Smudges, Cairns, Threshold Bridges, Breathing Knolls, Discovery Forks, and Trailside Havens. Additionally, Trails have numerous abrupt changes in elevation and direction, and at least some segments of the Trails are suitable for Barefoot Walking (see chapter 33, *Trail Certification,* for more details). Looking at the Trails as living organisms, these features are their vital organs. Their proper design, placement, and construction are crucial to your Trail's ability to function as a Nature portal, so spare no effort for the expertise needed.

Fifth: Consider Options

After basic requirements are met to qualify for Healing Nature Trail certification, there is quite a lot of room for adding creative touches and regional character to your Trail. Done well, they can help you meet the unique needs of your clientele, add depth to the Trail experience, make it more effective, draw people from different demographics, and inform your clientele of environmental issues related to the Trail experience. Check with your consultant to make sure your proposed modifications and additions will complement and contribute to your Trail's function. For more on options, please see the next chapter.

UTILIZE LOCALLY AVAILABLE AND RECYCLED RESOURCES

It keeps cost down, gives your Trail a local flavor, and engages the community in supporting and developing the Trail. It also reflects Nature's way of efficiency and direct recycling.

Designing for Special Needs

Each and all of us have special needs relating to our healing and Awakening. Most of those needs that Nature can fulfill are accommodated by a standard Healing Nature Trail.

Yet that may not be the case—or at least entirely the case—for many who are in recovery from surgery or a major illness, and those who use wheelchairs and crutches. They may be able to avail themselves of few, if any, Trail features.

Other people who are blind, sight-impaired, have limited mobility, and have certain psycho-emotional conditions may be able to use Trails with special accommodations. Here are the two basic approaches to providing those accommodations:

▶ Train Healing Nature Guides to be able to therapeutically support people to safely navigate the Trail and avail their clients of the Trail's special healing and Awakening-related features.

▶ Design safety and access features into the Trail, as specified by advocacy groups and resources such as the *Massachusetts Audubon Society Accessible Trails Manual.*[1]

Following is an overview of design features that can be incorporated into Trail systems for each special-needs group:

Wheelchair and Crutch Users

▶ Labyrinth-viewing platforms.

▶ Labyrinths with wheelchair and crutch-accessible Paths.

▶ Separate Trails, along with bridges and bough Smudges, that meet standards for wheelchair accessibility.

▶ Cairns, Zen Gardens, and Fire Pits set at heights accessible for individuals in wheelchairs and on crutches.

▶ Specially equipped canoes for Aquarinths.

▶ Wheelchair-accessible bathroom facilities.

Blind and Sight-Impaired

▶ Wider-than-normal Trails.

▶ Rope-guided Trails.

▶ Audio tours.

▶ Tactile Trail maps and handouts.

▶ Labyrinths with touch-detectable borders.

▶ Clearly signed high-risk Trail sections.

▶ Railings where needed.

▶ Nonslip surfaces.

Limited Mobility

▶ Loops and shortcuts to reduce distances.

▶ Key Trail features in close proximity to each other.

▶ Numerous periodically placed Trailside Benches.

▶ Strategically placed portable chair cribs.

▶ Bathroom facilities adjacent to remote sections of Trail.

Due to unique environmental conditions and municipal requirements, you may need to include additional special needs features in your Trail design. These features typically need to meet specific criteria, such as with minimum path width, maximum degree of slope, and railing placement for wheelchairs.

Begin by talking with agencies that work with special-needs populations. For ideas on creative approaches and nuances you might otherwise miss, see what other Healing Nature Trails have done. Your consultant will make sure you meet all requirements and tend to all details, large and small.

Just as important, your consultant is there to help you create an aesthetically pleasing presentation. Function needs to come first, yet those unquantifiable nuances that bring a sparkle to the eye and uplift the spirit are often what open the heart to healing presence. With everything you do, give attention to detail, so that you make a strong initial impression and set the ambience for the Trail experience.

CHAPTER THIRTY-ONE

Options: Cairns, Cosmorinths, and Coneflowers

All Healing Nature Trails share characteristics that make them easily recognizable as family. You can Walk a Trail in the Desert, then in a Forest, then in the Mountains, and they will all feel familiar to you because of those common traits. That is the major reason why all Healing Nature Trails share the ability to encourage healing.

Even so, each Trail has a personality of its own. The Trail founders and developers, the local culture, and Nature herself, all play roles in how a particular Trail uniquely blossoms on the landscape.

In designing your Trail, you have considerable liberty with what you would like to include beyond the basic required features. When pondering options, consider what will complement your Trail both aesthetically and functionally. Your consultant can help you with the final decision-making process, and you might find inspiration in what other Trail developers have done.

Following are three options that work well on a variety of Trails. Along with descriptions of the options, you'll find the stories of their origins and how they were historically used. It is included to give Guides, and those taking self-guided Walks, inspiration and ideas on how to use these special features.

The Remembering Cairn

Ancient rock holds the memories of the Earth's formational history and the history of life on Earth. When you hold a stone that's over a billion years old, you might be able to feel some of that story.

Many people believe that stones with specific colors, shapes, structural features, and mineral compositions have unique properties. Stones with some of those specific qualities are used for divining, healing, protection, and inspiration.

Piles of stone stacked by human hands can be found around the world. Tibetans call them *stupa*; in India, they are known as *chorten*; in Mongolia, they are *ovoo*; and the Inuit of the Arctic refer to them as *tukilik*.[1] In English, they are collectively called *Cairns*. Some Cairns are contemporary, and some are relics from the time before recorded history. They are one of humanity's earliest forms of communicating and preserving information.[2] In general, they serve as trail markers, survey points, boundary lines, burial site markers, landmarks for sacred places, and memorials. By traditional custom, Korean mothers construct Memorial Cairns for each of their children.

Of most importance to us is the sense of community that Cairns have historically given to travelers and explorers who have shared the same path.[3] Even today, people building a Cairn, or adding a stone to one, find connection with Nature, history, and clan.

A *Remembering Cairn* has been erected at the head of the original Healing Nature Trail. Walkers say it helps them connect with the land and keep connected with what they experienced on the land. Some say it gives them a feeling of kinship with those who visited the Cairn and Walked the Trail before them, and with those who will come after them.

Classical Roots

In Greek mythology, Hermes is known as a messenger associated with boundaries, paths, and travelers. Sometimes he serves as a guide for the dead. It turns out that his role as a messenger and

294

guide for travelers may have an ancient association with Cairns, as the root of the name Hermes is the Greek word *herma,* which means: *prop, heap of stones, boundary marker.*[4]

The Greek countryside reflected Hermes's role. In many areas, Cairns could be found at boundaries and road crossings. Passersby showed respect for these Cairns by adding stones or anointing them with oil.

In Scotland, there is a tradition of carrying a stone from the bottom of a hill to add to the Cairn at the top. Scottish folklore tells of Highland clans preparing for battle by having each man place a stone on a pile. Those who survived would return to remove a stone from the pile. They then conducted the ritual of building the remaining stones into a Cairn to honor and remember those who had fallen.

Cairns Today

The traditional Cairn has not only survived, but we find it alive and well in our modern era. Recently made Cairns can be found on many prominent elevations around the world. An example is Central Washington State's Manastash Ridge, which is a renowned destination for hikers. Memorial Point, at the very top of the Ridge, features a number of Cairns constructed as memorials to the dead.

The act of using our hands to gather natural elements such as stones, then piling them up in a simple, culturally meaningful formation, has from the earliest of times been a profound act of both letting go and staying connected to those whom we have lost. Sometimes we return to Nature to contemplate the mysteries of life and death because Nature—like the mysteries of life and death—lies beyond the frontier of our regular lives. There we can reconnect to the primal wellsprings of our creative spirit and how they manifest in basic, physical acts, such as the making of the Cairn, to express life's mysteries.[5]

At the Remembering Cairn on the original Healing Nature Trail, Walkers are invited to participate in the ancient giving and receiving tradition by bringing a stone to commemorate their Healing Journeys. Here are some guidelines:

- Bring a Stone with you and leave it at the Cairn at the start of your Walk. This acts as a metaphor for leaving your baggage behind and traveling light on the Trail, so that you will have open arms to receive whatever is given.

- At the end of your Walk, choose a new Stone to take home with you. This connects you to all who have Walked before you, and with all who will follow in your footsteps.

- Another option is to carry your Stone with you on the Trail, to infuse it with the energy of the Trail and help you to remember the experience.

Above all, a Cairn speaks *community*. Those stones came together through your desire for relationship with Nature and the wayward fragments of your psyche. Let the community of contributors to the Cairn be your community, as you walk the Trail of Life together.

The Cosmorinth: Labyrinth in the Sky

The night sky is the Maze known as the Cosmorinth. Endless configurations of celestial bodies, along with the voids between them, form the Pathways that the Skywalker takes on her Journey through the far reaches of inner space to find herself.

Unlike other Labyrinthine Trail adjuncts, the Cosmorinth is already provided for you. Your task is only to make a safe and comfortable lift-off pad for your intergalactic-traveling clients.

Here, Trail Guides and therapists have the bigger task—and often the most challenging of the Trail experience. They have to copilot their clients through the Great Unknown. Every other Maze has either a set Path or boundaries, and this one has neither. Nor does it have a set purpose.

Yet by having nothing, it has everything. The infinity of inner-outer space offers an infinity of possibilities. The Cosmorinthine experience could be the beginning and end of a Healing Journey.

Or it could provide the breakthrough that makes a heretofore grounded Healing Journey now flight-ready.

This section on Cosmorinths provides assistance for both the lift-off pad and the guided voyage.

Platform Features

There are three prime requirements for a Cosmorinth platform: comfort, convenience, and quiet. Meeting those requirements helps maintain the necessary stillness and isolation that the dark and quiet of the night provides. With sensory stimulation and outside disturbance kept to a minimum, the body-mind connection transforms the Earthly Journey into a Cosmic Journey.

Platform Design Criteria:

1. **Location.** Light pollution and visual obstructions are your primary considerations. Because clear visibility is essential, locating a platform in or near urban or industrial areas is a highly unlikely possibility. Local sources of light pollution can often be mitigated. Assess potential sites for Trees, towers, or utility poles that might tarnish a panoramic view of the night sky.

2. **Access.** With the range of risks involved in negotiating the dark, and with a lighted walkway not being possible (in order to maintain the nightly ambience), platform access ought to be short and easily navigable. Factor in proximity to parking and easy access in case of emergency. Healing Nature Guides are trained to safely lead people through the dark and handle nighttime emergencies. If you are without access to the services of a Guide, be sure that your attending staff are appropriately trained.

3. **Elevation.** Humidity, cold air, and biting Insects are all concentrated at ground level. Nocturnal animals can cause disturbance at ground level as well. In all but the most open and barren of habitats, an elevated platform or its equivalent is essential.

4. **Composition.** The platform could be a deck, pier over water, elevated walkway, rooftop, rock outcrop, or something similar. The two criteria to meet are minimum effective elevation and footprint dimensions. Based on local conditions and season, most platforms stand three to eight feet above ground. Platform size should be a minimum of eight-by-eight feet to ensure safe and adequate room for Guide/therapist and client. A minimum-size platform can accommodate only one client-Guide pair. With larger platforms, plan for around ten feet between clients.

The Cosmorinth Heritage

"So it comes to pass," says literary critic Bruno Schulz, "that, when we pursue an inquiry beyond a certain depth, we step out of the field of psychological categories and enter the sphere of the ultimate mysteries of life. The floorboards of the soul, to which we try to penetrate, fan open and reveal the starry firmament."[6, 7]

Penetrating the starry firmament has been the unending quest of our species. It takes on metaphorical form with the story of Minos, the legendary Athenian king who constructed the famed Cretan Labyrinth to house the monstrous Minotaur. Yet that was not enough to keep the Minotaur from wreaking destruction. Minos had to command that fourteen young men and women be sacrificed to the Minotaur every nine years.

The sacrifices brought anguish to the people of Athens. Yet there was no other way to keep the Minotaur content in his confinement.

Ariadne, daughter of Minos, was gravely disturbed by the grief of the people. She partnered with Theseus, who was sent to Crete to be sacrificed himself, to subdue the Minotaur. She gave Theseus a crown once belonging to the god Dionysus to aid him in his quest.

Theseus used the light of the crown to illuminate the Pathway out of the Labyrinth after slaying the Minotaur. To memorialize the end of the scourge, Dionysus placed her crown among the stars. We see her crown today as the Corona Borealis (or Northern Crown) constellation.

Corona Borealis is one of eighty-eight officially recognized constellations in the contemporary Euro-American world. Yet innumerable constellations have existed in other cultures throughout human history. In this day, the constellations of many extant peoples remain unknown to us. In the cosmology of the Ojibwe people indigenous to the Northern Wisconsin area where the original Healing Nature Trail is located, there is the story of the Elder who paddles the night skies in a stone canoe, and you can see his starry outline if you know where to look.[8]

Like the constellations, the origins of our relationship to the Cosmos are largely lost to the mists of time. Yet we do know that the Cosmos has been a constant companion to the evolution of our kind. We have long looked to the sky for light, warmth, direction, timekeeping, myth, and meaning. The constellations may be the earliest form of writing—the first answer to our need to convey the experiences, stories, and beliefs about the nature of the world around us. Is it any wonder, then, that we have found meaning in the forms celestial bodies take?

Walking the Celestial Maze

Due to the ethereal nature of the Cosmos and our species' long-standing symbolic and metaphorical relationship with it, a more in-depth exploration of the metaphysical aspects of the Cosmorinthine experience may be needed than with most other Trail features.

The greatest insights sometimes require only the smallest shifts in perspective. In all of its various forms, the Maze is capable of affecting that. By acting as a meditative and archetypal tool for contemplation, the Maze can help us alter perception and enhance presence.

The power for the Maze to do so comes from its body-mind linking geometry. It enables us—through the seemingly simple act of walking (literally or figuratively)—to leave behind our everyday stresses. We then have the needed psychic space to listen and contemplate life's greater questions.

Night skies do not yield their sacred geometry so easily to the conscious mind. It sees no relationship between the ordered Path of a Walking Labyrinth and the dizzying possibilities presented by the overwhelming Cosmos. Yet the begging questions that we are infinitely asking have no trouble negotiating the Boundless Void—once we step out of the way. As medieval Spanish writer Cervantes said, "Let the whole universe be for thee no more than the reflection of thine own heroic soul."[9]

This begs the question, "How do we utilize the Cosmos in such a way?"

One traditional way is to simply be present and observe. Allow yourself to ramble among the stars and let your imagination have its play with the forms they make. While doing so, gently hold onto your concerns and questions. Allow your psyche, mirrored in what you see above, to explore itself within.

The Cosmorinth has a quality unique amongst all Mazes: great awarenesses can come not only from connections made, but from the act of avoiding all connections. Flecks of light, the glow of the moon, and empty space are so unfathomable that we could cease to wonder and simply be.

A Sky-Walking Practice

In Tibetan Buddhism, there is a teaching known as *Dzogchen*, or *Great Perfection*, which is primordial awareness. We enter a state in which we recognize our essential nature and its inherent connection to everything else. It is a state of pure being, without boundaries between self and other, without accepting or rejecting anything in one's awareness. One settles into the space between thoughts, which is like darkness between stars.

Dzogchen has a meditative practice called *Sky Gazing*. Rather than using metaphor and imagination, as with *Walking the Celestial Maze* above, Sky Gazing eliminates both thought and active visualization, while maintaining presence within primordial awareness.

To practice Sky Gazing, day or night:

1. **Locate an elevated area** with an expansive view of the sky. Get comfortable, either sitting or lying on your back.

2. **Take a number of long, slow breaths,** to lower your pulse and calm your mind. Feel yourself soften.

3. **Gaze with full attention,** yet without focus, into the Great Expanse above.

4. **Become your breath** and follow it. Going out, your breath takes all thoughts with it, and they dissolve as they merge into the open sky. Coming in, your breath dissolves the thought-clouds of your inner sky.

5. **Bask in the awareness** that this expansive, clear state is you, and that it is your natural state of being.

6. **Keep following your breath,** until you realize that your inner space and outer space are one. Duality is then dissolved.

7. **Hold this state for as long as you can.** When you get distracted, breathe yourself back.

Pollinator Wildflower Beds

Flowers have a purpose: to produce the seed that perpetuates the species. And they serve a purpose for us: their beauty and perfumed essences grace our lives and uplift our spirits. From our perspective, these purposes make sense. They are utilitarian, and they are of benefit.

At the same time, the Flowers are entities unto themselves. Yes, they are here to serve both their species and us, yet they also have lives of their own, with Labyrinthine Paths to walk. Forming those Paths are Bees and Butterflies, Deer and Rabbits, wind and rain. Like us, Flowers sleep and rise, feel pain and ecstasy, and struggle with stress and trauma (see chapter 10). In their Walking, they find the clarity to continue, much as we do.

A Flower can guide a meditation, and a Flower can be a guiding example for our Healing Journey. Following is a way to bring the renewing gifts of Flowers to the Healing Nature Trail experience.

There are regional Wildflowers nearly everywhere, and there are Bees and Butterflies who have symbiotic relationships with those Flowers. The Insects bring pollen to fertilize the Flowers, and the Flowers in turn provide the Insects with nourishing nectar and pollen.

Both the Insects and the Flowers realize that they need to give in order to receive. The same is true with us. Earlier in the book, we discussed how the sounds, sights, and smells of beautiful Nature can reduce our stress and anxiety.[10] However, Nature is no longer so beautiful in areas where Wildflowers no longer grow. The loss of habitat due to agriculture and urbanization, climate change, and pesticides has led to a corresponding crash in pollinator species populations' health.[11]

Conspicuous pollinators like Butterflies and Bees act as indicator species for the well-being of Insects in general. Current research shows Insects in the main are declining at the rate of around 10 percent per year.[12, 13, 14] Protecting and restoring pollinator habitat benefits many other Insect species, along with the plants and animals who depend on them.

By planting native Wildflowers, we engage in a mutual healing relationship. It is an opportunity for us, along with the Insects and Flowers, to give, so that we may receive. Along with supporting pollinator Insect communities,[15] we bring ourselves the aromatherapeutic effects of floral essences and the uplifting aesthetic influence of blooming Flowers (see chapter 11).

We also benefit health-wise from planting the Flowers, which is a practice called *horticultural therapy*.[16] Mental and physical recovery is accelerated, and functional skills are improved.[17, 18] Abandoning the mechanical approach to planting seed that became common with commercial agriculture, we return to the aboriginal way, which is a conscious and sensual ritual of impregnating the earth.

Establishing Beds on the Trails

The developers of the original Healing Nature Trail established flowerbeds at the base of the entryway drive, so Wildflowers are the first thing you see upon arrival. The Gateway Labyrinth is essentially a Pathway through a Wildflower Meadow, and you will see other Wildflowers scattered randomly throughout the premises. The local populations of Butterflies and Bees have increased dramatically since the first Flowers were planted.

For assistance with establishing pollinator beds, contact your local Wildflower nursery. There are several good books on the topic to guide you as well. If you would like professional help with any or all phases, two of the developers of the original Trail run an environmental restoration consulting service, and one of their specialties is Wildflower reintroduction.

Whichever route you take, it is important that you choose Flower species that are indigenous to your locale. Flowers from other bioregions, even though they are technically wild, can become invasive and outcompete your native Flowers.

CHAPTER THIRTY-TWO

Invite and Inspire

"When should we start spreading the word, and what's the best way to do it?" are common questions fielded by consultants working with Healing Nature Trail creators.

"The best time to start is right along with your initial planning," says Trail cofounder Tamarack Song. "The dedication and enthusiasm behind everything you do is going to touch people, either directly or indirectly. They'll be taking notes and asking questions, which give you great opportunities to share one-on-one. If you take the time to connect with them on a heart level and listen to their stories, they'll tell you what they need from Nature, and how they can help Nature heal. They'll also give you clues on how you can reach people like them.

"Regarding the best forms of outreach," continues Tamarack, "the first thing to do is avoid the marketing approach. These days, we see everything from refrigerators to religions being commercially packaged and promoted. However, yearning people are not a market, and our Mother Earth is not a product to be marketed.

"We can do something different. Nature speaks well for herself, and the need is already there. So rather than persuade, we can just spread Nature's voice and let our Trail's presence and features be known."

Mindful Outreach

With something we believe in, reaching out to others becomes an easy—and even rewarding—task. Our enthusiasm and conviction are infectious; we have no need for promotion or selling tactics.

Yet our efforts to inform have to work. What we have to offer as a doorway to Nature's healing touch only matters if we can reach the people who need it, and that means we have to use media intelligently. Our outreach efforts are the bridge from Nature to them, which is so vitally important that it's why this is the longest chapter in the book.

Here are the four cornerstones of Mindful Outreach that we are going to cover in-depth in this chapter:

1. Meet people where they are at.

This is the essence of outreach. It doesn't matter how wonderful our Trail is if we don't speak a language people understand, or if we come across as having the One True Path to Wellness. Nature's language is understood by everybody, and Nature's touch is recognized by everybody. Our job is to give voice to what Nature is already whispering, and to shine light on Nature's outstretched arms.

2. Use a multimedia approach.

Not too long ago, radio, television, and the printed word were the only conventional options for reaching people. Now the possibilities seem endless. The initial approach is to utilize every media venue we can, to find out what best works for us.

3. Encourage word of mouth.

It's typically the best way to spread the word, as the enthusiasm of grateful people is infectious. They're anxious to share the stories of their transformative experiences in the Bosom of Nature. This is the kind and quality of outreach that cannot be purchased at any price. Along with being the cheapest method of outreach, it's the easiest, as it takes little additional effort.

4. Post where prospective Trail users frequent.

It's a message only if people see or hear it, and the second-easiest way to accomplish that (after word of mouth) is to post it where people regularly stop or gather. Posting saves energy and is cost effective because it keeps working as long as it's up.

The Three-Step Approach to Mindful Outreach

Imagine that you're going on a first date with a person you are just getting to know. You first reached out to him to see if he was interested. If so, you set a mutually agreeable date, time, and place to meet, along with something you'd both enjoy doing together.

All the while, the two of you are sensitive to each other's needs and desires. You want to have a mutually rewarding experience, which means you first need to get to know each other's personalities, likes and dislikes, beliefs, inspirations, and repulsions. And let's not forget, you want to have fun!

The same approach, goals, and sensitivities apply to Mindful Outreach. Here is a three-step method that has helped many succeed:

First: Set Your Intention

You and your associates are creating something special: a fresh out-of-the-box Nature-based approach to psycho-emotional healing. You are developing a Trail that has features conducive to self-reflection and healing, along with incorporating elements that distinguish your Trail from all others.

Bring this distinctiveness into your intention. It will help you take an outreach approach that reflects your uniqueness. In addition, it will help you recognize that what works outreach-wise for you may differ somewhat from what works for other healing, self-discovery, and meditative practices.

Here are three awarenesses to help develop your intention:

1. **What you offer has no direct parallels.**
2. **Healing Nature Trails serve as adjuncts** to other healing modalities.
3. **You may initially have few, if any, connections** with other services.

Yet, there is tremendous potential because what you offer will appeal to many people. Along with that, there is the potential for developing working relationships with other healing practitioners, as Nature's healing energies work synergistically with many approaches. All it takes to make it happen is a mindful approach to your mission coupled with smart outreach.

Now, develop your Mindful Outreach Mission Statement, based on how you define your uniqueness. That will be your intention. Display it prominently to guide and inspire you as you pursue your outreach goals.

Second: Address Your Basic Needs

If you are like most start-up Trails, you have five basic needs. They apply whether you are a new organization or tucking under the umbrella of an existing one, as a Trail is an entity unto itself. Your first-line outreach needs are:

1. **Name recognition**. The more people who see and hear your name, the more likely they are to utilize your services.

2. **A platform,** to establish your credibility and the efficacy of the services you offer.

3. **Networking,** which is essential for both mutual support with other organizations and to bring clients your way.

4. **Attracting a variety of clients,** which includes individuals unassociated with the network you create.

5. **Referrals.** You'll find that word of mouth and professional recommendations will continually be your best advertising.

To fulfill these needs as completely and efficiently as you can, make the following four criteria your mantra:

1. Connect one-on-one whenever possible.

2. Keep everything as low-budget as possible.

3. Use Maverick Outreach techniques (see page 313).

4. Cross-connect outreach as much as you can.

There is a lot contained in those twenty-five words. We'll take an in-depth look at each criteria under *The Four Outreach Strategies* later in the chapter.

Third: Personalize It

You can have a jaw-dropping Trail and the best outreach plan, but if you don't personalize your approach to prospective clients and help each one of them see how they are going to directly benefit, many people who could find wellness in Nature's embrace, will not. Following is an effective five-point way to individualize your outreach that originated with Jim Morningstar, PhD, founder of Transformations Worldwide Learning Community. You'll see that they are the same points you cover on a first date, and when building any meaningful relationship, for that matter.

The Five Steps to Personalized Outreach

1. You want to do this.

Clarity and conviction are needed, yet passion alone inevitably leads to blindness and danger. Listen to the doubts and fears of your staff, as they will do just as much to ensure success as your inspiration and hard work.

2. You want them to know about you.

Many people think that getting the word out means describing their philosophy and waxing poetic to create alluring images. It may read well and give a warm, fuzzy feeling; however, it does little to attract clients. They need to see *usable* information: bullet points on services offered, location, and contact information.

3. What's in it for them?

Here it's important to sound realistic. Express what someone can achieve without stretching the truth. Most clients are drawn to a pragmatically realistic goal, and many others are either intimidated by grandiose promises or have grown numb to them.

4. You seldom connect on first contact.

Most prospective clients respond to your third outreach effort. Here's how to orchestrate it:

First contact: A generic advertisement, which should focus largely on image-building, yet include some core information.

Second contact: Connect individually, by e-mail or letter.

Third contact: A phone call. Ask if they have any questions about the services you offer, then inform them about an upcoming event. To ensure continued contact, ask if they would like to receive your newsletter or be placed on your mailing list.

5. After the first meeting, cultivate a deeper sense of connection.

The kinetic energy and inspiration your clients receive from their time with you fades over time. Right away it is critical to establish the basis of a continuing relationship, because it may be your only opportunity. Here are the steps to take:

a. **Give something away.** Make it relevant to the experience, attractive to the client, and inexpensive for you.

b. **Make sure they reconnect with you.** Provide contact information and a defined format that fits your routine, without being intrusive.

c. **Ask what they got out of the experience.** Here is where some of the best testimonials come from, which are valuable tools for attracting new clients.

This personal attention helps clients feel valued, and it reinforces what they gained.

The Five Outreach Strategies

Now that you have defined your unique outreach approach, individualized it, and personalized it, you need methods for bringing your message to prospective clients. The most recommended or value-priced of outreach options can be the worst of choices if they do not reach your audience, even though they may be reaching large numbers of people. It's a common error committed by new organizations.

The usual reason for the poor return is that these organizations focused on people in general, rather than on specific demographics.

Even then, you are not guaranteed a good return. Along with reaching your specific audience, you have to touch them in a way that makes them want to come to you. To do both effectively—and have your efforts reflect who you are—hold the following three principles for effective outreach dear to you:

- **Go out on your edge** to explore unusual and overlooked outreach possibilities.

- **Envision the spectrum of prospective Trail users** and where to reach them.

- **Approach them in ways that will raise their eyebrows**.

Five Outreach Strategies for Putting the Three Principles to Practice

Following are the most highly effective, inexpensive, and least labor-intensive methods for applying the Three Principles.

1. One-On-One

Start by inviting therapists and other wellness practitioners for a special tour of the Trail. Send packets with this book and a couple of posters and handouts to selected professionals and other interested individuals. Set up a booth at a healing arts fair and talk with all the people you can. Participate in call-in radio programs and webinars. Do presentations in libraries, Nature centers, yoga centers, and wherever else you can arrange them. Post in natural food stores, Laundromats, and wherever else you can. Equip your vehicles with satchels of informational materials, so that they are on hand for any eventuality. Be aware that any random contact could potentially benefit from a closer relationship with Nature.

2. Community Networking

Experience shows that a new Healing Nature Trail has the potential to capture the imagination of a considerable number of people who are affiliated with like-minded organizations, such as natural healing, chiropractic, medical and mental health clinics, along with retreat and Zen centers. Each institution represents a community of people, which saves you time and makes your outreach cost effective. In addition, word of a new and innovative healing modality tends to spread on its own through the community of like-minded organizations.

Fringe benefits include volunteers and potential board and staff members for your organization, and reciprocal agreements for support, posting, and sharing resources.

One mistake some new organizations make is to focus primarily on networking nationally or internationally on the institutional level. Though it can be valuable for furthering professional goals, it contributes little or nothing to reaching prospective Trail users.

3. Low-Budget

No matter what level of outreach resources you have available to you, the low-budget approach helps you make intelligent and effective decisions. Keep in mind that *low-budget does not always mean doing things the cheapest possible way*. Reaching out by e-mail seems to be a cost-effective way to get the biggest bang for your time-and-energy buck. However, old-fashioned letters typically get ten times the response of e-mails.

Start by listening. There are likely people in your organization who have low-budget outreach experience. Do some research. Talk to the outreach people from other Trails to see what worked for them.

Next, gear your low-budget outreach to low-profile demographics. Consider that little independent bookstore on the other side of town, the sangha group that meets every Tuesday afternoon, your staff's Facebook friends. What you have to offer needs to be made known to the widest possible spectrum of people who are seeking solace, healing, and renewed connection with self and Nature. From there, the alluring Trail you have created will take care of the rest.

4. Maverick

Related to the low-budget approach, Maverick Outreach goes yet a step further. It is essentially using any unconventional way to reach people that you can dream up. It may incorporate the element of surprise, seldom-used techniques, or unusual platforms.

Take the owner of a new music store who had devoted a significant amount of his start-up budget to conventional advertising. The response was adequate to get him established; however, it didn't help him break into the market the way he thought he could. He knew more people would appreciate the quality and value of what he had to offer—if only he could get them in the door.

He decided to take his message directly to the people, by hiring high school kids to distribute flyers door-to-door in neighborhoods where his prospective clientele lived. He distributed coupons himself on a busy street, where he found that some people were impressed to meet the owner doing his own outreach.

In short order his business started to grow, with satisfied customers joining in his effort by spreading the word to their friends.

If a new outreach idea raises your eyebrow because it seems unconventional—even outlandish—or ridiculously simple, it has Maverick Outreach potential. When you react to a fresh approach with "Why didn't I think of that?" give it serious consideration.

5. Cross-Connect

Your goal here is to reach two or more audiences with the same effort, or mention additional products and services along with the primary item you are presenting. Here are some classic examples:

> *It's the latest thriller by Jane Austin, author of the heart-stopping cliffhanger* Murder On the Marrakesh Express.

> *Clover Farm Butter, which seems custom made for Quaker Farms Sourdough Bread.*

Cross-connect outreach opportunities are nearly endless; they are limited only by your imagination. To get you started, explore the possibility of tagging on to the outreach endeavors of the professional clients you serve. The reverse works as well: ask the clients who use your Trail if they would like to piggyback on your outreach efforts.

Unfortunately, the approach is seldom used, unless someone is selling supplemental advertising space on their promotional material. Most people worry that they would be watering down their outreach efforts if they were to include others.

In actuality, one hand feeds another. Whether you are an addendum on another's outreach efforts or vice versa, the relationship is mutually beneficial. The association helps to establish a sense of credibility and enhanced value for both organizations, in ways that go beyond what either organization could accomplish on its own.

The five Mindful Outreach approaches we just covered hold four values in common:

▶ **Unconventional**

▶ **Highly effective**

▶ **Economical**

▶ **Efficient**

Not so coincidentally, these are the values of Nature-immersion healing as well. When you apply the same approach and principles to both your outreach and healing-support efforts, you'll see that they work together synergistically. The distinction between them fades, and they become part of the same deep upwelling to return to the Mother for nurturance and renewal.

Ten-Plus-Two Outreach Secrets

1. **Make it fun or it won't get done.** Without humor, what you do accomplish will not have the spirit it could. To keep your work on outreach both entertaining and fulfilling:

    ▶ **Do it with others,** even if it's just to gain some outside perspective.

    ▶ **Maintain a sense of humor,** to keep from taking yourselves too seriously.

    ▶ **Have your litmus test be the sense of satisfaction** you gain from sharing your heart and supporting others on their Healing Journeys.

2. **Keep it simple, so that it simply gets done.** Save the frills for later, or for your own edification. Most people are going to relate to only the essence anyway.

3. **Build it and they will come.** In the 1989 movie *Field of Dreams*, an Iowa corn farmer named Ray (played by Kevin Costner) is guided by a mysterious voice to somehow bring back a professional baseball team from 1919 who were unfairly banished from the game they loved, so they could again play. Ray's neighbors thought he was crazy, yet he went ahead and built a baseball diamond in the middle of his cornfield. And the team—along with Ray's estranged father—came to play. It's a story of belief in yourself and your dream, and the healing it can bring. If this is your story, build your Trail, and they will come.

4. **Keep centered; the most important time in outreach is the silence after.** What often happens—especially with new ventures—is that you're not getting the flood of responses you had hoped for. Doubt creeps in, and you want to erase the slate and do it differently. The antidote: Keep centered and believing in yourselves and what you have to offer. Go back to your Outreach Mission Statement and renew your initial inspiration, and you'll do fine.

5. **Brainstorm for prospective clients.** Sit down with your staff and friends to generate a list of prospective Trail users—both individuals and groups. Start with mental health practitioners, natural healing clinics, massage therapists, breath-workers, support groups, veterans' organizations . . .

6. **Use posters.** These old-fashioned marketing tools still work because they reach people where they frequent, and they catch those who are not tuned into other media. Post in coffee shops, natural food stores, Laundromats, book-stores, waiting rooms, and anywhere else you can think of. Post online as well.

7. **Fill empty mailboxes.** Unlike most other media out-reach, a stamp costs everyone the same amount, no matter how effective the message it carries. With the onslaught of online advertising and how easy it is to delete, direct mail has quietly regained effectiveness. It must be handled, and it has little competition; so if it is well-designed, it will grab attention. And don't forget coupons or special offers—they work!

8. **Take advantage of news releases.** An in-house parallel is putting five-minute informational videos describing an upcoming course or event up on your internet homepage.

9. **Make every contact mutually valuable.** The burnout factor is high for people who only give. See yourself in your clients and expand along with them.

10. **Focus on what works.** Most outreach is wasted energy—unless you understand and abide by the *80/20 Rule* (which is also known as the *Pareto Principle*). It states that 80 percent **of** your **results** typically come from 20 percent of your efforts. Take time to determine which of your outreach endeavors are the effective ones, then focus your time, energy, and monetary resources on them, and watch your results improve with notably less effort than before.[1]

11. **Remember, first impressions are lasting impressions.** When they're bad, they are hard to overcome; however, when they're good, they are easy to expand upon.

12. **End on a high note.** We tend to forget how bad an experience was—or how long it lasted—and recall it positively if it ended on a high note. This is known as *peak-end theory*, which was developed by Daniel Kahneman, recipient of the 2002 Nobel Prize in Economics.[2] Put the theory to practice in these ways:

- When a process involves pain or anguish, focus on the positive result.

- Wrap up every experience on a high note.

- When you know an experience will take a downturn at the end, skip the ending.

- A sad ending feels better when you look at how much worse it could have been.

VOLUNTEER POWER

You might not typically think of volunteers as members of your outreach team, yet they are some of your best ambassadors. They're not engaged because it's their job, but rather because they believe in your Trail and have a heartfelt stake in it. They'll enthusiastically spread the word about the Trail to family, friends, and others who they think could benefit from it. Be sure to honor your volunteers, as they serve your mission in many valuable ways.

Developing Outreach Material

Just like your Trail has qualities that distinguish it from other Trails, your prospective clients have qualities that set them apart. You can best reach them by avoiding a one-size-fits-all approach, and instead generate your own outreach materials specifically for your own type of client base.

This doesn't mean that you can't utilize the exceptional materials that other organizations have developed. It certainly makes more sense to do so than to expend energy trying to reinvent the wheel. Yet you want to customize those materials, so they'll best speak to *your* prospective clients.

Get the Information You Need

You best know who you are and what you have to offer; you are the best people to either develop or customize your outreach material. Even if you enlist an outside agency for outreach assistance, the raw material the agency needs comes from you.

To help you develop that material, ask yourselves the following eight questions.[3] The answers will tell you how to let others know who you are and what you have to offer. Along with that, you will clarify your clients' needs, and how to meet them.

1. What makes your Trail different from just walking in the Woods?
2. What makes it uniquely healing?
3. What makes it accessible to individuals and groups?
4. What makes it affordable?
5. What makes it enjoyable?
6. How do I envision myself getting there and having a highly valuable experience?
7. What other resources in the area make the trip worth the time and effort?
8. Who has done it and what do they say about it?

Use the information you have generated from this process for descriptive materials and promotion of all kinds, including signs, websites, social media, interviews, presentations, newspaper and radio ads, flyers, and videos.

Outreach That Keeps on Working

Following is a sampling of flyers and posters generated by Trail organizations using material created by the above process. Please feel free to use whatever you like, and to revise it to meet your needs.

Effective posters are simple and catchy. You need to do two things: catch people in passing, and give them a good reason to follow up. For ideas on layout and design, look at posters and flyers that catch your attention.

You'll see a couple of examples below that employ humor or a clever twist of phrase. Comic relief can be therapeutic, as we sometimes take ourselves too seriously—especially when working with the fallout of our wayward culture and tortured Earth. Yet, so as not to offend anyone, we must be careful to employ wit tastefully and sparsely.

When Have You Last ...
taken the time to listen
to the voices of Nature
and bathe
in her breathtaking beauty?
Come and walk
the Healing Nature Trail.

**www.healingnatureparis.org
620-000-0000**

**Are you haunted
by the memory ...**
of trauma or childhood abuse?
Do you keep repeating the same
self-destructive patterns?

Are you caught in a time warp
and unable to move on?

There is hope ...

**The Healing Nature Trail
www.healingnaturemadison.org
620-000-0000**

The Forest Is Expecting You

Come and be reborn
in the cradle of Nature
Inhale healing essences
Exhale pain and grief
Forget what you remember
Remember what you've
forgotten

The Healing Nature Trail
www.healingnatureashland.org
620-000-0000

For a Breath of Fresh Air ...

that can give you a new lease on
life come and walk the Healing
Nature Trail
www.healingnaturemayville.org
620-000-0000

Warning: Do not breathe in Nature
if you want to go on being confused,
depressed, or unfulfilled.

Side Effects: Breathing in Nature has
been associated with increased risk
of inner peace, vitality, gratitude, and
insight.

In Case of Overdose: Immediately consult the nearest Elder Tree.

Do You Get More Depressed ...

because you're always depressed?

Do you get mad at yourself
for being so angry?

What if ...
you could start to change that?

The Healing Nature Trail
www.healingnatureseattle.org
620-000-0000

When sorrow
nearly drowns you ...

and pain has got you down
There is a place where you can go
A haven tried and true
With Elder Trees to lean on

The Healing Nature Trail
www.healingnatureboston.org
620-000-0000

Now to Get Started

Follow these three guiding principles and, with no extra effort,
you will extend your reach and magnify its effect:

- ❱ Be specific with your message and identifying your audience.
- ❱ Improve efficiency by eliminating duplication and consoli-
  dating efforts.

▶ Create an outreach blitz by releasing everything you have at once.

THE FINAL WORD ON OUTREACH

You now have a well-equipped outreach workshop with a wide selection of tools. You may never need them all, yet the fact that you have them greatly increases the odds that you're going to choose the methods that will reach the people who could benefit from your Trail. Choose wisely, and you will do well in fulfilling your mission.

After Outreach, Then What?

You've done well at letting people know about the Trail and what it has to offer them, and now they're coming. This is a critical time, as they're going to give you only one chance to help them commune with Nature. Adding to that, you carry the responsibility you assumed when you offered to play a role in their Healing Journeys.

At this point, it's all about presentation. Whether you are guiding a Trail Walk, giving a workshop, or conducting a seminar, the same four steps will help you do your best and ensure that your clients gain the most from the experience.

The Four Steps to a Successful Presentation

1. Tell them what you are going to do.
2. Do it.
3. Tell them what you did.
4. Ask them to acknowledge what they received.

This is essentially an empowering and retaining exercise. If you say, *I'm going to throw this ball as far as I can*, you'll be able to toss it farther than if you said nothing. When you summarize a presentation you just heard, you're going to retain more of it than if you just went on to your next activity.

Going a step further, to reflect on the presentation with some-body (step 4) helps validate it and give it more value. This magni-fies the effect of your efforts.

An added bonus is the potential valuable outreach aid your clients give you when they describe what they gained from their experience with you. It gives prospective clients a firsthand feel for what you have to offer.

If you wish to use a client's description, ask for permission to quote him or her.

When Things Go Wrong

And they will at times, in spite of your best efforts. You are work-ing with wounded people: some come in crisis, some have trauma memories surface on the Trail, and others have desperation-driven high expectations. You will not be able to help all of them to their satisfaction, and now and then someone could become resentful or accusatory because of it.

This could create issues that go beyond the scope of this book. Here we are looking only at outreach effects.

Earlier in the chapter we covered the power of word-of-mouth publicity, which is typically very effective. Unfortunately, it's true whether the talk is positive or negative. So as much as you want to encourage warming flames, you want to calm chilling winds.

If They Aren't Satisfied

Your ethical responsibility is to address an unsatisfactory Trail experience, no matter what the reason. If someone is in crisis, you must immediately defer to the proper authorities. For noncrisis cases, follow these three steps:

First: listen empathetically and take notes.

Second: address the issue and come to a mutually agreeable resolution.

Third: defer to superiors when a resolution is not achievable.

If They Don't Come

Your clients are not the only ones with expectations. After all the work you and your staff have put into developing your Trail, how could you not be hopeful that people would come?

With Trails that are established by existing organizations, there is often a line waiting at the grand opening, as there is an established clientele to draw from. However, Trails sponsored by start-up organizations might get off to a slow start. The reason is covered earlier in this chapter under *The Five Steps to Personalized Outreach: #4. You seldom connect on first contact.*

This is a good and necessary part of the establishment process of a Trail, as it forces you to listen to your prospective clients and be sure you are addressing their needs. Momentum is bound to build. In the end, you will benefit from a slow start because it will help you establish solid roots and sustainable practices.

In the meantime, you need to keep believing. In *Field of Dreams* (see #3 under *Ten-Plus-Two Outreach Secrets* earlier in the chapter), it took undying belief for the dream to come true. It might help adopt these words of poet Wallace Stevens as your mantra: "After the final no there comes a yes, and on that yes the future world depends."[4]

"Yet what if they don't come?" says a nagging voice that you can't help but hear. To be realistic, there is the odd chance that your Trail will not succeed. And even if that turned out to be the case, perhaps you needed to create the Trail anyway—for your own Healing Journey.

Instead of listening to fear, listen to your heart, and others will feel it. Those who need to come, will come.

CHAPTER THIRTY-THREE

Trail Certification

Nature works to heal us and keep us healthy, whether or not we consciously engage in the process. Yet we can increase that healing potential by taking advantage of landscape features that maximize exposure to Nature's healing gifts. We could further enhance the healing effect by improving access with a trail that is specially designed for the purpose.

To ensure that trails of this specialized type meet the standards for site selection, design features, safety, effectiveness, environmental stewardship, and responsible management established by the parent organization, the Healing Nature Center of Wisconsin (www.healingnaturecenter.org), they must be currently certified by said organization. If they meet the criteria for certification, they may bear the name *Healing Nature Trail* (a registered trademark).

Following are the primary features of a certified Healing Nature Trail system that encourage public and professional confidence.

What Certification Assures

▶ **Professional Trail management** and a solid sponsoring organization.

▶ **An easy-to-navigate, safe, and aesthetically appealing Trail** with the required research-validated features conducive to healing.

- **Appropriate informational material** and gear for client comfort and safety.

- **Trail Guides certified for assisting clients** on their Healing/Awakening Journeys.

- **Maintaining a standard** that can get compromised when new healing modalities become popular.

- **Client and healing practitioner accessibility** without discrimination.

- **Listing on the online National Healing Nature Trail Registry,** where clients and healing practitioners can confidently go to find certified Trails.

- **The uniform quality and consistency of features** found in all Healing Nature Trails. Shared family traits make Healing Nature Trails easy to identify and ensure that all Trails possess the reasons for the effectiveness of Healing Nature Trails.

Certification Requirements

A Healing Nature Center certifying agent evaluates Trail systems applying for certification, using the method described under *Certification Rating System* later in this chapter. Certification is verified by a sign posted at the head of a Trail, by a certificate displayed in the Trail office/welcome center, and by being listed on the National Healing Nature Trail Registry.

Provisional certification may be granted to existing trails being revamped into Healing Nature Trails, and to new trails that are within a few points of qualifying. All provisional certifications are granted with the condition that full certification be achieved by a specified date, or the provisional certification will be revoked.

Certification is subject to biannual renewal (see *Biannual Recertification* at end of this chapter). In special circumstances, a certification requirement can be modified or waived, at the discretion of the certifying agent, in consultation with the Trail director.

For-profit organizations need to demonstrate their altruistic intent with a clause delineating their protocols for allowing access to individuals, professionals, and organizations with limited financial resources. Such clause is a necessary addendum to their Trail Certification Contract.

Following are the Trail features that a certifying agent assesses.

Required Features for Evaluation

I Organizational

1. **A sponsoring organization** that is responsible and stable.

2. **A management system** that is competent.

3. **A support network,** including volunteers, benefactors, legacy funds, and grants.

4. **Trained staff,** including at least one mental health professional and one Healing Nature Guide (HNG). Option: an independent HNG who lives in the vicinity.

5. **A code of ethics** and grievance procedures.

6. **A nondiscrimination clause,** to assure that the Trail and attendant services are available to all.

7. **A statement of province,** similar to the one found in chapter 29.

8. **An accessibility policy,** to open the Trail to those of limited financial means.

9. **An outreach plan** designed to reach prospective clients.

10. **Meeting local zoning requirements.**

11. **A commitment to environmental stewardship** and a reduce-reuse-recycle policy.

12. **An invasive species management program.**

II Location

1. **Four acres or more** of varied natural landscape.

2. **A visible barrier** from distracting sights.

3. **A low ratio of intruding noise** to natural background sound.

4. **A safe setting** where clients, practitioners, and staff can both feel and be out of harm's way.

5. **A Trail design that is sensitive** to indigenous flora and fauna, particularly endangered species.

6. **A grove of mature Trees.**

7. **Minimum Trail length** of one-half mile.

8. **Water of some sort,** which could be Wetland, Stream, Pond, Lake, or Ocean.

9. **Adequate parking.**

10. **No conflict of interest** with neighbors or others with jurisdictional authority.

III *General Trail*

1. **Dedicated exclusively to Nature Healing** and meditation. **Option: a multi-use trail** with posted times for exclusive use as a Healing Nature Trail.

2. **An office/welcome center** that is conveniently located, inviting, and adequately stocked with gear and accessories.

3. **A written history** of the land, the Trail, and their healing story. It also should include a history of local predecessor trails.

4. **The story of local naturalists,** past and present, who encouraged time in Nature for its health benefits, and how their legacy reflects in your efforts.

5. **Bathroom facilities** at the trailhead or an adjacent facility. For Trails over one-half mile long, a latrine within a five-minute walk from any point on the Trail.

6. **Suitability for barefoot** and light-footwear walking.

7. **Accommodations for special-needs clients.**

8. **Posted carrying capacity** and *Entrance by registration only* notice.

9. **Posted Trail map,** with designated features and distances.

10. **Posted contact numbers** for medical emergencies, law enforcement, fire, and Trail management/maintenance.

11. **Brochure rack** for fold-out Trail map and brochures on Breathing in Nature and Aromatherapy.

12. **Certification sign** designating an approved Healing Nature Trail.

IV Specific Trail

1. **Initial impact.** At the onset, Trail design and appearance must be both inviting and aesthetically pleasing, as first impressions set the tone for a Trail Walk.

2. **Safety features.** A clearly delineated Trail with protection from potential environmental hazards, and with features enabling those who step off the path to reorient themselves.

3. **An Entry Threshold** at the beginning of the Trail, yet far enough in that it is immersed in the ambience of Nature. The best Thresholds are, in this order:

    a. **Bridges** spanning Ravines, Streams, or the narrows of a Pond or Wetland.

    b. **Sudden elevation changes,** such as bluffs leading up to plateaus or down into river bottoms.

    c. **Switchbacks,** where a Trail suddenly disappears into a canyon or valley.

4. **Havens,** which are nooks for solace and reflection, located just off of the Trail. To assure privacy, a gate of some sort is used. There are to be two types of Havens:

    a. **Expansive,** to encourage openness and perspective. These sites provide either panoramic or deep-Forest views.

    b. **Reflective,** to support introspection and listening. They are tucked into dense groves or clefts in ledges, or amongst boulders or large Tree trunks.

5. **Group meeting areas.** Similar to Reflective Havens, they provide privacy and a closed-in feeling. A minimum of three meeting areas is recommended, to accommodate groups of two-to-five, six-to-ten, and up to twenty.

6. **Benches in high-energy areas,** such as in the midst of a grove of Elder Trees or a patch of lush Wildflowers, or adjacent to Rapids and Waterfalls.

7. **Abrupt changes in direction,** gradient, walking surface, and habitat.

8. **Aromatherapy sites,** to practice Conscious Breathing in patches of medicinal Herbs and groves of aromatic Bushes or Trees.

9. **Informative signs** on how indigenous people use particular Trees and Herbs for healing and craftwork, and how clients can do the same. Signs are posted in areas other than the Trail proper, so as not to be distractive.

10. **Discovery Forks** are branches on a Trail that serve as metaphors for the choices we face on our Healing Journey. There should be a minimum of three per Trail.

11. **Zen Untangle** is a clutter of stumps and boulders the size of a large room. Designed for mindless meandering, which helps clear nagging thoughts and feelings.

12. **Zen Garden** is a table-size patch of bare sand, with an assortment of sticks and stones, for creating a virtual refuge or depicting a mental landscape.

13. **Trail Shelter,** such as a gazebo or pagoda, midway on Trails over a half-mile long. For rest and refuge in the event of a sudden storm.

14. **Reintegration Strip** is a nondescript section of Trail at the very end of the Walk, for winding down and preparing for reentry. Has adjacent picnic tables.

15. **Trail's-End Nook** is a secluded meeting/reflection area at the end of the Trail, with a fire pit for closing rituals. Has a view that inspires and encourages contemplation.

16. **Return Threshold.** At the very end of a Trail, it meets the same criteria for an Entry Threshold (see #3), which could double for a Return Threshold.

Optional Features

Any Trail adjunct that contributes to its efficacy, but is not a required feature, is eligible for inclusion as an optional feature. The certifying agent determines whether or not a feature qualifies.

Those that do not qualify as either required or optional features may still be allowed as Trail adjuncts. The main determining factor is whether or not they detract from a Trail's stated mission.

Optional features (some of which are described in chapter 31) can include, but are not limited to:

▶ Walking Labyrinths (Turf, Hedge, Cobble, or otherwise)

▶ Stump Labyrinths

▶ Aquarinths

▶ Finger Labyrinths

▶ Cosmorinths

▶ Walk-through Smudges

▶ Remembering Cairns

▶ Additional footbridges

▶ Wildflower Beds

▶ A rare and endangered species reintroduction program

Certification Rating System

Required Features

▶ Each required feature is rated on a 0-to-10 point scale, with 0 being totally inadequate and 10 being perfect.

▶ Each required feature must score a minimum of 6 points.

Optional Features

▶ Each optional feature included in the Trail is rated on a 0-to-7 point scale, with 0 being totally unsatisfactory and 7 being perfect.

▶ Each optional feature included in the Trail must score a minimum of 4 points.

Trail Scoring

The assigned points for all required and optional features are added together. If the aggregate score equals 75 percent or more, a Trail qualifies for certification.

Certification for Already Existing Trails

Any trail is eligible for consideration as a Healing Nature Trail. It must undergo the same assessment process as a newly designed Healing Nature Trail. To determine whether an existing trail holds potential, and to efficiently and economically revamp a trail, begin by enlisting the services of a Healing Nature Trail consultant.

Here is the usual process:

1. Contact the Healing Nature Center to arrange for an initial trail assessment.

2. You will be given recommendations for any improvements or additions needed to meet certification requirements.

3. Once work is completed, your trail will receive a certification assessment.

4. The assessor will give you a scorecard, along with either your certification or recommendations for any final work that needs to be completed for certification.

Biannual Recertification

All Healing Nature Trails are assessed for recertification every two years, on the anniversary of their initial certification. This keeps Trails maintained to standard, and it assures consistency of service when there are changes in tenure or management.

On-site inspection by a certifying agent may or may not be necessary. At the discretion of the agent, the assessment could be conducted by remote interview, along with the submission of video footage or digital images of selected required and optional features.

CHAPTER THIRTY-FOUR

Trail Certification for Trauma Healing

Healing Nature Trails provide a metaphor for the Trauma-Healing Journey. Many Trails can gain the additional certification for trauma healing as they stand. Some Trails will need minor modifications or additions in order to exhibit all of the features for catalyzing the ten crucial Healing Steps listed in the box at the end of the chapter.

To show how a Trail can be a vehicle for trauma healing, this chapter gives an overview of the Trauma-Healing Journey (based on the author's book, *Breaking the Trauma Code*). Let's start with a definition of terms:

Stress: a state of psycho-emotional strain sufficient to activate the fight-flight-freeze response. The cause of stress can be either actual or imagined.

Chronic Stress: a protracted state of stress resulting from either recurring cause or failed stress release.

Trauma: the nervous system's capacity for release becoming overwhelmed by a highly disturbing experience, circumstance, or state of stress. Indelibly imprints the individual and permanently alters his or her life. Can produce distorted thoughts, feelings, and/or behaviors.

Trauma Memory: an unresolved actual or imagined high-stress episode that metastasizes. It is lifelong and unresolvable, and it remains latent until triggered.

Trauma-Memory Response (TMR): the largely uncontrollable acting out of Trauma Memory. Can manifest as flashbacks, reenacting, role casting, nightmares, withdrawal, emotional extremes, mistrust, panic attacks, agitation, jumpiness, stuttering. Also known as *post-traumatic stress disorder* or PTSD.

Story: The narrative by which a traumatic episode is related. The episode, its time of occurrence, and its various components may or may not have transpired.

Script: the screenplay enacted when a Trauma Memory is triggered. Evolves over time in response to coping efforts, new information, and life experience. Can be rewritten, but not eliminated.

Trigger: any reminder, conscious or subconscious, that creates an association with the traumatic episode. Often precipitates a TMR.

For a clearer understanding of how these terms relate to one another, here is the trauma pathway: **Stress –> Trauma –> Trauma Memory –> TMR**

The Trauma-Healing Journey

Here is a general overview of the objectives to reach for transforming trauma into a benign presence—and perhaps even a strength:

The first goal: take personal responsibility.

I no longer blame others for my trauma memories and TMRs, and I don't expect someone else to fix it. When I can do that, I am no longer limited by the *who*, *what*, and *why*. My healing is now my work, not somebody else's. I have eliminated the inevitable dead ends that I come to when relying on others. The reality is that the people involved in my trauma change over time, their memories often differ from mine, and some of them are either unavailable or no longer alive.

The second goal: separate my trauma memory from its story.

The two mix like oil and water—my trauma memory is somatic, wordless, and permanent, while my trauma story is conscious, verbal, and changeable. The story distracts from the necessary deep healing by keeping me focused on who did what to whom and why.

Stories are based on memories, which are by nature inaccurate or incomplete, at least to some degree. Circumstances change, and so do I. The longer it's been, the more my memory alters the story.

When I release the story, I allow myself to see things differently. My trauma memory is no longer directly connected to the people involved, or to the circumstances. That lets me embrace my trauma for what it *now* is to me.

The third goal: revise the script.

When I rewrite the lines I've been reading when I have a TMR, I can transform it from hurtful to respectful and supportive. I can then consciously engage in my healing process, by using my TMR as a portal to go down deep into my timeless, wordless self, where my trauma memory dwells.

How Nature Can Trigger Trauma Memories

As much as most people are drawn to Nature, many experience some level of stress when outdoors and away from familiar comforts. The stress could be caused by annoying bugs, fear of wild animals, or disagreeable weather.

Healing Nature Trails can add to the stress because they have a low-yet-discernible level of physical challenge designed into them. Abrupt changes in direction and elevation, along with transitions from one habitat type to another, stimulate the body-mind connection. When we can enact something physically atypical, it encourages the enactment of its psycho-emotional counterpart, which facilitates the release of repressed emotions and encourages new avenues of perception (see chapter 20 for more on this topic).

Any of those stressors can potentially trigger TMRs. When we recognize that TMRs are not caused by something we experience, but rather by our nervous system's response to what we experience, we can take advantage of Nature-related TMRs by using them as openings for deep healing. Otherwise, many people tend to limit their time in Nature in order to avoid stress and TMRs.

To be effective in working with clients experiencing Nature-triggered TMRs, it helps for healthcare practitioners to understand the types of stressors that typically affect people in Nature. They are referred to as *Threshold Experiences*, and they fall into four categories:

1. Unfinished Business

After a few days of camping or canoeing, the freshness and feelings of escape into the wilds become replaced with doubts, fears, and regrets. I could've stayed home and gotten that project finished, or I should've worked this week so we can afford that new car we need.

2. Tolerance

At around two to three weeks, physical discomfort becomes more noticeable; familiar surroundings, routines, and foods are missed; and we struggle to be fully present. We feel fatigued, emotionally flat, and we get absorbed in daydreaming.

3. Doubt

A month passes, and we enter a state of existential crisis: We feel disoriented, depressed, and self-critical. We start questioning our beliefs and the decisions that have brought us here.

4. Cultural Transition

Two to three months into the experience, memories of loved ones back home are no longer enough to sustain us. We miss our old routines, and we don't have trusted friends to confide in.

For more on the topic of Thresholds, please see chapters 3 and 4 of *Wilderness Stress and Trauma: Management Protocols for Therapy Programs, Outdoor Schools, and Expeditions* by Tamarack Song.

The stated onset times for the Threshold Experiences are averages, and people experience the Thresholds in environments other than the outdoors. Right away on a Healing Nature Trail, some Walkers begin feeling one or more of the Thresholds loom. Life transitions, struggles with addictions, and relationship issues may have had them already immersed in the Thresholds. For them, the gate is wide open for what the Trail has to offer.

The Trail as a Healing Metaphor

The power and resilience of the body-mind connection is the key to using a Healing Nature Trail for trauma healing. Here, in more detail, are the inner steps on the Trauma-Healing Journey that get empowered by physically enacting them on a Healing Nature Trail:

HEALING STEP	TRAIL STEP
1. Take personal responsibility.	Putting foot on the Trail.
2. Enter wordlessness, the Void.	Walking the Labyrinth, Finger Labyrinth, Cosmorinth; and viewing panoramic vistas.
3. Abandon abandonment.	Returning to Mother Nature's embrace; sitting between Elder Trees and beside Water.
4. Leave stressors, traumatizers behind.	Smudging; crossing the Threshold Bridge.
5. Empower the experience.	Leaving/taking a Cairn stone; choosing Discovery Forks; spending time in Reflective Havens.
6. Reintegrate with life.	Conscious Breathing, touching, feeling; Aromatherapy.
7. Drop the trauma story.	Walking the Zen Untangle; tending the Zen Garden.

HEALING STEP	TRAIL STEP
8. Work out immediate stress.	Walking the Trail, especially barefoot.
9. Enter trance; heal with fire.	Gazing into the Trail's-End Fire; Trance Dancing.
10. Rewrite the script.	Working with my therapist in the Trail's-End Nook.

CHAPTER THIRTY-FIVE

Associate and Senior Healing Nature Guide Degree Programs

M any healing practitioners, groups, and individuals choose to guide themselves on a Healing Nature Trail. With the map and supplemental materials provided, a self-guided tour can be an Awakening—i.e., life-changing—experience.

Yet we need to remember that everyone has blind spots. When we struggle with overwhelming emotions and trauma memories, or when we've lost our way and have burning questions, our perceptiveness and sense of presence can be compromised. In addition, the energy it takes to organize ourselves and focus on the task at hand often detracts from getting centered and gaining as much as possible from the Trail experience.

Healing Nature Guides can alleviate much of the stress of preparation and greatly enhance a Trail Walk. Here is what Healing Nature Guides have to offer clients:

▶ **Assistance with booking** and personal preparation.

▶ **Tailored Trail Walks,** based on sensitivity to clients' particular needs, combined with intimate knowledge of the Trail and Nature's healing forces.

▶ **A sense of peace** for clients, who, knowing that somebody is tending to details and there for them if needed, can fully immerse themselves in the Trail experience.

▶ **Quiet, empathetic presence,** along with someone to listen or talk to, if desired.

- **A sentry,** to assure privacy when utilizing the Trail's various features.
- **Guidance** in recognizing and processing what came from the Trail Walk.

In addition, Senior Healing Nature Guides come to clients with advanced education and training in the healing arts, which are comprised of all conventional, alternative, and indigenous practices dedicated to maintaining and restoring physical or psycho-emotional well-being. This includes, but is not limited to, standard mental and physical health disciplines (including Traditional Chinese), Shamanism, Chiropractic, Nursing, Breathwork, Physical Therapy, Massage, Herbology, Pharmacology, and the Esoteric Healing Arts.

Senior Guides provide uniquely tailored Trail Walks that meld Nature's healing powers synergistically with their own professional healing modalities. Trained to translate clients' Trail experiences into metaphors and awareness-raising stories, Senior Guides show how to use the Trail as a means of better understanding relationship dynamics, change, death, and other aspects of life's Journey.

A GUIDING PRINCIPLE

To be deeply affecting, a Healing Journey must be client-driven. The Healing Nature Guide Degree Programs train Guides to play consultative rather than directing roles for their clients. The foundation for that is provided by two core skills learned in the courses: listening and asking questions.

Suicide Prevention

Both Associate and Senior Healing Nature Guides, along with Instructors, are trained in suicide prevention and carry Outdoor Suicide Prevention certification. Their training helps them identify prospective clients who fall into the unique category of suicide-prone individuals who turn to Nature for either rescuing or a place to release their last breath.

In the training, Guides and Instructors learn to identify active and passive suicide types, walking suicides, and those who come to either plan or commit suicide in Nature.

Programs Offered

For those called to be Healing Nature Guides or program Instructors, the Healing Nature Center offers four accredited degree programs:

- Associate Healing Nature Guide (AHNG)
- Senior Healing Nature Guide (SHNG)
- Off-Trail Healing Nature Guide (AHNG-O or SHNG-O)
- Healing Nature Guide Instructor

To ensure that a uniform standard of education is maintained that gives Healing Nature Guides a solid base of applicable knowledge and experience, only graduates of the appropriate accredited Healing Nature Center degree programs have the right to use the associated titles and acronyms, as listed above. Certified diplomas must be publicly displayed in the office of the practitioner.

To maintain certification, all Healing Nature Guides must enroll in a Healing Nature Center accredited eight-contact hour refresher course every two years, to maintain their skill level and keep them abreast of the latest developments in their profession. The refresher course certificates of completion are to be publicly displayed beside their diplomas.

Under each of the following program descriptions, prerequisites are listed. One of them is a four-year degree or *equivalent*. The Healing Nature Center wants to assure the accessibility of its programs to all who are called to serve in Nature healing, including those who are educated nontraditionally, have other-culture backgrounds, and learned through experience and self-study.

STUDY AND PROFESSIONAL SUPPORT

Students can elect to participate remotely in the Study Buddy Program, and there is an online classroom for the at-home study and internship portions of courses. Instructors are available by phone or e-mail during posted office hours. Guides, Instructors, and Directors have the Healing Nature Professionals E-group, where they go for support and advice and to stay updated on new therapies and research.

Program Instructors

All Instructors are graduates of the Healing Nature Center's Instructor Degree Program, or they are specialists in related fields. Assistant Instructors are Healing Nature Guides who have received Instructor training. The current Head Instructor is Tamarack Song, the present executive director of the Healing Nature Center, and the cofounder of Healing Nature Trails (see bio at end of book).

The Associate Healing Nature Guide Degree Program

Prerequisites

- A four-year degree or license in one of the healing arts.
- Degree equivalents and work experience will be considered.
- Successful completion of the application process.

Associate graduates are authorized to:

- Display the diplomas they are awarded.
- Use the title *Certified Healing Nature Guide*, and the acronym AHNG after their names.
- Guide clients independently on Healing Nature Trails.
- Guide clients on noncertified trails, provided:
  1. The trails meet or nearly meet the minimum requirements for a Healing Nature Trail (see chapter 33).

2. The trails are scouted out immediately prior to the guided Walk to ensure that there is nothing that would disrupt the client's experience.

▶ Assist Senior HNGs and healthcare professionals on Trail Walks.

▶ Mentor Associate students in Module III of their course.

> An Associate Healing Nature Guide degree alone does **not** qualify a Guide to diagnose conditions or prescribe treatments for clients. AHNGs **can** practice on clients the healing systems for which they are trained and licensed.

Associate HNG Course Outline

The course is comprised of three modules, beginning with six weeks of at-home study, followed by four days of on-Trail training, and concluding with six supervised Trail Walks.

Module I: At-Home Study

A six-week at-home unit, it is comprised of sixty hours of reading, research, and dialogue. Here is the unit framework:

1. A study of selected material from *The Healing Nature Trail* book and other sources.

2. Naturalist training, for in-depth understanding of Nature's healing attributes, and for examples from Nature to use as healing metaphors and to help personalize the Trail experience.

3. Training in ethical guidelines and grievance procedures.

4. Suicide-prevention training.

5. Conscious Breathing training.

6. Online discussion of materials in an e-group format.

7. A survey of Nature-based healing programs and practices from around the world.

Module II: Foundational Guide Training

This four-day unit takes place on location at a Healing Nature Trail. It consists of:

1. A review of the at-home study.

2. A presentation of Trail development, use, and management.

3. A guided tour of the Trail, detailing each of the Trail's design and healing features, the science behind them, and how they can be best utilized.

4. Instruction for guiding special-needs clients, including the blind, those with limited mobility, and those in wheelchairs.

5. Training in Conscious Walking and Blindfold Trail Walking.

6. Each student is taken on a Trail Walk by a Healing Nature Guide.

7. Students team up to take each other on a total of three guided Trail Walks, each time with a different partner. The Walks are supervised by a Healing Nature Guide, who takes detailed notes of the student's performance.

8. In-group assessments of the Trail Walks.

Module III: Guiding Trail Walks Training

Part 1 of this module consists of conducting six Trail Walks over a six-month period on a certified Healing Nature Trail, supervised by an Instructor-approved Healing Nature Guide. The Trail Walks are to be conducted in this fashion:

1. The client whom the student guides must be made fully aware of the fact that this is a training session, and that it is being overseen by a Healing Nature Guide.

2. One of the six Walks must be video recorded.

3. The series of Walks is to include a minimum of two solo client Walks and two group client Walks.

4. The six Walks are to be spread out over the six-month period to give the student the opportunity to reflect on each experience.

5. The Guide who oversees each Walk is to hand his or her written critique of the Walk over to the student within twenty-four hours of the completion of each Walk.

6. The student is to write a concise 600- to 800-word report on each Walk, which is to cover: an overview of the Trail Walk; what went well for the student; what the student missed or overlooked; and how the student can improve his or her next Walk.

Part 2 of this module consists of shadowing a Healing Nature Guide on six Trail Walks, interspersed between the Part 1 Walks the student conducts. The shadowings are to be conducted in this fashion:

1. The Guide is to request the consent of his or her client to have a student shadow him or her on the Trail Walk.

2. The student is to shadow the entire Trail Walk, from greeting the client to the client's departure.

3. The student shadows in silence, without interfering or interjecting in any way.

4. The student may assist only if specifically requested to do so by the Guide.

5. The student is to write a concise 300- to 400-word review of each Guide shadowing, which is to cover: an overview of the Trail Walk; what the student learned; and what the student would do differently.

Within thirty days of completion of Module III, copies of the six reports and six shadowing reviews, along with the video recording of one Walk, are to be turned in to the Instructor for review.

Assuming the successful completion of all three Modules, the student receives an Associate Healing Nature Guide diploma from the Healing Nature Center, which grants the graduate the

THE HEALING NATURE TRAIL

full rights and privileges of the title Associate Healing Nature Guide, as specified above.

The Senior Healing Nature Guide Degree Program

After gaining their Associate Degree, graduates can apply for the Senior Dissertation.

Prerequisites

▶ A postgraduate degree, or a four-year degree with an additional degree or certification in the healing arts.

▶ Degree equivalents and work experience will be considered.

▶ Associate HNG diploma status.

▶ Practice as an Associate HNG for a minimum of six months, guiding a minimum of fifteen clients in that time period.

▶ Successful completion of the application process.

Senior graduates are authorized to:

▶ Execute the following rights and privileges in addition to those authorized for Associate graduates.

▶ Use the title *Senior Healing Nature Guide*, and the acronym SHNG after their names.

▶ Practice, on Healing Nature Trails and equivalents, the healing modalities for which the Senior Guide is trained and licensed, which could include diagnosing conditions and prescribing treatments.

▶ Use Healing Nature Trail materials in their professional practices. This includes books and other printed/online materials, and aids such as Finger Labyrinths and Tokens.

▶ Offer workshops to the public in the specific Nature-immersion modalities for which they are HNG certified, such as The Labyrinthine Experience, Breathing in Nature, Primal Aromatherapy, Grounding, and Conscious Walking.

▶ Assist Instructors in trainings, courses, and workshops.

Senior HNG Dissertation Outline

1. **Form a Dissertation Committee,** Instructor and student together select members to form the committee, which is to consist of the Instructor, a Healing Nature Guide, and a mental health therapist.

2. **The student prepares a dissertation,** to be comprised of a 5,000-word written or oral presentation, with citations, consisting of three parts:

    ▶ What a Healing Nature Trail means to me personally.

    ▶ The potential I see for Healing Nature Trails to help clients.

    ▶ How I perceive my role as a Guide, now and in the foreseeable future.

3. **The student circulates the dissertation for review,** to a minimum of five Senior Healing Nature Guides. Student then revises the dissertation, based on reviews.

4. **The student presents and defends the dissertation** in front of the Dissertation Committee. The committee seeks to establish the student's passion to serve, topical depth of knowledge, and ability to convey the spirit of a Healing Nature Trail.

5. **The Dissertation Committee deliberates in private.** There are three possible conclusions, listed below. All conclusions but *Fail* must be unanimous.

    ▶ **Pass** Both the dissertation and defense are satisfactory.

    ▶ **Re-defend** Not satisfied with the dissertation and/or defense, the committee yet believes that a satisfactory re-presenting and defense is possible.

    ▶ **Fail** At least one committee member is unsatisfied with the dissertation and/or defense and concludes that a re-presentation would be unsatisfactory.

6. **The committee posts its conclusion** in writing to the student within forty-eight hours of his or her defense.

7. **With a re-defend conclusion, the student has sixty days** to re-present and defend.

Assuming the successful presentation and defense of the dissertation, the student receives a Senior Healing Nature Guide diploma from the Healing Nature Center, which grants the graduate the full rights and privileges of the title Senior Healing Nature Guide, as specified above.

The Off-Trail HNG Certification Course

There is pleasure in the pathless woods, says Lord Byron; and Off-Trail Healing Nature Guides show there is healing as well. Associate and Senior Healing Nature Guides are eligible to receive an additional certification that qualifies them to guide clients off-trail in any natural area that has features suitable for catalyzing the Healing Nature experience.

Prerequisites

- Associate or Senior HNG diploma status.
- One year having transpired since receiving their diploma.
- Guiding a minimum of ten clients since receiving their diploma.
- Successful completion of the application process.

Off-Trail certification authorizes the holder to:

- Display the certification they are awarded.
- Use the title *Off-Trail Healing Nature Guide*, and the acronym of HNG-O after their names.
- Take clients on guided Walks in trail-free natural areas, provided that the areas have a high proportion of the features common to Healing Nature Trails.

Off-Trail HNG Training Outline

1. **The student selects five trail-free natural areas** (or trail-free sectors of natural areas) that have a high proportion of

the features needed for Healing Nature Trail certification (see chapter 33).

2. **The student self-critiques each selection** for the Instructor.

3. **A minimum of three natural areas must meet Instructor approval,** or the student continues to search for areas.

4. **The student guides one client or group,** accompanied by the Instructor, on a Healing Nature Walk in one of the areas mutually agreed upon by the student and Instructor.

5. **The student self-critiques his or her Walk** for the Instructor.

6. **The Instructor assesses the student's overall performance**, including self-critiques.

Assuming the successful completion of the training, an Off-Trail certification is affixed to the Healing Nature Guide's diploma by the Healing Nature Center, which grants the Guide the full rights and privileges of Off-Trail certification, as specified above.

CHAPTER THIRTY-SIX

The Healing Nature
Instructor Degree Course

Exceptional graduates of the Senior HNG course may be invited by their instructor to become Instructors themselves by enrolling in the Healing Nature Instructor Degree Course.

Prerequisites

 ▶ Senior HNG diploma status.

 ▶ A serious dedication to Nature healing and helping to make Nature's healing gifts available to others.

 ▶ Possessing the attendant communication, social, and organizational skills required for effective instructing.

Successful completion of the application process.

Instructors are authorized to:

 ▶ Independently organize and teach Associate and Senior Healing Nature Guide diploma courses and Off-Trail certification trainings.

 ▶ Train Assistant Instructors.

 ▶ Design and develop Healing Nature Trails.

 ▶ Serve as consultants and certifying agents for Healing Nature Trails.

Instructor Course Outline

The curriculum consists of four semesters devoted to Nature Studies, earning a Healing Nature Guide Degree, and mentored training, followed by the submission of a thesis.

Semesters 1 and 2

The Wilderness Guide Program (WGP) or equivalent. The WGP is an eleven-month wilderness-immersion program presented jointly by the Healing Nature Center and the Teaching Drum Outdoor School. Areas of study include animal language, tracking, edible and medicinal plants, primitive shelter building, basket making, orienteering, weather forecasting, canoeing, conflict resolution methods, dream interpretation, and other living-with-Nature skills.

Semester 3

Earning a Senior Healing Nature Guide Degree.

Semester 4

A six-month internship as an Assistant Instructor and intern to a Healing Nature Trail Director.

Thesis

The purpose of the thesis is to demonstrate depth of understanding in the field of Nature-based healing, mastery of relevant literature and scholarship, and the ability to contribute to the field. The thesis is to be constructed and evaluated thusly:

1. **Abstract** Roughly one-page long, it serves two purposes: to give an overview of the thesis and to encourage reader interest.

2. **Introduction** Gives a general overview of the Healing Nature field, historical and contemporary; then it shows a gap where a significant contribution can be made. Includes

the **Thesis Outline** and the **Thesis Statement**, which is one or two sentences stating the student's proposed novel approach to filling the gap.

3. **Appraisal** An assessment of topical literature and current programs that is intended to expose the gap.

4. **Approach** The student's proposal on how the gap could be filled, with a chronology of how the student developed the proposal.

5. **Discussion** What the proposal could mean to the Healing Nature community—both practitioners and clients—if implemented.

6. **Conclusion** In the student's estimation, how well was the thesis statement achieved? What are the limitations of the proposal? What suggestions does the student have for further development? How does the thesis fit in the arena of topical literature? Show a strong connection between introduction and conclusion.

7. **Peer Review** The course Instructor circulates the thesis to a minimum of five professionals in the Healing Nature field for peer review.

8. **Manifest** The student implements his or her proposal in at least one successful application.

Assuming a positive peer review and manifest, the Instructor Degree Course graduate is awarded a document by the Healing Nature Center conferring the title of Healing Nature Instructor, which grants the graduate the full rights and privileges of such title, as specified above.

Additional Training

Healing Nature Guides and Instructors are encouraged to continue their educations, for self-enrichment and to increase their professional depth of knowledge and experience. This adds to the range of what they have to offer clients, and to their ability to personalize their contributions.

Areas of pursuit have included Aromatherapy, Art Therapy, Breathwork, Communication Skills, Creative Writing, Environmental Restoration, Native Lifeway, Naturalist Training, Outdoor Skills, Psychology, Storytelling, Tree Climbing, Zen, and various healing arts.

Acknowledgments

I have written a number of books, but not one with near this many contributors. If the front cover was large enough, I would list all of their names along with mine. Yet honoring them here instead has a beautiful advantage—I have the space to acknowledge their contributions as well as them.

Jim Arneson of JAAD Book Design crafted the cover and interior; Amber Braun provided the Gateway Labyrinth design and researched Labyrinth history; Baerbel Ehrig gave an overview of pollinator Bee and Butterfly habitat restoration; Michael Fox researched Cairns and rendered the Trail map; Susan Gilman offered her experience in Grounding; Jim Morningstar, PhD, and Steve Moe, LMT, contributed to the sections on Conscious Breathing and the psychology of movement; Michael Patterson shared material on healing trails, Zen Gardens, and Labyrinths; Brett Schwartz formatted all the citations and numbered the index; Brittany Servent researched our Nature Guide legacy; Claire Sweeney interviewed people on Forest Therapy; Sami True offered her knowledge of Aromatherapy; Steve Yahr (author of *Letters from the Sanctuary: The Sam Campbell Story*) and Katie Kirby (curator of the Three Lakes Historical Museum) provided valuable archival information on the local pioneer Trail Guides; and a person who wishes to remain anonymous researched Nature-based healing and designed our logo.

Working beside me on nearly every phase of this project was my longtime collaborator and editor Andrew Huff. He conducted considerable research, set up the citations, and generated the index. Both he and Stephanie Phibbs, PhD, gave the manuscript a solid proofread.

Sherry Roberts of The Roberts Group Editorial & Design, LLC applied her talents to lend the text its final polish.

Even with the strong and fruitful partnership that coalesced, writing this healing trail presentation still turned out to be a largely solo venture. I needed quiet space and uninterrupted time, which was provided by friends and neighbors Luke and Myriam Brault, and the Edward U. Demmer Memorial Library of Three Lakes, Wisconsin.

Prior to this book project, I did not own a laptop computer, and I needed one for my remote writing venues. Early one afternoon, a delivery service brought a brand-new laptop to my doorstep, straight from the manufacturer. To this day, I do not know the responsible party.

To each and every one of these valued friends, collaborators, and phantom supporters, I extend my deepest gratitude. Without them, I'd still be lost in some fuzzy dream about what could be and how to achieve it.

Then again, there is one person who would never leave me floating around in my fantasies, pleasant as that might be. My bosom friend, loving mate, and creative partner Lety Seibel was an integral part of every phase of not only this book's creation, but also the birthing of the wondrous woodland trail that this book attempts to reflect. It is here that words must stop, as I have no way other than cherishing her every breath and movement to convey what her all-embracing presence means to me.

INDEX

A

Accommodations 246-50, 289-91, 328

ADD/ADHD 179, 249, 374. See also mental health; psycho-emotional health.

Adrenaline 31, 59

Affirmation 257

Air, ion-charged 17, 35, 46, 375

Alcove 18. *See also* Nook; Haven; Trail.

Alebrije tokens 137-39, 390

Algonquian people 173-4

Alzheimer's 39

American Indian 10, 71, 92, 159, 396

Amulets 115, 118, . See also shaman.

Ancient Ones 25

Animal 2, 6, 9, 15, 16, 18, 25, 39, 49, 52, 53, 54, 56, 62, 82, 91-5, 97, 98-103, 105, 106, 116, 127, 128, 132, 140, 141, 159, 163, 164, 167, 179, 197, 217, 233, 249, 250, 268, 297, 302, 337, 354, 387, 401

Animal Guide 99-100. See also Dodem.

Animal Guide workshops 270

Animal transformation 100. See shapeshifting. See also Dodem.

Appalachian Mountains 15

Aquarinths 79, 88, 130, 138, 191, 210, 211, 213, 214-16, 247, 250, 252, 290, 331. See also Labyrinth; Labyrinthine experience; Water.

Aristotle 17

Aromatherapy 23, 45, 46, 105-13, 139, 196, 198, 202, 239, 240, 248, 249, 250, 251, 252, 268, 329, 330, 339, 356, 357, 388, 389, 395. Primal Aromatherapy 94, 105, 109, 113, 161, 348 ; Tree Canopy Aromatherapy 113, 198-99. See also decongestion; diffusers/diffusion; direct inhalation; incense; Forest, Fragrance; oil, olfactory system; resin; smudge.

Artress, Reverend Dr. Lauren 81

Association of Nature and Forest Therapy Guides and Programs 371, 376,

Association of Therapeutic Effects of Forests 12

asthma 35

attention span 8, 38, 117

Auspacken 223, 225, 229

Autism 39, 249

Autoimmune disorders 34, 36, 381

Autonomic nervous system 72, 382

Awakening 29, 32, 43, 59, 77, 78, 120, 130, 147, 149, 249, 289, 290, 341, 396

Awakening journeys 2, 82, 326. See Journey.

Awakening the senses 258

Awareness 7, 38, 42, 53, 56, 66, 68, 78, 87, 88, 138, 159, 190, 197, 198, 214, 220, 221, 241, 256, 300-1, 307, 401

Awe 9, 37-8, 209, 375

B

Backpack/backpacking 136, 139

Balance 25, 30, 80, 98, 117, 141, 152, 162, 190, 247,

Baldwin, James 192

Barefooting 1, 17, 18, 22, 23, 34, 65-71, 127, 146, 185, 289, 328, 340,

Bates, Margaret 52

Becoming Nature 39, 91, 264, 387

Benyus, Janine M 8, 370

Baumbestauttung 131. *See* Tree Burial.

Bestattungswald 131. *See* Forest Burial.

Bioregion 9, 303

Biorhythms 66

Blindfold Sitting 149. *See* sensory deprivation.

Blindfold Rooting 71, 149

Blindfold Walking 44, 45, 147-51, 346

Blood glucose levels 34

Blood pressure 32, 34, 55, 58, 377, 382

Board of directors 265, 276-7, 282,

Body 1, 30, 38, 56-8, 60, 66, 72, 78, 94, 101, 108, 111, 117, 119, 145, 146, 159, 171, 186, 192-4, 195, 197, 200, 218, 233, 256, 257, 378, 379, 381, 385, 388, 390

Body-mind connection vi, 32, 38-9, 43-4, 46, 53, 61, 79, 80, 121, 134, 146, 149, 188, 191-4, 199, 217, 219, 224, 225, 226, 230, 248, 267, 337, 339

Bog ix, 128, 140, 160, 167, 187, 195, 196, 206, 210, 212, 284

Bonsai 11, 212, 371

Boundaries 13, 43, 119, 178, 184, 193, 216, 217, 218, 294-6, 300,

Boundary waters canoe area 157, 161

Brain 39, 58, 61, 80, 92, 109, 144, 145, 174, 194, 233, 371, 374, 375, 376, 380, 382, 387, 390, 391, 394.

Brain Spotting 46

Breaking the Trauma Code 401

Breath/breathing. Breathing in Nature v, 1, 23, 51-3, 56-7, 110, 151, 249, 319, 329, 348; Breath of Life 64, 87, 109; Breathing Knoll vi, 135, 195, 201, 210, 288; circular breathing 60-1; Conscious Breathing 17, 23, 52-64, 71, 87, 108, 138, 151, 198, 225, 248, 253, 330, 339, 345, 357, 378, 379, 380; Dragon's Breath 233-4; Fast Breathing 59; Nasal breathing 194; Slow breathing 58, 151, 379; Therapeutic Breathwork 238, 270, 316, 342, 356, 378, 379, 401; Timeless Breath 196.

Bridge. Bridge of No Return 188; Foot Bridge 130, 331; Threshold Bridge 23, 128, 130, 131, 135, 179, 187, 207, 235, 241, 247, 253, 255, 265, 271, 288, 329, 339.

Brother Wolf Foundation 268, 397

Brush-down smudge 186

Buddha 56, 57, 128, 231

Burial Extraction 70

Burroughs, John 21, 230

Butterfly 390, 398

C

Cabin in the Woods 92, 160

Cairn vii, 18, 82, 120, 135, 137, 172, 176, 186, 236, 247, 253, 288, 290, 293-6, 339, 357, 398 . Memorial Cairn 294; Remembering Cairn 130, 186, 294, 331.

Cancer 23, 33-4, 72, 369, 370, 373, 375, 389

Campbell, Joseph 25, 208, 396

Campbell, Sam 11, 15, 160-1, 163-5, 166, 168, 357, 371, 392, 393

Camping 5, 27, 164, 238-9, 338,

Canoe 5, 140, 157, 161, 169, 211, 214, 215, 247, 290, 299, 338, 354, 398

Cardiovascular stress 22, 32, 41, 379, 381, 382

Celestial maze 178-9, 299-300,

Center for environment, health and field services, at chiba university 35

Centering 18, 55, 111

Centering tools 116

Ceremonial fire pit 130

Ceremony/ceremonial 19, 55, sweat lodge ceremony 55

Certification . Trail Certification 288, 325-33; Trail certification contract 327; trail certification for trauma healing 335-40; certification and diploma programs 270, 343, 344, 347, 348, 350, 351, 353; certification rating system 326, 331-2; biannual recertification 333.

Charms 102, 118

Chequamegon-nicolet national forest 125, 160, 161, 267,

Childhood 22, 26, 56, 75, 157, 320, 372

Chopra, Deepak 135

Chorten 294

Circadian clock 96-7, 373, 387, 394

Circle way 75-6

Circle of life 209

Circulatory system 66

Circumambulation 75-6

Claves 117

Client/clients 16, 21, 42, 43, 45-8, 53, 58, 69, 135, 147, 205, 206, 210, 211, 225, 226, 252, 257, 269, 280, 289, 290, 296, 298, 305-23, 326, 327, 328, 330, 338, 341-2, 344-51, 355

Clothing 63, 69, 98, 99, 111, 136, 140, 185, 203

Co-intelligence 9, 371

288, 290, 401; Wilderness Guide Program 354

H

Habitat 5, 7, 16, 39, 107, 126, 178, 270, 287, 302, 357

Handouts 53, 138, 143, 262, 290, 311

Hanh, Thich Nhat 193, 378, 394, 396

Haven. Reflective 240, 329, 339; safe 16, 24; Trailside 149, **208-11**, 247, 271, 288

Headaches 44, 203, 281, 387

Headnets 139

Head instructor 344

Health xi, 6, 7, 8, 11, 12, 15, 22, 29, 30, 32, 36, 38, 41, 42, 44, 65, 110, 126, 162, 255, 302, 328, 369, 370, 371, 373, 374, 375, 376, 377, 378, 379, 380, 381, 382, 388, 389, 390, 394, 395, 398, 399

Health resorts 9

Healthcare providers/practitioners xi, 1, 21, 44, 45, 70, 135, 171, 181, 212, 248, 261, 267, 338, 345

Healing. Alternative healing 23, 78, 342, 390, 398; emergence nature healing 17; healing alchemy 23; healing arts 73, 311, 342, 348, 356; healing balm 9, 31, 197; healing catalyst 18, 23, 42, 45; healing gardens 128, 222, 371, 372, 390, 398; healing gifts 280; healing journey 2, 15, 16, 17, 23, 45, 81, 130, 140, 141-43, 180, 193, 215, 225, 238, 257, 296, 297, 302, 315, 321, 323, 330, 335, 336; healing nature preserve 128, 130, 131, **267-70**; healing nature walk 239, 351; healing touch xi, 1, 22, 27, 306, 372; healing water garden 128; nature healing 11, 12, 17, 328, 353; nature-based healing 2, 9, 12, 345, 354; personal journeys of healing or self-discovery 16, 23, 207; shamanic trance healing 148, 233, 388, 401; trail certification for trauma healing vii, **335-40**; trauma healing journey 45, 335-6, 339

Healing Nature Center vii, 11, 19, 89, 126, 127, 143, 173, 179, 241, 246, 263, 265, **267-70**, 325, 326, 343, 344, 347, 401

Healing Nature Guide. Associate, certified, off-trail, senior. 270, **341-51**

Healing nature instructor , 341-51, **353-6**

Healing nature guide instructor 343

Healing nature professionals 344

Healing nature trail v, vii, xi, 1-2, 3, 10-11, **15-9**, 22, 24, 27, 29, 39, 42-6, 48,

53-5, 67-70, 72-73, 81-2, 88, 98, 100, 110-3, 120, 123, 128-9, 131, 139, 148, 157, 160, 162-7, 172, 181, 183-4, 191-4, 238-9, 245-6, 249, 255, 258, 261-5, 267-70, 271, 273, 287-91, 293-6, 299, 302, 303, 305, 307, 312, 319-20, 325-33, 335, 337, 339, 341, 344-51, 353-4, 401

Healing nature trail board 276

Healing nature trail experience 17, 22, 53, 70, 73, 75, 112, 125, 302

Heart rate variability 34, 381

Heart-rhythm 116

Heartbeat 116-7

Herb 101, 110, 173-4, 201, 330, 342, 389, 395, 396, 401

Hippocrates 49, 232

Hodag 137, 390

Holland, John Henry 17

Hopi 54, 177

Hunter-gatherer ancestors 91, 98

I

Immune system 41, 65-6, 107, 111, 201, 373

Incense 18, 76, 106, 186, 388

Indigenous 9-10, 38, 66, 72, 84, 91, 118, 137, 190, 342, 401

Inflammation 381

Indoor 5-6, 7, 66, 88-9, 110

Inner nature 13, 15, 232

Insect 101, 105, 107, 111-2, 136, 139, 202-3, 297, 302, 398

Integrative 2, 38, 39, 376, 389

Intelligence 8, 38

Internal governing architecture 274

International Dark-Sky Association 179

Internal Society of Nature and Forest Medicine 12, 29, 371, 372

International Union of Forest Research Organizations 29

Interpersonal Neurobiology Model 42, 376

Intuition/intuitive 16, 23, 39, 78, 88, 102, 130, 159, 220

Invasive species 127, 270, 303, 327

Iroquois 54

Isolation 7, 22

J

Japan 11, 12, 18, 31, 222, 371, 373, 374, 375, 382

Endnotes

Chapter One

1   Kahlil Gibran, *The Prophet* (Alfred A. Knopf, 1923), 36.

Chapter Two

1   John Muir, "The Wild Parks and Forest Reservations of the West," *The Atlantic Monthly* (January 1898): 15, http://ebooks.library.cornell.edu/cgi/t/text/text-idx?c=atla;idno=atla0081-1.

2   D.E. Bowler, L.M. Buyung-Ali, T.M. Knight, and A.S. Pullin, "A Systematic Review of Evidence for the Added Benefits to Health of Exposure to Natural Environments," *BMC Public Health* 10 (2010): 456.

3   John Wilmoth, "World's Population Increasingly Urban with More than Half Living in Urban Areas," (July 2014).

4   Christine Haaland and Cecil Konijnendijk van den Bosch, "Challenges and Strategies for Urban Green Space Planning in Cities Undergoing Densification: A Review," *Urban Forestry & Urban Greening* 14.4 (2015): 760-71.

5   M.C. Hansen, P.V. Potapov et al., "High-Resolution Global Maps of 21st-Century Forest Cover Change," *Science* 342, no. 6160 (November 15, 2013): 850-853, DOI:10.1126/science.1244693.

6   John P Robinson, "The National Human Activity Pattern Survey (NHAPS): A Resource for Assessing Exposure to Environmental Pollutants," *Journal of Exposure Analysis and Environmental Epidemiology* 11 (2001): 231-52, DOI:10.1038/sj.jea.7500165.

7   Neil Klepeis, (correspondence), Lawrence Berkeley National Laboratory: Berkeley, CA. E-mail: neklepeis@lbl.gov. www.nature.com/jes/journal/v11/n3/full/7500165a.html.

8   Richard Louv, *Last Child in the Woods: Saving Our Children from Nature-Deficit Disorder* (Chapel Hill, NC: Algonquin Books, 2008), 36.

9   Robert Michael Pyle, *The Thunder Tree: Lessons from an Urban Wildland*, (Lyons Press, 1998). Taken from the publicity synopsis found on major websites such as Goodreads and Amazon.

10   Qing Li et al., "Visiting a Forest, But Not a City, Increases Human

Natural Killer Activity and Expression of Anti-Cancer Proteins," *International Journal of Immunopathology and Pharmacology* 21, no. 1 (2008): 117-27.

11   Rebekah Levine Coley, William C. Sullivan, and Frances E. Kuo, "Where Does Community Grow? The Social Context Created by Nature in Urban Public Housing," *Environment and Behavior* 29, no. 4 (1997): 468-94.

12   Richard Louv, *Last Child in the Woods: Saving Our Children from Nature-Deficit Disorder*, 66.

13   H.L. Burdette and R.L. Whitaker, "Resurrecting Free Play in Young Children: Looking Beyond Fitness and Fatness to Attention, Affiliation and Effect," *American Medical Association* (2005).

14   Andrea Faber Taylor and Frances E. Kuo, "Children with Attention Deficits Concentrate Better After Walk in the Park," *Journal of Attention Disorders,* 12.5 (2009): 402-409.

15   N.M. Wells, "At Home with Nature: Effects of 'Greenness' on Children's Cognitive Function," *Environment and Behavior* 32, no. 6 (2000): 775-95.

16   V. Seymour, "The Human–Nature Relationship and Its Impact on Health: A Critical Review," *Frontiers in Public Health* 4 (2016): 260, http://doi.org/10.3389/fpubh.2016.00260.

17   Janine M. Benyus, *Biomimicry: Innovation Inspired by Nature* (New York: Harper Collins, 1997), 297.

18   Charles Cook, *Awakening to Nature: Renewing Your Life by Connecting with the Natural World*, 1st ed., (McGraw-Hill, 2001), vii.

19   Hanna Loewy, *Einstein Biography* by A&E Television, VPI International, 1991, television.

20   Qing Li et al., "Visiting a Forest, But Not a City, Increases Human Natural Killer Activity and Expression of Anti-Cancer Proteins," *International Journal of Immunopathology and Pharmacology* 21, no. 1 (2008): 117-27.

21   Renate Cervinka, Kathrin Röderer, and Elisabeth Hefler, "Are Nature Lovers Happy? On Various Indicators of Well-Being and Connectedness with Nature," *Journal of Health Psychology* 17.3 (2012): 379-88.

22   Ruth Ann Atchley, David L. Strayer, and Paul Atchley, "Creativity in the Wild: Improving Creative Reasoning Through Immersion in Natural Settings," *PloS one* 7, no. 12 (2012): e51474.

23   Emi Morita et al., "A Before and After Comparison of the Effects of Forest Walking on the Sleep of a Community—Based on Sample of People with Sleep Complaints," *Biopsychosocial Medicine* 5 (2011): 13.

24   Jia Wei Zhang et al., "An occasion for unselfing: Beautiful nature leads to prosociality," *Journal of Environmental Psychology* 37 (2014): 61-72.

25   Netta Weinstein, Andrew K. Przybylski, and Richard M. Ryan, "Can

Nature Make Us More Caring? Effects of Immersion in Nature on Intrinsic Aspirations and Generosity," *Personality and Social Psychology Bulletin* 35, no. 10 (2009): 1315-29.

26   V. Seymour, "The Human-Nature Relationship and Its Impact on Health: A Critical Review," 260.

27   Eva M. Selhub, MD, and Alan C. Logan, ND, *Your Brain On Nature: The Science of Nature's Influence on Your Health, Happiness, and Vitality* (Canada: John Wiley & Sons Ltd., 2012), 22.

28   "What is Co-Intelligence?" *The Co-Intelligence Institute*, last modified 2017, http://www.co-intelligence.org/CIWhatsCI.html.

29   *The Zen of Bonsai: Tending Your Tree of Life,* by Tamarack Song, unpublished.

30   Bun Jin Park, Y. Miyazaki et al., "The Physiological Effects of Shinrin-yoku (Taking in the Forest Atmosphere or Forest Bathing): Evidence from Field Experiments in 24 Forests Across Japan," *Enviro Health Prev Med.* (January 2010): 18-26, DOI:10.1007/s12199-009-0086-9.

31   Ibid.

32   "Key Words," *Ministry of Agriculture, Forestry, and Fisheries,* http://www.maff.go.jp/e/keyword/index.html.

33   *Association of Nature and Forest Therapy Guides and Programs,* http://www.natureandforesttherapy.org/the-association.html.

34   Asmita Patel et al., "General Practitioners' Views and Experiences of Counseling for Physical Activity Through the New Zealand Green Prescription Program," *BMC Family Practice* 12, no. 1 (2011): 119.

35   Boyd A. Swinburn et al., "Green Prescriptions: Attitudes and Perceptions of General Practitioners Towards Prescribing Exercise," *Br J Gen Pract* 47, no. 422 (1997): 567-69.

36   M.J. Hamlin et al., "Long-Term Effectiveness of the New Zealand Green Prescription Primary Health Care Exercise Initiative," *Public Health* 140 (2016): 102-8.

37   Elise Yule, "The Long-Term Effectiveness of the New Zealand Green Prescription Primary Health Care Intervention on Christchurch Residents," *Lincoln University* (2015).

38   "What Is the History of INFOM?" *International Society of Nature and Forest Medicine*, last modified 2010, http://infom.org/faq/.

Chapter Three

1   Chapter 9 in *Mormon Lilies* in *Steep Trails: Nature Essays* (World Library Classics, 2009).

2   Chris Gage, *How to Hike the Appalachian Trail: A Comprehensive Guide to Plan and Prepare for a Successful Thru-Hike* (Independently published, 2017).

3   Three Lakes Historical Museum, *Sam's Trees: A Guide to the Sam Campbell Memorial Trail*, revised edition (Three Lakes, WI: 2016).

4   Clare Cooper Marcus and Naomi A Sachs, *Therapeutic Landscapes: An Evidence-Based Approach to Designing Healing Gardens and Restorative Outdoor Spaces* (Wiley, 2013).

5   https://www.takingcharge.csh.umn.edu/explore-healing-practices/ healing-environment/what-are-healing-gardens.

6   Of his many books relating to the subject matter, Emergence from Chaos to Order, Oxford University Press, (1998), ISBN 0-7382-0142-1, is the most concise.

Chapter Four

1   Robert Allister, "Yama-no-Uchi," *House and Garden* 20 (September 1911): 158.

2   Corey Floyd, PhD, "What Lack of Affection Can Do to You," *Psychology Today* (August 31, 2013).

3   Larry Chang, *Wisdom for the Soul: Five Millennia of Prescriptions for Spiritual Healing* (Gnosophia, 2006), Front cover.

4   Tiffany Field, "Touch for Socioemotional and Physical Well-Being: A Review," *Developmental Review* 30, no. 4, (December 2010): 367-83.

5   Ralph Waldo Emerson, "Nature" in *Nature: Addresses and Lectures* (Hard Press Publishing, 2013), 10.

6   D. Ricketson and A. Ricketson, *Daniel Ricketson and His Friends: Letters, Poems, Sketches etc.* (New York: AMS Press, 1985), 77.

7   A.R. Edwards and D.M. Adams, *Thriving Beyond Sustainability Pathways to a Resilient Society* (New Westminster, B.C.: Post Hypnotic Press, 2011), 149.

8   I. Fjørtoft, *Early Childhood Education Journal* 29 (2001): 111, https://doi. org/10.1023/A:1012576913074.

9   Richard Louv, *Last Child in the Woods: Saving Our children from Nature-Deficit Disorder*.

10   "The History of Audubon," *Audubon*, accessed 4 June 2018, www.audubon.org/about/history-audubon-and-waterbird-conservation.

11   "2017 Median Pay," *US Bureau of Labor Statistics*, US Bureau of Labor Statistics, accessed 13 April 2018, www.bls.gov/ooh/life-physical-and-social-science/home.htm.

12   K. Bricker, "Trends and Issues For Ecotourism and Sustainable Tourism, accessed July 28, 2018, https://sustainabledevelopment.un.org/content/ documents/4099Presentation 0.1 Kelly Bricker-full presentation.pdf.

Chapter Five

1   Retrieved from https://www.medscape.com/viewarticle/864050_3.

2   "What is the history of INFOM?" *The International Society of Nature and*

Forest Medicine, last modified 2010, http://infom.org/faq.

3   Benjamin Franklin, "On Protection of Towns from Fire, 4 February 1735," *Founders Online*, National Archives, last modified March 30, 2017, http://founders.archives.gov/documents/Franklin/01-02-02-0002.

4   *The Papers of Benjamin Franklin, vol. 2*, January 1, 1735, through December 31, 1744, ed. Leonard W. Labaree, (New Haven: Yale University Press, 1961), 12-15.

5   M.A. Bonmati-Carrion et al., "Protecting the Melatonin Rhythm through Circadian Healthy Light Exposure," *International Journal of Molecular Sciences* 15, no. 12 (2014): 23448–500.

6   "Overview of the Annual Health, Labour, and Welfare Report 2016," MHLW Japan, http://www.mhlw.go.jp/english/wp/wp-hw8/dl/summary.pdf.

7   Qing Li, Toshiaki Otsuka et al., "Acute Effects of Walking in Forest Environments on Cardiovascular and Metabolic Parameters," *Springer-Verlag* (March 23, 2011): 2848, DOI 10.1007/s00421-011-1918-z 123.

8   Bum Jin Park, Y. Miyazaki et al, "The Physiological Effects of Shinrin-Yoku (Taking in the Forest Atmosphere or Forest Bathing): Evidence from Field Experiments in 24 Forests Across Japan," *Enviro Health Prev Med.* (January 2010): 18-26, DOI:10.1007/s12199-009-0086-9.

9   Ibid.

10 Ibid.

11 Qing Li et al., "Acute Effects of Walking in Forest Environments on Cardiovascular and Metabolic Parameters," 2850.

12 "Stanford Study Finds Walking Improves Creativity," *Stanford News* (April 24, 2014).

13 M. Oppezzo and D.L. Schwartz, "Give Your Ideas Some Legs: The Positive Effect of Walking and Creative Thinking," *Journal of Experimental Psychology* 40, no. 4 (July 2014): 1142-52.

14 Thomas Münzel et al., "Environmental Noise and the Cardiovascular System," *Journal of the American College of Cardiology* 71, no. 6 (February 2018), DOI:10.1016/j.jacc.2017.12.015.

15 "Data and Statistics," *World Health Organization*, last modified 2018, http://www.euro.who.int/en/health-topics/environment-and-health/noise/data-and-statistics.

16 Florence Williams, "Eight Amazing Ways Nature Can Heal You," *Rodale's Organic Life* (February 2017), https://www.rodalesorganiclife.com/wellbeing/8-amazing-ways-nature-can-heal-you/slide/1.

17 Qing Li et al., "Forest Bathing Enhances Human Natural Killer Activity and Expression of Anti-Cancer Proteins," *International Journal of Immunopathology and Pharmacology* 20 (2007): 3-8.

18 Qing Li et al., "A Forest Bathing Trip Increases Human Natural

Killer Activity and Expression of Anti-Cancer Proteins in Female Subjects," *Journal of Biological Regulatory & Homeostatic Agents* 22, no. 1 (2008): 45-55.

19 Qing Li, "Effect of Forest Bathing Trips on Human Immune Function," *Environmental Health and Preventive Medicine* 15, no. 1 (2010): 9–17, http://doi.org/10.1007/s12199-008-0068-3.

20 Juyoung Lee et al., "Nature Therapy and Preventive Medicine, Public Health," *Social and Behavioral Health* (2012): 326-336, ISBN: 978-953-51-0620-3, www.intechopen.com/books/public-health-social-and-behavioral-health/nature-therapy-and-preventivemedicine.

21 M. Velarde et al., "Health Effects of Viewing Landscapes—Landscape Types in Environmental Psychology," *Urban Forestry & Urban Greening* 6, no. 4 (2007): 199-212.

22 R.S. Ulrich, "View Through a Window May Influence Recovery," *Science* (1984): 224-25, https://www.ncbi.nlm.nih.gov/pubmed/6143402/.

23 Juyoung Lee et al., "Nature Therapy and Preventive Medicine, Public Health."

24 Yoshifumi Miyazaki, Harumi Ikei, and Chorong Song, "Forest Medicine Research in Japan," *Japanese Journal of Hygiene* 69, no. 2 (2014): 122-35.

25 Ibid.

26 Qing Li et al., "Acute Effects of Walking in Forest Environments on Cardiovascular and Metabolic Parameters," *Springer-Verlag* (March 2011): 2848, DOI 10.1007/s00421-011-1918-z 123.

27 Juyoung Lee et al., "Nature Therapy and Preventive Medicine, Public Health," 329, 333-34, 338.

28 Ibid, 330.

29 Yuko Tsunetsugu, Bum-Jin Park, and Yoshifumi Miyazaki, "The Trends on the Research of Forest Bathing in Japan, Korea and in the World Trends in research related to 'Shinrin-yoku' (taking in the forest atmosphere or forest bathing) in Japan," *The Japanese Society for Hygiene* (July 2009): 33.

30 Rathish Nair and Arun Maseeh, "Vitamin D: The 'Sunshine' Vitamin," *Journal of Pharmacology and Pharmacotherapeutics* 3, no. 2 (April 2012): 118-126, DOI:10.4103/0976-500X.95506, PMCID: PMC3356951, www.ncbi.nlm.nih.gov/pmc/articles/PMC3356951/.

31 Josie Glausiuz, "Mind and Brain/Depression and Happiness—Raw Data 'Is Dirt the New Prozac?'," *Discover Magazine* (July 2007), http://discovermagazine.com/2007/jul/raw-data-is-dirt-the-new-prozac.

32 F.E Kuo and A.F. Taylor, "A Potential Natural Treatment for Attention-Deficit/Hyperactivity Disorder: Evidence from a National Study," *American Journal of Public Health* 94, no. 9 (2004): 1580-86, www.nps.gov/choh/

learn/news/upload/Park-Rx-One-Pager-2.pdf.

33 Anne Frank, *The Diary of a Young Girl: The Definitive Edition* (New York: Doubleday, 1995), 196.

34 N. Goel et al., "Controlled Trial of Bright Light and Negative Air Ions for Chronic Depression," *Psychol. Med.* 7 (2005): 945–955, DOI:10.1017/S0033291705005027.

35 Vanessa Perez, Dominik D. Alexander, and William H. Bailey, "Air Ions and Mood Outcomes: A Review and Meta-Analysis," *BMC Psychiatry* 13 (2013): 29.

36 Roppei Yamada et al., "Water-Generated Negative Air Ions Activate NK Cell and Inhibit Carcinogenesis in Mice," *Cancer Letters* 239, no. 2 (2006): 190-97.

37 T.D. Bracken and G.B. Johnson, "In: Air Ions: Physical and Biological Aspects," Small Air Ion Environments (1987): 13-21.

38 Yuko Tsunetsugu, Bum-Jin Park, and Yoshifumi Miyazaki, "The Trends on the Research of Forest Bathing in Japan, Korea and in the World Trends in Research Related to 'Shinrin-Yoku' (Taking in the Forest Atmosphere or Forest Bathing) in Japan," *The Japanese Society for Hygiene* (July 2009): 33.

39 Josie Glausiuz, "Mind and Brain/Depression and Happiness—Raw Data 'Is Dirt the New Prozac?'," *Discover Magazine* (July 2007), http://discovermagazine.com/2007/jul/raw-data-is-dirt-the-new-prozac.

40 E. Morita et al., "A Before and After Comparison of the Effects of Forest Walking on the Sleep of a Community—Based on a Sample of People with Sleep Complaints," *US National Library of Medicine National Institutes of Health* (Oct 2011), DOI:10.1186/1751-0759-5-13.

41 David B. Yaden et al., "The Overview Effect: Awe and Self-Transcendent Experience in Space Flight," *Psychology of Consciousness: Theory, Research, and Practice* 3, no. 1 (March 2016): 1-11, URL: http://dx.doi.org/10.1037/cns0000086.

42 Ibid.

43 Adam Hoffman, "How Awe Makes Us Generous: A New Study Finds that Feeling Small in Nature Makes Us More Generous to Other Humans," *Greater Good Magazine* (August 3, 2015), https://greatergood.berkeley.edu/article/item/how_awe_makes_us_generous.

44 Ibid.

45 Christopher Bergland, "The Power of Awe: A Sense of Wonder Promotes Loving-Kindness," *Psychology Today*, last modified May 20, 2015, https://www.psychologytoday.com/blog/the-athletes-way/201505/the-power-awe-sense-wonder-promotes-loving-kindness.

46 M. Townsend and R. Weerasuriya, *Beyond Blue to Green: The Benefits of Contact with Nature for Mental Health and Well-Being* (Melbourne, Australia:

Beyond Blue Limited, 2010), 15.

47 S.M.E. Van Dillen et al., "Green Space in Urban Neighbourhoods and Residents' Health: Adding Quality to Quantity," *Journal of Epidemiology and Community Health* 66 (2012): e8.

48 M. Townsend and R. Weerasuriya, *Beyond Blue to Green: The Benefits of Contact with Nature for Mental Health and Well-Being*, 21.

49 Larry Merculieff, Aleut elder and member of Board of Advisors for The Association of Nature and Forest Therapy Guides and Programs, http://www.natureandforesttherapy.org/about.html.

50 R.A. Atchley, D.L. Strayer, and P. Atchley, "Creativity in the Wild: Improving Creative Reasoning through Immersion in Natural Settings," *PLoS ONE* 7, no. 12 (2012): e51474, DOI:10.1371/journal.pone.0051474.

51 K. Korpela et al., "Restorative Experience and Self-Regulation in Favorite Places," *Environment and Behaviour* 33, no. 4 (2001): 575-76.

52 R.L. Buckner, J.R. Andrews-Hanna, and D.L. Schacter, "The Brain's Default Network," *Annals of the New York Academy of Sciences* 1124 (2008): 1-38, DOI:10.1196/annals.1440.011.

Chapter Six

1 "2018 Outdoor Participation Report," *Outdoor Industry Association*, last modified July 17, 2018, https://outdoorindustry.org/resource/2018-outdoor-participation-report/.

2 Ibid.

3 C. Charles, PhD, and Richard Louv, "Children's Nature Deficit: What We Know—and Don't Know," *Association of Nature and Forest Therapy*, accessed July 31, 2018, http://www.natureandforesttherapy.org/uploads/8/1/4/4/8144400/childrens_nature_deficit_disorder_2009.pdf.

4 Ibid.

5 Oliver Pergams and Patricia A. Zaradic, "Evidence for a Fundamental and Pervasive Shift Away from Nature-Based Recreation," *Proceedings of the National Academy of Sciences* (2008).

6 Derek Yach, David Stuckler, and Kelly D. Brownell, "Epidemiologic and Economic Consequences of the Global Epidemics of Obesity and Diabetes," *Nature Medicine* 12, no. 1 (2006): 62.

7 H. Weinberger et al., "Trends in Depression Prevalence in the USA from 2005 to 2015: Widening Disparities in Vulnerable Groups," *Psychological Medicine* 1 (2017), DOI:10.1017/S0033291717002781.

8 M. Velarde et al., "Health Effects of Viewing Landscapes—Landscape Types in Environmental Psychology," *Urban Forestry & Urban Greening* 6, no. 4 (2007): 199-212, DOI:10.1016/j.ufug.2007.07.001.

9 M. Nathaniel Mead, "Benefits of Sunlight: A Bright Spot for Human

Health," *Environmental Health Perspectives* 116, no. 4 (2008): A160-67.

10 Ming Kuo, "How Might Contact with Nature Promote Human Health? Promising Mechanisms and a Possible Central Pathway," *Frontiers in Psychology* 6 (2015): 1093.

11 D.J. Siegel, *Pocket Guide to Interpersonal Neurobiology: An Integrative Handbook of the Mind* (New York: W.W. Norton & Company, 2012).

12 Jeanne M. Bulgin, Arreed F. Barabasz, and W. Rand Walker, "Restricted Environmental Stimulation Therapy," *Encyclopedia of Psychotherapy* (2002): 565-69.

13 Anette Kjellgren and Jessica Westman, "Beneficial Effects of Treatment with Sensory Isolation in Flotation-Tank as a Preventive Health-Care Intervention—A Randomized Controlled Pilot Trial," *BMC Complementary and Alternative Medicine* 14 (2014): 417.

14 Fátima Aparecida Caromano et al., "Effects of Modified Restricted Environmental Stimulation Therapy on Relaxation, Heart Rate, Blood Pressure and Flexibility," *International Archives of Medicine* 8 (2015).

15 Sven Bood et al., "Effects of Flotation-Restricted Environmental Stimulation Technique on Stress-Related Muscle Pain: What Makes the Difference in Therapy-Attention-Placebo or the Relaxation Response?" *Pain Research and Management* 10, no. 4 (2005): 201-9.

16 Sven Bood, Anette Kjellgren, and Torsten Norlander, "Treating Stress-Related Pain with the Flotation Restricted Environmental Stimulation Technique: Are There Differences Between Women and Men?" *Pain Research and Management* 14, no. 4 (2009): 293-98.

17 Kristoffer Jonsson and Anette Kjellgren, "Promising Effects of Treatment with Flotation-REST (Restricted Environmental Stimulation Technique) as an Intervention for Generalized Anxiety Disorder (GAD): A Randomized Controlled Pilot Trial," *BMC Complementary and Alternative Medicine* 16, no. 1 (2016): 108.

18 Peter and Frederick F. Ikard, "Use of Sensory Deprivation in Facilitating the Reduction of Cigarette Smoking," *Journal of Consulting and Clinical Psychology* 42, no. 6 (1974): 888.

19 Helen Christensen and E. Di Giusto, "The Effects of Sensory Deprivation on Cigarette Craving and Smoking Behavior," *Addictive Behaviors* 7, no. 3 (1982): 281-84.

20 P. Suedfeld, J.W. Turner, and T.H. Fine, "Restricted Environmental Stimulation," *Recent Research in Psychology,* 245-54.

21 P. Suedfeld and J.L. Kristeller, "Stimulus Reduction as a Technique in Health Psychology," Health Psychology 1, no. 4 (1982): 337-57.

22 "Depression, Too, Is a Thing with Feathers," *Contemporary Psychoanalysis* 44, no. 4 (2008).

Chapter Seven

1 J.D. Oliver, *Contemplative Living* (New York: Random House International, 2001), 61.

2 Andrew Weil, *Spontaneous Healing* (New York: Random House, 1995), 204.

3 J.D. Oliver, *Contemplative Living*, 61.

4 Andrew Weil, *Spontaneous Healing*, 203-5.

5 Shahriar Sheikhbahaei and Jeffrey C. Smith, "Breathing to Inspire and Arouse," *Science* 355, no. 6332 (2017): 1370-71.

6 Gay Hendricks, *Conscious Breathing: Breathwork for Health, Stress Release, and Personal Mastery* (New York: Bantam Books, 1995), 11-13, 25-31.

7 D. Farhi and B. Young, *The Breathing Book: Good Health and Vitality through Essential Breath Work* (East Roseville, N.S.W.: Simon & Schuster, 1997), 166.

8 Ibid, 7.

9 Ibid.

10 Ibid, 6.

11 Mehri Bozorg-Nejad et al., "The Effect of Rhythmic Breathing on Pain of Dressing Change in Patients with Burns Referred to Ayatollah Mousavi Hospital," *World Journal of Plastic Surgery* 7, no.1 (2018): 51.

12 Gay Hendricks, *Conscious Breathing: Breathwork for Health, Stress Release, and Personal Mastery*, 23-25.

13 D.W. Quellette et al., *Heal Yourself with Breath, Light, Sound and Water ...* (Nature Life News, 2006), 12-13.

14 Thich Nhat Hanh, *Transformation and Healing* (Berkeley, CA: Parallax Press, 1990).

15 D.W. Quellette et al., *Heal Yourself with Breath, Light, Sound and Water ...*, 2.

16 Ibid, 1.

17 Ibid.

18 Elke Vlemincx, Ilse Van Diest, and Omer Van den Bergh, "A Sigh of Relief or a Sigh to Relieve: The Psychological and Physiological Relief Effect of Deep Breaths," *Physiology & Behavior* 165 (2016): 127-35.

19 Elke Vlemincx, Michel Meulders, and James L. Abelson, "Sigh Rate During Emotional Transitions: More Evidence for a Sigh of Relief," *Biological Psychology* 125 (2017): 163-72.

20 C. Caldwell, *Getting in Touch: The Guide to New Body-Centered Therapies* (Wheaton, IL: Quest Books, 1997), 37.

21 Gay Hendricks, *Conscious Breathing: Breathwork for Health, Stress Release, and Personal Mastery*, 7, 30.

22 D.W. Quellette et al., *Heal Yourself with Breath, Light, Sound and Water ...*, 10.

23 Gay Hendricks, *Conscious Breathing: Breathwork for Health, Stress Release, and Personal Mastery*, 11-18.

24 Kevin Yackle et al., "Breathing Control Center Neurons that Promote Arousal in Mice," *Science* 355, no. 6332 (2017): 1411-15.

25 Vera Eva Zamoscik et al., "Respiration Pattern Variability and Related Default Mode Network Connectivity are Altered in Remitted Depression," *Psychological Medicine* (2018): 1-11.

26 Anup Sharma et al., "A Breathing-Based Meditation Intervention for Patients with Major Depressive Disorder Following Inadequate Response to Antidepressants: A Randomized Pilot Study," *The Journal of Clinical Psychiatry* 78, no. 1 (2017): e59-e63.

27 D. Adler et al., "Breathing and the Sense of Self: Visuo-respiratory Conflicts Alter Body Self-Consciousness: p111," *Respiration* 87, no. 6 (2014): 546.

28 Gay Hendricks, *Conscious Breathing: Breathwork for Health, Stress Release, and Personal Mastery*, 25-31.

29 G.K. Pal and S. Velkumary, "Effect of Short-Term Practice of Breathing Exercises on Autonomic Functions in Normal Human Volunteers," *Indian Journal of Medical Research* 120, no. 2 (2004): 115.

30 J.D. Oliver, *Contemplative Living*, 61.

31 D.W. Quellette et al., *Heal Yourself with Breath, Light, Sound and Water ...*, 8-9.

32 G.K. Pal and S. Velkumary, "Effect of Short-Term Practice of Breathing Exercises on Autonomic Functions in Normal Human Volunteers," 115.

33 G. Naik, G.S. Sunil, and G.K. Pal, "Effect of Modified Slow Breathing Exercise on Perceived Stress and Basal Cardiovascular Parameters," *International Journal of Yoga* 11, no. 1 (2018): 53-58.

34 D.W. Quellette et al., *Heal Yourself with Breath, Light, Sound and Water ...*, 9.

35 G.K. Pal and S. Velkumary, "Effect of Short-Term Practice of Breathing Exercises on Autonomic Functions in Normal Human Volunteers," 115.

36 G. Naik, G.S. Sunil, and G.K. Pal, "Effect of Modified Slow Breathing Exercise on Perceived Stress and Basal Cardiovascular Parameters," 53-58.

37 D.W. Quellette et al., *Heal Yourself with Breath, Light, Sound and Water ...*, 4.

38 Donald J. Noble et al., "Slow Breathing Can Be Operantly Conditioned in the Rat and May Reduce Sensitivity to Experimental Stressors," *Frontiers in Physiology* 8 (2017).

39 G.K. Pal and S. Velkumary, "Effect of Short-Term Practice of Breathing Exercises on Autonomic Functions in Normal Human Volunteers," 115.

40 Donald J. Noble et al., "Slow Breathing Can Be Operantly Conditioned in the Rat and May Reduce Sensitivity to Experimental Stressors."

41 Gay Hendricks, *Conscious Breathing: Breathwork for Health, Stress Release, and Personal Mastery*, 8.

42 Donald J. Noble et al., "Slow Breathing Can Be Operantly Conditioned in the Rat and May Reduce Sensitivity to Experimental Stressors."

43 D. Farhi and B. Young, *The Breathing Book: Good Health and Vitality Through Essential Breath Work*, 7.

44 Vivek Kumar Sharma et al., "Effect of Fast and Slow Pranayama Practice on Cognitive Functions in Healthy Volunteers," *Journal of Clinical and Diagnostic Research* 8, no. 1 (2014): 10.

45 Ibid.

46 Ibid.

47 Ibid.

48 Gay Hendricks, *Conscious Breathing: Breathwork for Health, Stress Release, and Personal Mastery*, 12-14, 37-38.

49 James Beard, *Pranayama and Breath Work Workbook* (Sacred Systems, 2017), 8.

50 Fahimeh Mohammadi Fakhar, Forough Rafii, and Roohangiz Jamshidi Orak, "The Effect of Jaw Relaxation on Pain Anxiety During Burn Dressings: Randomised Clinical Trial," *Burns* 39, no. 1 (2013): 61-67.

51 Gay Hendricks, *Conscious Breathing: Breathwork for Health, Stress Release, and Personal Mastery*, 23-25.

52 D. Farhi and B. Young, *The Breathing Book: Good Health and Vitality Through Essential Breath Work*, 8.

53 C. Zelano et al., "Nasal Respiration Entrains Human Limbic Oscillations and Modulates Cognitive Function," *Journal of Neuroscience* 36 (2016): 12448-467.

54 J.E. LeDoux, "Emotion circuits in the brain," *Annual Reviews Neuroscience* 23 (2000): 155-84.

55 P. Lakatos et al., "An oscillatory hierarchy controlling neuronal excitability and stimulus processing in the auditory cortex," *Journal of Neurophysiology* 94, no. 3 (Sept 2005): 1904-11.

56 Kevin Yackle et al., "Breathing Control Center Neurons that Promote Arousal in Mice," *Science* 355, no. 6332 (2017): 1411-15.

57 D.W. Quellette et al., *Heal Yourself with Breath, Light, Sound and Water ...*, 11-13.

58 Ibid, 1.

59 Ibid, 2.

60 Gay Hendricks, *Conscious Breathing: Breathwork for Health, Stress Release, and Personal Mastery*, 24, 30-31.

61 D.W. Quellette et al., *Heal Yourself with Breath, Light, Sound and Water ...*, 2.

62 D. Farhi and B. Young, *The Breathing Book: Good Health and Vitality Through Essential Breath Work*, 9.

63 Ibid, 10.

64 Ibid, 5.

Chapter Eight

1 Roger Gottlieb, *This Sacred Earth: Religion, Nature, Environment* (Routledge, 2004), 39.

2 Stephen T. Sinatra et al., "Electric Nutrition: The Surprising Health and Healing Benefits of Biological Grounding (Earthing)," *Alternative Therapies in Health & Medicine* 23, no. 5 (2017).

3 James L. Oschman, Gaétan Chevalier, and Richard Brown, "The Effects of Grounding (Earthing) on Inflammation, the Immune Response, Wound Healing, and Prevention and Treatment of Chronic Inflammatory and Autoimmune Diseases," *Journal of Inflammation Research* 8 (2015): 83-96.

4 G. Chevalier et al., "Earthing: Health Implications of Reconnecting the Human Body to the Earth's Surface Electrons," *Journal of Environmental Public Health* (2012): 291541.

5 Passi et al., "Electrical Grounding Improves Vagal Tone in Preterm Infants," *Neonatology* 112, no. 2 (2017): 187-92.

6 James L. Oschman, Gaétan Chevalier, and Richard Brown, "The Effects of Grounding (Earthing) on Inflammation, the Immune Response, Wound Healing, and Prevention and Treatment of Chronic Inflammatory and Autoimmune Diseases," 83–96.

7 Neil E. Klepeis et al., "The National Human Activity Pattern Survey (NHAPS): A Resource for Assessing Exposure to Environmental Pollutants," *Journal of Exposure Science and Environmental Epidemiology* 11, no. 3 (2001): 231.

8 "The Medicine Wheel and the Four Directions—Medicine Ways: Traditional Healers and Healing—Healing Ways—Exhibition—Native Voices," *US National Library of Medicine*, National Institutes of Health, www.nlm.nih.gov/nativevoices/exhibition/healing-ways/medicine-ways/medicine-wheel.html.

9 N.H. Johari et al., "A Behaviour Study on Ablution Ritual Among Muslim in Malaysia," *Procedia— Social and Behavioral Sciences*, 106 (2013): 6-9.

10 Gary Chamberlain, "From Holy Water to Holy Waters," *Water Resources IMPACT* 14, no. 2 (2012): 6-9.

11 K. Nair, "Role of Water in the Development of Civilization in India—A Review of Ancient Literature, Traditional Practices and Beliefs," *IAHS PUBLICATION* 286 (2004): 160-66.

12 David Paul Smith, "Chapter 17: The Sweat Lodge as Psychotherapy," *Integrating Traditional Healing Practices into Counseling and Psychotherapy* (2005): 196-209.

13 "How Much Water Is There on, in, and above the Earth?" *US Department of the Interior and the US Geological Survey*, last modified 2016, https://water.usgs.gov/edu/earthhowmuch.html.

14   Peter Suedfeld, Elizabeth J. Ballard, and Margaux Murphy, "Water Immersion and Flotation: From Stress Experiment to Stress Treatment," *Journal of Environmental Psychology* 3, no. 2 (1983): 147-55.

15   B. Ditto, M. Eclache, and N. Goldman, "Short-Term Autonomic and Cardiovascular Effects of Mindfulness Body Scan Meditation," *Annals of Behavioral Medicine* 32, no. 3 (2006): 227-34.

16   R. Perini and A. Veicsteinas, "Heart Rate Variability and Autonomic Activity at Rest and During Exercise in Various Physiological Conditions," *European Journal of Applied Physiology* 90, no. 3-4 (2003): 317-25.

17   R.C. Ziegelstein, "Acute Emotional Stress and Cardiac Arrhythmias," *Journal of the American Medical Association* 298, no. 3 (2007): 324-29.

18   L. Mourot et al., "Cardiovascular Autonomic Control During Short-Term Thermoneutral and Cool Head-Out Immersion," *Aviation, Space, and Environmental Medicine* 79, no. 1 (2008): 14-20.

19   L. Mourot et al., "Conditions of Autonomic Reciprocal Interplay Versus Autonomic Co-Activation: Effects on Non-Linear Heart Rate Dynamics," *Autonomic Neuroscience,* 137, no. 1 (2007): 27-36.

20   Y. Nagasawa et al., "Effects of Hot Bath Immersion on Autonomic Activity and Hemodynamics: Comparison of the Elderly Patient and the Healthy Young," *Japanese Circulation Journal* 65, no. 7 (2001): 587-92.

21   M. Nishimura and S. Onodera, "Effects of Supine Floating on Heart Rate, Blood Pressure and Cardiac Autonomic Nervous System Activity," *Journal of Gravitational Physiology* 7, no. 2 (2000): 171-72.

22   M. Nishimura and S. Onodera, "Effects of Water Temperature on Cardiac Autonomic Nervous System Modulation During Supine Floating," *Journal of Gravitational Physiology* 8, no. 1 (2001): 65-66.

23   C. Miwa et al., "Sympatho-Vagal Responses in Humans to Thermoneutral Head-Out Water Immersion," *Aviation, Space, and Environmental Medicine* 68, no. 12 (1997): 1109-114.

24   T. Mano et al., "Sympathetic Nervous Adjustments in Man to Simulated Weightlessness Induced by Water Immersion," *Journal of UOEH* 7 (1985): 215-27.

25   J.F. Thayer and J.F. Brosschot, "Psychosomatics and Psychopathology: Looking Up and Down from the Brain," *Psychoneuroendocrinology* 30, no. 10 (2005): 1050-58.

26   M. Toda et al., "Change in Salivary Physiological Stress Markers by Spa Bathing," *Biomedical Research* 27 (2006): 11-14.

27   D. Marazziti et al., "Thermal Balneotherapy Induces Changes of the Platelet Serotonin Transporter in Healthy Subjects," *Progress in Neuro-Psychopharmacology & Biological Psychiatry* 1, no. 3 (2007): 1436–439.

28   N.A. Shevchuk, "Adapted Cold Shower as a Potential Treatment for Depression," *Med Hypotheses* 70, no. 5 (2008): 995-1001.

29   R. Rhoades and D.R. Bell, *Medical Physiology: Principles for Clinical*

Medicine (Philadelphia: Wolters Kluwer, 2018), 68.

30 Ibid.

31 Steven D. Waldman, "Functional Anatomy of the Thermoreceptors," chap. 109 in *Pain Review E-Book* (Elsevier Health Sciences, 2016).

32 K. Yamamoto et al., "Autonomic, Neuro-Immunological and Psychological Responses to Wrapped Warm Footbaths—a Pilot Study," *Complementary Therapies in Clinical Practice* 14 (2008): 195–203.

33 E. Ferguson, *Baptism in the Early Church: History, Theology, and Liturgy in the First Five Centuries* (Grand Rapids: 2009).

34 Ian Bradley, *Water: A Spiritual History* (A&C Black, 2012), 14-15.

35 E. Ferguson, *Baptism in the Early Church: History, Theology, and Liturgy in the First Five Centuries.*

Chapter Nine

1 *Webster's Third New International Dictionary, Volume 1* (Chicago: Encyclopedia Britannica Incorporated, 1993), 409, ISBN 0-87779-201-1.

2 Tamarack Song and Moses Beaver, *Whispers of the Ancients: Native Tales for Teaching and Healing in Our Time* (University of Michigan Press, 2010), 48-52.

3 Ibid, 95-96.

4 John Bowker, The Oxford Dictionary of World Religions (New York: Oxford University Press, 1999), 224. ISBN 0-19-866242-4.

5 "On This Day, Even Torah Dances in a Circle," *Jewish Exponent*, last modified June 2013, http://jewishexponent.com/2013/06/07/on-this-day-even-torah-dances-in-a-circle/.

6 "Jewish Wedding Dance," https://weddings.lovetoknow.com/wiki/Jewish_Wedding_Dance.

7 Madhu Bazaz Wangu, *World Religions: Hinduism* (Chelsea House, 2009), 107.

8 Johannes H. Emminghaus, *The Eucharist: Essence, Form, Celebration* (Liturgical Press, 1978), 110.

9 Ziauddin Sardar, *Mecca: the Sacred City* (Bloomsbury, 2014), xviii-xix.

10 John Bowker, The Oxford Dictionary of World Religions, 224.

11 Malcolm Duncan, *Duncan's Ritual of Freemasonry*, 8.

12 Robert Ferré, *Classical Labyrinths: Construction Manual* (Labyrinth Enterprises, 2001), 87.

13 W. Matthews, *Mazes and Labyrinths: Their History and Development* (New York: Dover Publications, 1970), 153.

14 E.E. Hogan, *Way of the Winding Path: A Map for the Labyrinth of Life* (Ashland, OR: White Cloud Press, 2003), 9.

15 Ibid, 5.

16 Robert Ferré, *Classical Labyrinths: Construction Manual*, 13.

17 Ibid, 15.

18 Ibid, 13.

19 Ibid, 18.

20 W. Matthews, *Mazes and Labyrinths: Their History and Development*, 59-64.

21 Ibid, 91.

22 Ibid, 137.

23 Ibid, 7-8.

24 Ibid, 28.

25 Ibid, 75.

26 R. Ferré, *Chartres Labyrinth: Construction Manual* (St. Louis, MO: Labyrinth Enterprises, 2014), 42.

27 Ibid, 38.

28 Stephen Skinner, *Sacred Geometry: Deciphering the Code* (Sterling Publishing Company, Inc., 2009).

29 Robert Lawlor, *Sacred Geometry: Philosophy and Practice* (Crossroad, 1982).

30 R. Ferré, *Chartres Labyrinth: Construction Manual*, 38.

31 Ibid, 144.

32 Patricia Fara, *Science: A Four Thousand Year History* (2009), 3.

33 R. Ferré, *Chartres Labyrinth: Construction Manual*, 151.

34 E.E. Hogan, *Way of the Winding Path: A Map for the Labyrinth of Life*, 17.

35 W. Matthews, *Mazes and Labyrinths: Their History and Development*, 184.

36 Ibid.

37 R. Ferré, *Chartres Labyrinth: Construction Manual*, 50.

38 W. Matthews, *Mazes and Labyrinths: Their History and Development*, 204.

39 Ibid, 184.

40 E.E. Hogan, *Way of the Winding Path: A Map for the Labyrinth of Life*, 11.

41 Ibid.

42 W. Matthews, *Mazes and Labyrinths: Their History and Development*, 18.

43 Ibid, 19.

44 Ibid, 44.

45 R. Ferré, *Classical Labyrinths: Construction Manual*, 14-15.

46 Ibid, 11.

47 Ibid, 38.

48 W. Matthews, *Mazes and Labyrinths: Their History and Development*, 30.

49 Ibid, 153.

50 "Stone Age Carvings in Goa," *Team Digital Goa*, Goa Digest, last modified December 28, 2015, https://digitalgoa.com/stone-age-carvings-in-goa.

51 Clive Ruggles and Nicholas J. Saunders, *Desert Labyrinth: Lines, Landscape and Meaning at Nazca, Peru* (Antiquity Publications, 2012), 1128-135.

52 W. Matthews, *Mazes and Labyrinths: Their History and Development*, 153.

53 Ibid, 44.

54 Ibid, 6.

55 Ibid, 7.

56 R. Ferré, *Classical Labyrinths: Construction Manual*, 14.

57 Ibid, 19.

58 Johari Harish, *Ayurvedic Massage: Traditional Indian Techniques for Balancing Body and Mind* (Healing Arts Press, 1996), 116.

59 R. Ferré, *Classical Labyrinths: Construction Manual*, 91.

60 E.E. Hogan, *Way of the Winding Path: A Map for the Labyrinth of Life*, 6.

61 Ibid.

62 Ibid.

63 Marilyn Thomas Faulkenburg, *Church, City, and Labyrinth in Brontë, Dickens, Hardy, and Butor* (Peter Lang Pub Incorporated, 1993), 21.

64 W. Matthews, *Mazes and Labyrinths: Their History and Development*, 6-9.

65 Ibid, 1.

66 E.E. Hogan, *Way of the Winding Path: A Map for the Labyrinth of Life*, 4.

67 Ibid, 35.

68 Ibid.

69 R. Ferré, *Classical Labyrinths: Construction Manual*, 154.

70 Ibid, 153.

71 "Books About Labyrinths," *Labyrinth Community Network*, accessed 9 November 2018, http://www.labyrinthnetwork.ca/books-about-labyrinths/.

Chapter Ten

1 Kahlil Gibran, *The Prophet* (Alfred A. Knopf, 1923), 40.

2 Daniel Chamovitz et al., *What a Plant Knows: A Field Guide to the Senses* (Scientific American, 2012), 6.

3 Daniel Chamovitz et al., *What a Plant Knows: A Field Guide to the Senses*, 5.

4 Daniel Chamovitz et al., "The COP9 Complex, a Novel Multisubunit Nuclear Regulator Involved in Light Control of a Plant Developmental Switch," *Cell* 82, no. 1 (1996): 115-21.

5 Alyson Knowles et al., "The COP9 Signalosome Is Required for Light-Dependent Timeless Degradation and *Drosophila* Clock Resetting," *Journal of Neuroscience* 29, no. 4 (2009): 1152-62.

6 Ning Wei, Giovanni Serino, and Xing-Wang Deng, "The COP9 Signalosome: More Than a Protease," *Trends in Biochemical Sciences* 33, no. 12 (2008): 592-600.

7 Daniel Chamovitz et al., *What a Plant Knows: A Field Guide to the Senses*, 4.

8 Ibid, 9.

9 Ibid, 10.

10 Ibid, 9-10.

11 Marion W. Parker et al., "Action Spectrum for the Photoperiodic Control of Floral Initiation in Biloxi Soybean," *Science* 102, no. 2641 (1945): 152-55.

12 Warren L. Butler et al., "Detection, Assay, and Preliminary Purification of the Pigment Controlling Photo Responsive Development of Plants," *Proceedings of the National Academy of Sciences of the United States of America* 45, no. 12 (1959): 1703-8.

13 Joanne Chory, "Light Signal Transduction: An Infinite Spectrum of Possibilities," *Plant Journal* 61, no. 6 (2010): 982-91.

14 Daniel Chamovitz et al., *What a Plant Knows: A Field Guide to the Senses*, 24.

15 Ibid, 22-23.

16 Ibid, 24.

17 Ibid, 20.

18 Ian T. Baldwin and Jack C. Schultz, "Rapid Changes in Tree Leaf Chemistry Induced by Damage: Evidence for Communication Between Plants," *Science* 221, no. 4607 (1983): 277-79.

19 Vladimir Shulaev, Paul Silverman, and Ilya Raskin, "Airborne Signaling by Methyl Salicylate in Plant Pathogen Resistance," *Nature* 385, no. 6618 (1997): 718-21.

20 Mirjana Seskar, Vladmir Shulaev, and Ilya Raskin, "Endogenous Methyl Salicylate in Pathogen-Inoculated Tobacco Plants," *Plant Physiology* 116, no. 1 (1998): 387-92.

21 Michael Pollan, *The Botany of Desire: A Plant's-Eye View of the World* (New York: Random House, 2001).

22 Erik E. Filsinger and Richard A. Fabes, "Odor Communication, Pheromones, and Human Families," *Journal of Marriage and Family* 47, no. 2 (May 1985): 349-59.

23 Shani Gelstein et al., "Human Tears Contain a Chemosignal," *Science* 331, no. 6014 (2011): 226-30.

24 Daniel Chamovitz et al., *What a Plant Knows: A Field Guide to the Senses*, 50.

25 Denis Lee, Diana H. Polisensky, and Janet Braam, "Genome-Wide Identification of Touch- and Darkness- Regulated Arabidopsis Genes: A Focus on Calmodulin-like and XTH Genes," *New Phytologist* 165, no. 2 (2005): 429-44.

26 Mark J. Jaffe, "Thigmomorphogenesis: The Response of Plant Growth and Development to Mechanical Stimulation—with Special Reference to *Bryonia dioica*," *Planta* 114, no. 2 (1973): 143-57.

27 David C. Wildon et al., "Electrical Signaling and Systematic Proteinase-Inhibitor Induction in the Wounded Plant," *Nature* 360, no. 6399 (1992): 62-65.

28 Daniel Chamovitz et al., *What a Plant Knows: A Field Guide to the Senses,* 106.

29 Ibid, 113.

30 Ibid, 114.

31 Ibid, 120-21.

32 Ales Pecinka et al., "Transgenerational Stress Memory Is Not a General Response in Arabidopsis," *PLoS One 5,* no. 3 (2010): e9514.

33 Jean Molinier et al., "Transgenerational Memory of Stress in Plants," *Nature* 442, no. 7106 (2206): 1046-49.

34 Eric D. Brenner et al., "Arabidopsis Mutants Resistant to S(+)-Beta-Methyl-Alpha, Beta-Diaminopropionic Acid, a Cycad-Derived Glutamate Receptor Agonist," *Plant Physiology* 124, no. 4 (2000): 1615-24.

35 Hon Ming Lam et al., "Glutamate-Receptor Genes in Plants," *Nature* 396, no. 6707 (1998): 125-26.

36 Erwan Michard et al., "Glutamate Receptor-like Genes Form Ca2+ Channels in Pollen Tubes and Are Regulated by Pistil D-Serine," *Science* 332, no. 434 (2011).

37 J. Fromm and S. Lautner, "Electrical Signals and Their Physiological Significance in Plants," *Plant, Cell & Environment* 30, no. 3 (2006): 249-57, DOI:10.1111/j.1365-3040.2006.01614.x.

38 Jonathan Gressel, "Blue-Light Photoreception," *Photochemistry and Photobiology* 30, no. 6 (1979): 749-51.

39 Margaret Ahmad and Anthony Cashmore, "HY4 Gene of *A. thaliana* Encodes a Protein with Characteristics of a Blue-Light Photoreceptor," *Nature* 366, no. 6451 (1993): 162-66.

40 Anthony Cashmore, "Cryptochromes: Enabling Plants and Animals to Determine Circadian Time," *Cell* 114, no.5 (2003): 537-43.

41 Daniel Chamovitz et al., *What a Plant Knows: A Field Guide to the Senses,* 140.

42 Ibid, 141.

43 John J. Bonica, "Need of a Taxonomy," *Pain* 6, no. 3 (1979): 247-52.

44 Michael C. Lee and Irene Tracey, "Unraveling the Mystery of Pain, Suffering, and Relief with Brain Imaging," *Current Pain and Headache Reports* 14, no. 2 (2010): 124-31.

45 Tamarack Song, *Becoming Nature: Learning the Language of Wild Animals and Plants* (Bear & Company, 2016), 9-12.

46 Examples in Tamarack Song, *Whispers of the Ancients* (University of Michigan Press, 2010), where animals play prominent roles in all twenty-five of the stories.

47 Maxime Aubert et al., "Pleistocene Cave Art from Sulawesi, Indonesia," *Nature* 514, no. 7521 (2014): 223.
Larry V. Benson et al., "Dating North America's Oldest Petroglyphs, Winnemucca Lake Subbasin, Nevada." *Journal of Archaeological Science* 40, no. 12 (2013): 4466-76.

48 Brad Pillans and L. Keith Fifield, "Erosion Rates and Weathering History of Rock Surfaces Associated with Aboriginal Rock Art Engravings (Petroglyphs) on Burrup Peninsula, Western Australia, from Cosmogenic Nuclide Measurements," *Quaternary Science Reviews* 69 (2013): 98–106.

49 http://news.nationalgeographic.com/news/2013/08/130815-lake-winnemucca-petroglyphs-ancient-rock-art-nevada/.

50 Xiaohong Wu et al., "Early Pottery at 20,000 Years Ago in Xianrendong Cave, China," *Science* 336, no. 6089 (2012): 1696–700.

51 For more on Shamanism and Shamanic Healing, see Tamarack Song, *Trance Trauma Release.*

52 R. Gibson, *My Body, My Earth: The Practice of Somatic Archaeology* (Bloomington, IN: IUniverse, 2008), 40.

53 Personal comment from Debbra Anne Jacobson, Wisconsin.

Chapter Eleven

1 Robert Louis Stevenson et al., *The Novels and Tales of Robert Louis Stevenson* (Charles Scribner's Sons, 1909), 172.

2 Daniel Chamovitz et al., *What a Plant Knows: A Field Guide to the Senses,* 27–28.

3 Martin Heil and Richard Karban, "Explaining Evolution of Plant Communication by Airborne Signals," *Trends in Ecology & Evolution* 25, no. 3 (2010): 137–44.

4 Richard Karban and Kaori Shiojiri, "Self Recognition Affects Plant Communication and Defense," *Ecology Letters* 12, no. 6 (2009): 502–6.

5 Richard Karban et al., "Communication Between Plants: Induced Resistance in Wild Tobacco Plants Following Clipping of Neighboring Sagebrush," *Oecologia* 125, no. 1 (2000): 66–71.

6 Richard Karban, "Plant Behaviour and Communication," *Ecology Letters* 11, no. 7 (2008): 727–39.

7 Richard Karban et al., "Deciphering the Language of Plant Communication: Volatile Chemotypes of Sagebrush," *New Phytologist* 204, no. 2 (2014): 380–85.

8 "The Story of Frankincense," *Middle East Institute,* www.mei.edu/sqcc/frankincense.

9 Nigel Groom, "Frankincense and Myrrh. A Study of the Arabian Incense Trade," *Longman: London & New York* 285 (1981).

10 Maria Lis-Balchin, "Essential Oils and 'Aromatherapy': Their Modern Role in Healing," *Journal of the Royal Society of Health* 117, no. 5 (1997): 324–29.

11 Shingo Ueki et al., "Effectiveness of Aromatherapy in Decreasing Maternal Anxiety for a Sick Child Undergoing Infusion in a Paediatric Clinic," *Complementary Therapies in Medicine* 22, no. 6 (2014): 1019–26.

12 Mi-kyoung Lee et al., "The Effects of Aromatherapy Essential Oil Inhalation on Stress, Sleep Quality, and Immunity in Healthy Adults: Randomized Controlled Trial," *European Journal of Integrative Medicine* 12 (2017): 79–86.

13 Ibid.

14 Babar Ali et al., "Essential Oils Used in Aromatherapy: A Systemic Review," *Asian Pacific Journal of Tropical Biomedicine* 5, no. 8 (2015): 601–11.

15 T. Dunning, "Aromatherapy: Overview, Safety, and Quality Issues." *OA Alternative Medicine* 1, no. 1 (2013): 6.

16 Ibid.

17 *PDQ® Integrative, Alternative, and Complementary Therapies Editorial Board,* National Cancer Institute, https://www.cancer.gov/about-cancer/treatment/cam/hp/Aromatherapy-pdq.

18 https://plants.usda.gov/core/profile?symbol=IMCA.

19 https://plants.usda.gov/core/profile?symbol=cope80.

20 Lynn DeVries, "Sweet Fern," *Sweet Fern—Medicinal Herb Info*, Medicinal Herb Info, medicinalherbinfo.org/herbs/SweetFern.html.

21 Ibid.

22 Bianca Bosker, *Cork Dork: A Wine-Fuelled Adventure Among the Obsessive Sommeliers, Big Bottle Hunters, and Rogue Scientists Who Taught Me to Live for Taste* (Penguin Random House, 2017).

23 Roppei Yamada et al., "Water-Generated Negative Air Ions Activate NK Cell and Inhibit Carcinogenesis in Mice," *Cancer Letters* 239, no. 2 (2006): 190–97.

24 L.M. Livanova et al., "The Protective Effects of Negative Air Ions in Acute Stress in Rats with Different Typological Behavioral Characteristics," *Neuroscience and Behavioral Physiology* 29, no. 4 (1999): 393–95.

25 Jim English, "The Positive Health Benefits of Negative Ions," *Nutri Rev* (2013).

26 T. Reilly and I.C. Stevenson, "An Investigation of the Effects of Negative Air Ions on Responses to Submaximae Exercise at Different Times of Day," *Journal of Human Ergology* 22, no. 1 (1993): 1–9.

27 Namni Goel et al., "Controlled Trial of Bright Light and Negative Air Ions for Chronic Depression," *Psychological Medicine* 35, no. 7 (2005): 945–55.

28 T. Dunning, "Aromatherapy: Overview, Safety, and Quality Issues," *OA Alternative Medicine* 1, no. 1 (2013): 6.

Chapter Twelve

1 *Webster's Third New International Dictionary of the English Language, Unabridged* (Encyclopedia Britannica, Inc., 1993), 2404.

Chapter Thirteen

1   "Nicolet–Wolf River Scenic Byway," accessed August 2, 2018, https://www.nicolet-wolfriver-scenicbyway.com/.

2   S.G. Potts et al., "Global Pollinator Declines: Trends, Impacts, and Drivers," *Trends in Ecology and Evolution* (2010): 345-53.

3   A.E. Waltz and W.W. Covington, "Butterfly Response and Successional Change Following Ecosystem Restoration," *USDA Forest Service Proceedings* (2001).

4   *American Horticultural Therapy Association*, last modified 2017, http://www.ahta.org/what-is-horticultural-therapy.

5   Martin L. Verra et al., "Horticultural Therapy for Patients with Chronic Musculoscelatal Pain: A Pilot Study," *Alternative Therapies in Health and Medicine* (2012): 44-50.

6   I. Soederback et al., "Horticultural Therapy: The 'Healing Garden' and Gardening in Rehabilitation Measures at Danderyd Hospital Rehabilitation Clinic, Sweden," *Pediatric Rehabilitation* (2004).

7   Britta Bauer, *Tree burials in Germany: Social Science Study of an Alternative Burial Form* (Hamburg: Verlag Dr. Med. Kovac, 2015).

8   Martin Prechtel, *The Unlikely Peace at Cuchumaquic* (North Atlantic Books, 2012), 155-56.

Chapter Fourteen

1   D. Salwak, *The Wonders of Solitude* (Novato, CA: New World Library, 1998), 69.

2   "Alebrijes: Surreal Oaxacan Folk Art," *National Park Service*, US Department of the Interior, last modified 2015, https://www.nps.gov/cham/learn/historyculture/oaxacan-art.htm.

3   M. Chibnik, "Advertising Oaxacan Woodcarvings," *Human Organization* 67, no. 4 (2008): 362-72, http://www.jstor.org/stable/44127801.

4   L.S. Kearney, *The Hodag and Other Tales of the Logging Camps* (Democrat Printing Company, 1928).

5   E. Morgan, *Change for Health: Volume II Making Positive Changes in Your Life and Health with Brief Inspirational Messages*, Lulu.com (2016).

Chapter Fifteen

1   Aydin Tozeren, *Human Body Dynamics: Classical Mechanics and Human Movement* (Springer, 1999), 1.

2   James A. Blumenthal et al., "Lifestyle and Neurocognition in Older Adults with Cognitive Impairments," *Neurology* (December 19, 2018).

3   Thich Nhat Hanh, *Touching the Earth: 46 Guided Meditations for Mindfulness Practice* (Parallax Press, 2008), 103.

4   M. Jenice Goldston and Laura Downey, *Your Science Classroom* (Sage Publications, 2013), 132.

5   Kenneth Hugdahl et al., "Blind Individuals Show Enhanced Perceptual and Attentional Sensitivity for Identification of Speech Sounds," *Cognitive Brain Research* 19, no. 1 (2004): 28-32.

6   Catherine Y. Wan et al., "Early but Not Late-Blindness Leads to Enhanced Auditory Perception," *Neuropsychologia* 48, no. 1 (2010): 344-48.

7   Kirsten Hötting and Brigitte Röder, "Hearing Cheats Touch, But Less in Congenitally Blind than in Sighted Individuals," *Psychological Science* 15, no. 1 (2004): 60-64.

8   André Dufour, Olivier Després, and Victor Candas, "Enhanced Sensitivity to Echo Cues in Blind Subjects," *Experimental Brain Research* 165, no. 4 (2005): 515-19.

9   Andrew J. Kolarik et al., "A Summary of Research Investigating Echolocation Abilities of Blind and Sighted Humans," *Hearing Research* 310 (2014): 60-68.

10 Ron Kupers and Maurice Ptito, "Compensatory Plasticity and Cross-Modal Reorganization Following Early Visual Deprivation," *Neuroscience & Biobehavioral Reviews* 41 (2014): 36-52.

11 Josef P. Rauschecker, "Cortical Plasticity and Music," *Annals of the New York Academy of Sciences* 930, no. 1 (2001): 330-36.

12 Ron Kupers and Maurice Ptito, "Compensatory Plasticity and Cross-Modal Reorganization Following Early Visual Deprivation," 36-52.

13 Josef P. Rauschecker, "Cortical Plasticity and Music," 330-36.

14 Laurent Renier, Anne G. De Volder, and Josef P. Rauschecker, "Cortical Plasticity and Preserved Function in Early Blindness," *Neuroscience & Biobehavioral Reviews* 41 (2014): 53-63.

15 Atsuko Yoshimura et al., "Blind Humans Rely on Muscle Sense More than Normally Sighted Humans for Guiding Goal-Directed Movement," *Neuroscience Letters* 471, no. 3 (2010): 171-74.

16 E.G. Ekdale, "Comparative Anatomy of the Bony Labyrinth (Inner Ear) of Placental Mammals," *PLoS One* 8, no. 6 (2013): e66624.

17 A.J. Hudspeth, "The Hair Cells of the Inner Ear," *Scientific American* 248, no. 1 (1983): 54-65.

18 "Inner Ear," *Inner Ear: Anatomy*, Encyclopædia Britannica, Inc., last modified 12 Feb. 2015, www.britannica.com/science/inner-ear.

Chapter Seventeen

1   *Keeper of the Wild: The Life of Ernest Oberholtzer* (Minnesota Historical Society Press, 2001), 14.

2   C. Maser, *Forest Primeval: The Natural History of an Ancient Forest*, (Corvallis, OR: Oregon State University Press, 2001), 230.

3   Mahatma Gandhi, *All Men Are Brothers* (A&C Black, 2005), 114.

4   Mahatma Gandhi and Judith M. Brown, *The Essential Writings* (New York: Oxford University Press, 2008), 41.

5   *The Collected Works of Mahatma Gandhi, Volume 77* (Ministry of Information and Broadcasting, Government of India, 1958), 5.

6   M.K. Gandhi, *Ramanama* (Ahmedabad, India: Navajivan Publishing House, 1949), 25.

7   Curt Meine, "Wherefore Wildlife Ecology?" in *Aldo Leopold: His Life and Work* (University of Wisconsin Press, 2010).

8   Aldo Leopold, *Round River* (New York: Oxford University Press, 1993), 145-46.

9   "Jaunts with Jamie," *Rhinelander Daily News* (August 22, 1960), 3.

10 Steven W. Yahr, chap. 4 in *Letters from the Sanctuary: The Sam Campbell Story* (Ithaca, MI: AB Pub., 2018).

11 "North Woods Naturalist Fears Demise of Forest Land," *Milwaukee Sentinel* (June 4, 1982).

12 Tamarack Song, "For Love of Community: The Story of Doris and the Late Walt Goldsworthy," *The Three Lakes News* (August 22, 2007), 3B.

13 W. Goldsworthy and C.C. Gonring, *Wilderness Reflections* (Milwaukee, WI: Ideals Pub., 1977), 28.

14 Tamarack Song, "For Love of Community: The Story of Doris and the Late Walt Goldsworthy," 3B.

15 Shandelle Henson, *Sam Campbell, Philosopher of the Forest* (Three Lakes Historical Society, 2001), 81-84.

16 Ibid.

17 W. Goldsworthy and C.C. Gonring, *Wilderness Reflections* (Milwaukee, WI: Ideals Pub., 1977), 33.

18 Ibid, 54.

19 Ibid, 42.

20 Ibid, 13.

21 Ibid, 12.

22 Steven W. Yahr, chap. 4 in *Letters from the Sanctuary: The Sam Campbell Story*.

23 A. Derleth, *Mr. Conservation: Carl Marty and His Forest Orphans* (Park Falls, WI: MacGregor Litho, 1971), 9.

24 A. Derleth, *Mr. Conservation: Carl Marty and His Forest Orphans*, 51.

25 E.L. Johnson, *Mother Is a Saint Bernard* (Park Falls, WI: MacGregor Litho, 1970), back cover.

26 A. Derleth, *Mr. Conservation: Carl Marty and His Forest Orphans*, 94.

27 C. Marty, *Northernaire's Ginger and Her Woodland Orphans* (Park Falls, WI: MacGregor Litho, 1953), 9.

28 Steven W. Yahr, chap. 3 in *Letters from the Sanctuary: The Sam Campbell Story*.

29 Ibid.

30 Sam Campbell, interview with the *Milwaukee Journal*, October 9, 1941.

31 Three Lakes Historical Society, *Come Explore the Sam Campbell Memorial Forest and Hiking Trail Complex* (Three Lakes, Wisconsin).

32 S.M. Henson, *Sam Campbell: Philosopher of the Forest* (Brushton, NY: TEACH Services, 1995), 12.

33 Ibid, 81.

34 Sam Campbell, *Woodland Portraits* (Ideals Publishing Company, 1976), 11.

35 Steven W. Yahr, chap. 10 in *Letters from the Sanctuary: The Sam Campbell Story*.

36 Ibid.

37 Sam Campbell, *Let Life Begin,* 1934.

38 Sam Campbell, *Sanctuary letters: Being a Collection of Nature Writings* (Three Lakes, WI: 1933), 34.

39 Sam Campbell, *Moose Country* (Pacific Press Publishing Association, 1950), 133.

40 Sam Campbell, *Naturalness*.

41 Three Lakes Historical Museum, *Sam's Trees: A Guide to the Sam Campbell Memorial Trail* (Three Lakes, WI: 2016).

42 Sam Campbell, *On Wings of Cheer* (Pacific Press Publishing Association, 1948), 61.

43 Sam Campbell, *Sanctuary Letters: Being a Collection of Nature Writings,* 38.

44 S.M. Henson, *Sam Campbell: Philosopher of the Forest*, 1.

45 Sam Campbell, *November Come to the North Country*, 25.

46 Sam Campbell, *On Wings of Cheer*, 45.

47 S.M. Henson, *Sam Campbell: Philosopher of the Forest*, 1.

48 Sam Campbell, *Ebony Mansions*, 19.

49 Sam Campbell, *Sanctuary Letters: Being a Collection of Nature Writings*, 38.

50 Sam Campbell, *Naturalness*, 45.

51 Sam Campbell, *Sanctuary Letters: Being a Collection of Nature Writings*, 27.

52 Sam Campbell, *Let Life Begin,* 1934.

53 *Rhinelander Daily News* (August 22, 1960), 3.

54 Tamarack Song, "For Love of Community: The Story of Doris and the Late Walt Goldsworthy," 3B.

55 Harvey Hanson, "Memorial Trail Dedicated to Author Sam Campbell," *The Herald* (September 1989), 9.

56 *C&NW Newsliners*, Chicago & Northwestern Historical Society, http://www.cnwhs.org.

57 Wendy Robinson (correspondence), Three Lakes, WI, July 2018.

58 Tamarack Song, "For Love of Community: The Story of Doris and the Late Walt Goldsworthy," 3B.

59 *Rhinelander Daily News* (August 22, 1960), 3.

60 R. Browning, *Selections from the Poems and Plays of Robert Browning* (S.l.: Tredition Classics, 2012), 54.

Chapter Eighteen

1 M. Pauley Stephen, *"Lighting for the Human Circadian Clock: Recent Research Indicates that Lighting has Become a Public Health Issue,"* Medical Hypotheses 63, no. 4 (2004): 588–96, DOI:10.1016/j.mehy.2004.03.020.

2 Sharon Guynup, "Light Pollution Taking Toll on Wildlife, Eco-Groups Say," *National Geographic Today* (April 17, 2003).

Chapter Nineteen

1 Robin Wall Kimmerer, "Braiding Sweet Grass," *Milkweed* (2013), 301.

Chapter Twenty

1 William Russell White, Leadership Abridged, *Meador* (1956), 710.

2 Larry Chang, *Wisdom for the Soul: Five Millennia of Prescriptions for Spiritual Healing* (Gnosophia, 2006), 768.

3 Elizabeth R. Grant and Michael J. Spivey, "Eye Movements and Problem Solving: Guiding Attention Guides Thought," *Psychological Science* 14, no. 5 (2003): 462-66.

4 Chris L. Kleinke, Thomas R. Peterson, and Thomas R. Rutledge, "Effects of Self-Generated Facial Expressions on Mood," *Journal of Personality and Social Psychology* 74, no. 1 (1998): 272.

5 Tal Shafir et al., "Emotion Regulation Through Execution, Observation, and Imagery of Emotional Movements," *Brain and Cognition* 82, no. 2 (2013): 219-27.

6 Laura E. Thomas and Alejandro Lleras, "Swinging into Thought: Directed Movement Guides Insight in Problem Solving," *Psychonomic Bulletin & Review* 16, no. 4 (2009): 719-23.

7 Thich Nhat Hanh, *The Miracle of Mindfulness: An Introduction to the Practice of Meditation* (Beacon, 1999), 22.

8 Thich Nhat Hanh, *The Miracle of Mindfulness: An Introduction to the Practice of Meditation,* 15.

9 S.T. Carmichael et al., "Central Olfactory Connections in the Macaque Monkey," *Journal of Comparative Neurology* 346, no. 3 (1994): 403-34.

10 J.E. LeDoux, *Annual Reviews Neuroscience* 23 (2000): 155-84.

11 H. Eichenbaum et al., *Annual Reviews Neuroscience* 30 (2007): 123-52.

12 P. Lakatos et al., "An oscillatory hierarchy controlling neuronal excitability and stimulus processing in the auditory cortex," *Journal of Neurophysiology* 94, no. 3 (2005): 1904-11.

13 Shirley Agostinho et al., "Giving Learning a Helping Hand: Finger Tracing of Temperature Graphs on an iPad," *Educational Psychology Review* 27, no. 3 (2015): 427-43.

14 Neon Brooks and Susan Goldin-Meadow, "Moving to Learn: How Guiding the Hands Can Set the Stage for Learning," *Cognitive Science* 40, no. 7 (2016): 1831-49.

15 Susan Wagner Cook, Zachary Mitchell, and Susan Goldin-Meadow, "Gesturing Makes Learning Last," *Cognition* 106, no. 2 (2008): 1047-58.

16 Susan Goldin-Meadow, "How Gesture Works to Change our Minds," *Trends in Neuroscience and Education* 3, no. 1 (2014): 4-6.

17 Myrto-Foteini Mavilidi et al., "Effects of Integrated Physical Exercises and Gestures on Preschool Children's Foreign Language Vocabulary Learning," *Educational Psychology Review* 27, no. 3 (2015): 413-26.

18 Miriam A. Novack et al., "From Action to Abstraction: Using the Hands to Learn Math," *Psychological Science* 25, no. 4 (2014): 903-10.

Chapter Twenty-One

1 Leonard Lyons, "The Lyons Den," Column 2, *The Pittsburgh Press* (March 1956).

2 Lety Seibel (correspondence), Three Lakes, WI, August 2018.

3 Albert Einstein, *The World As I See It* (The Book Tree, 2007), 66.

4 Steven Foster, "Herbs for Health: Health Benefits of Evening Primrose," *Mother Earth Living*, last modified October 1995, www.motherearthliving.com/Health-and-Wellness/herbs-for-health-health-benefits-of-evening-primrose.

5 Lynn DeVries, "Sweet Fern," *Sweet Fern—Medicinal Herb Info*, Medicinal Herb Info, medicinalherbinfo.org/herbs/SweetFern.html.

6 "Wintergreen," *Healthy Ingredients: Wintergreen*, American Botanical Council, cms.herbalgram.org/healthyingredients/Wintergreen.html?ts=1497021423.

7 "Balsam Fir," *Herbal Encyclopedia*, Cloverleaf Farm, accessed 29 Apr. 2017, www.cloverleaffarmherbs.com/balsam-fir/.

8 Marlene Ericksen, *Healing With Aromatherapy* (New York: McGraw-Hill, 2000), 9.

9 Sonia Hines et al., "Aromatherapy for Treatment of Postoperative Nausea and Vomiting," *Cochrane Database of Systematic Reviews* (April 2012), DOI:10.1002/14651858.cd007598.pub2.

10 "*University of Maryland Medical Center – Aromatherapy*," University of Maryland Medical Center.

11 L. Mason et al., "Systematic Review of Efficacy of Topical Rubefacients Containing Salicylates for the Treatment of Acute and Chronic Pain," British Medical Journal 328, no. 7446 (2005): 995.

12 "Trees of the Adirondacks: Yellow Birch (Betula Alleghaniensis),"*Trees of the Adirondacks: Yellow Birch|Betula Alleghaniensis*, Adirondacks Forever Wild, last modified 2017, wildadirondacks.org/trees-of-the-adiron-dacks-yellow-birch-betula-alleghaniensis.html.

13 Albert B. Reagan, "Plants Used by the Bois Fort Chippewa (Ojibwa) Indians of Minnesota," *Wisconsin Archeologist* 7, no. 4 (1928): 231.

14 E. Martini, "Jacques Cartier Witnesses a Treatment for Scurvy," Vesalius 8, no. 1 (2002): 2-6.

15 Don J. Durzan, "Arginine, Scurvy, and Cartier's 'Tree of Life,'" *Journal of Ethnobiology and Ethnomedicine* 5 (2009): 5.

16 B. Schick, "A Tea Prepared from Needles of Pine Trees Against Scurvy," *Science* 98 (1943): 241–42.

17 C. Macnamara, "Vitamin C in Evergreen Tree Needles," *Science* 98 (1943): 242.

18 H.H. Smith, "Ethnobotany of the Menomini Indians," *Bulletin of the Public Museum of the City of Milwaukee* 4 (1923): 1-174.

Chapter Twenty-Two

1 Chris H. Hardy, *The Sacred Network: Megaliths, Cathedrals, Ley Lines, and the Power of Shared Consciousness* (Inner Traditions, 2011), 4.

2 Richard Louv, *Last Child in the Woods: Saving Our Children from Nature-Deficit Disorder*, 109.

3 *Reflections on the Art of Living: A Joseph Campbell Companion*, ed. Diane K. Osbon (New York: HarperCollins, 1991), 8, 18.

4 *The Poetical Works of Robert Southey: Complete in One Volume* (Paris: A. and W. Galignani, 1829), 5.

Endnotes Chapter Twenty-Three

1 Larry Chang, *Wisdom for the Soul: Five Millennia of Prescriptions for Spiritual Healing*, front cover.

2 E. Barrie Kavasch and Karen Baar, *American Indian Healing Arts: Herbs, Rituals, and Remedies for Every Season of Life* (Bantam, 1999), 31-32.

Chapter Twenty-Four

1 H. Lindlahr, *Nature Cure: Philosophy and Practice Based on the Unity of Disease and Cure* (Charleston, SC: BiblioBazaar, 2006), 227.

2 Patterned after the text on the front cover of the guestbook at the Cedar Valley Conference Center in West Bend, WI, 2017.

Chapter Twenty-Six

1 C. Dohnal, *Columbia River Gorge: Natural Treasure on the Old Oregon Trail* (Charleston, SC: Arcadia, 2003), 152.

2   Steve Moe (correspondence), Rhinelander WI, 2016.

3   Thich Nhat Hahn, *Awakening of the Heart: Essential Buddhist Sutras and Commentaries* (Parallax, 2012), 78.

Chapter Twenty-Eight

1   *Brother Wolf Foundation*, www.brotherwolffoundation.org.

Chapter Twenty-Nine

1   Paul Axtell, "The Most Productive Meetings Have Fewer Than Eight People," *Harvard Business Review*, June 22, 2018.

2   Cyril Northcote Parkinson, *Parkinson's Law, and Other Studies in Administration* (Houghton Mifflin Harcourt, 1957).

3   John M. Polimeni, Kozo Mayumi, Mario Giampietro, and Blake Alcott, *The Jevons Paradox and the Myth of Resource Efficiency Improvements* (Routledge, 2007).

4   Stephen G. Dimmock, William C. Gerken, and Nathaniel P. Graham, "Is Fraud Contagious? Co-Worker Influence on Misconduct by Financial Advisors," *Journal of Finance* (February 3, 2018): 18, DOI:10.1111/jofi.12613.

5   Ibid.

6   Ibid.

7   Ibid.

8   Ibid.

9   Stephen R. Block and Steven Rosenberg, "Toward an Understanding of Founder's Syndrome: An Assessment of Power and Privilege Among Founders of Nonprofit Organizations," *Nonprofit Management and Leadership* 12 (2002): 353.

10   Stephen R. Block and Steven Rosenberg, "Toward an Understanding of Founder's Syndrome: An Assessment of Power and Privilege Among Founders of Nonprofit Organizations," 354.

11   Elizabeth Schmidt, "Rediagnosing 'Founder's Syndrome': Moving Beyond Stereotypes to Improve Nonprofit Performance," *Nonprofit Quarterly* (December 6, 2017).

12   Stephen R. Block and Steven Rosenberg, "Toward an Understanding of Founder's Syndrome: An Assessment of Power and Privilege Among Founders of Nonprofit Organizations," 354.

13   M. Wood, "Is Governing Board Behavior Cyclical?" *Nonprofit Management and Leadership* 3, no. 2 (1992): 139–63.

14   Stephen R. Block and Steven Rosenberg, "Toward an Understanding of Founder's Syndrome: An Assessment of Power and Privilege Among Founders of Nonprofit Organizations," 362.

Chapter Thirty

1   "Accessible Trails Manual," https://www.massaudubon.org/get-outdoors/accessibility/accessible-projects-and-partners/accessible-trails-manual.

Chapter Thirty-One

1   Norman Hallendy, *Tukiliit: The Stone People Who Live in the Wind* (University of Alaska Press, 2009), 9, 28.

2   David Williams, *Cairns: Messengers in Stone* (Mountaineers Books, 2012), 16–17.

3   Ibid.

4   Liddel Herma et al., *A Greek-English Lexicon at the Perseus Project*.

5   Mark Auslander, "Memorials in Nature," last modified 2012, culturalenvironments.blogspot.com.

6   *Letters and Drawings of Bruno Schulz, with Selected Prose,* ed. J. Ficowski, trans. W. Arndt with V. Nelson (New York: Harper & Row, 1988).

7   John Updike, "The Visionary of Brohobycz," *The New York Times Book Review* (October 1988).

8   Tamarack Song and Moses Beaver, "The Grandfather and the Stone Canoe" story in *Whispers of the Ancients: Native Tales for Teaching and Healing in Our Time,* 164–70.

9   Anatole France, *The Crime of Sylvestre Bonnard* (Dodd-Mead & Company, 1890), 136.

10 C.C. Marcus and M. Barnes, "Effects of Gardens on Health Outcomes: Theory and Research" in *Healing Gardens—Therapeutic Benefits and Design Recommendations* (New York: John Wiley and Sons, 1999), 27–86.

11 S.G. Potts et al., "Global Pollinator Declines: Trends, Impacts, and Drivers," *Trends in Ecology and Evolution* (2010): 345–53.

12 Caspar A. Hallmann et al., "More than 75 percent decline over 27 years in total flying insect biomass in protected areas," *PLOS* (October 2017).

13 Bradford C. Lister and Andres Garcia, "Climate-driven declines in arthropod abundance restructure a rainforest food web," *PNAS* 115, no. 44 (October 2018).

14 Gretchen Vogel, "Where have all the insects gone?" *Science* (May 2017).

15 A.E. Waltz and W.W. Covington, "Butterfly Response and Successional Change Following Ecosystem Restoration," *USDA Forest Service Proceedings* (2001).

16 *American Horticultural Therapy Association*, last modified 2017, http://www.ahta.org/what-is-horticultural-therapy.

17 Martin L. Verra et al., "Horticultural Therapy for Patients with Chronic Musculoscelatal Pain: A Pilot Study," *Alternative Therapies in Health and Medicine* (2012): 44–50.

18 I. Soederback et al., "Horticultural Therapy: The 'Healing Garden' and Gardening in Rehabilitation Measures at Danderyd Hospital Rehabilitation Clinic, Sweden," *Pediatric Rehabilitation* (2004).

Chapter Thirty-Two

1 Richard Koch, *The 80/20 Principle: The Secret to Achieving More with Less* (Currency, 1999), 21-3.

2 Joel Kahneman et al., "When More Pain Is Preferred to Less: Adding a Better End," *Psychological Science* 4, no. 6 (November 1993).

3 Jim Morningstar, PhD (correspondence), December 13, 2017.

4 Wallace Stevens, "The Well Dressed Man With a Beard," in *Parts of a World* (1942), in *Collected Poetry and Prose of Wallace Stevens* (Library of America ed.), 224.

Chapter Thirty-Three

1 *Guidelines for Community Noise*, ed. Birgitta Bergelund, Thomas Lindevall, and Dietrich H Schwela (Geneva: World Health Organization, April 1999), xvii.

About the Author

Tamarack Song learned about the healing powers of Nature through academic study, apprenticing to Native shamans and herbalists, living with a pack of Wolves, and residing in the wilds for most of his life. He currently lives in the Nicolet National Forest, where he keeps in touch with the Wolves and other medicine animals and plants with whom he works.

Tamarack serves as executive director of the Healing Nature Center, and he cofounded Healing Nature Trails. He has academic training in Stress Management, Ethics, Therapeutic Breathwork, Conservation, and Nonprofit Corporation Management. This book, *The Healing Nature Trail*, is based on his Nature-based Healing and Trauma Recovery PhD research. The author of books on shamanic trance healing, suicide prevention, spirit animal guides, animal tracking, Truthspeaking, Native-inspired childrearing, and Zen, he also serves as an environmental restoration and outdoor expedition consultant.

As founder of the Teaching Drum Outdoor School, he has developed management strategies for the psycho-emotional challenges unique to wilderness experiences. He has taught conflict resolution and indigenous living skills, herbalism, and dream therapy for forty years.